SPORT IN THE 80's

SPORT IN THE 80's
First Published in Great Britain in 1989 by

CENTURION BOOKS LIMITED
52 George Street, London W1H 5RF

Designed by Neville Uden

Photocredits:
Photographs on the dust jacket of HRH Princess Anne, Steffi Graf, Carl Lewis, Diego Maradona, Nigel Mansell, Dennis Conner and Seve Ballesteros, were obtained from **All Sport** as were the photos appearing on pages: 29, 32, 75, 76, 78, 96, 98 and 163.
The photograph of Ian Botham appearing on the dust jacket was obtained from **Coloursport** as were the photos on pages: 10, 12, 20 and 105.
The photograph on page 122 is courtesy of **The Burnley Express** and all other photographs used are courtesy of **The Daily Mail.**

British Library Cataloguing in Publication Data
Wooldridge, Ian
Sport in the 80's
1. Sports
I. Title
796

ISBN 0-948500-01-8

Typeset by Senator Graphics, London

Printed and Bound in Great Britain by Centurion Press Ltd

SPORT IN THE 80's

A PERSONAL VIEW

Ian Wooldridge

CENTURION

CONTENTS

FOREWORD

I have known Ian Wooldridge for some 30 years and now read him more avidly than ever. Sport has not become any more straightforward with the passing years but Ian addresses himself to the most difficult topics of the day with humour and with an unerring grasp of the main point of an argument.

Sports columnists are to some extent jacks of all trades and masters of none but I never recall having caught Ian out on the games of which I know a bit and I doubt if he gets much wrong in the many others which he tackles.

With all his success he remains the very opposite of a hard faced cynical journalist and is someone whom it is always good to see. I am sure that this book of Ian's masterpieces in the 1980s will give immense pleasure to many.

He is kind enough to say that he was a fan of mine when I was playing cricket. I can truthfully say that now I am a fan of his and have been for many years.

Denis Compton

INTRODUCTION

The Eighties saw sport soar to new zeniths of heroic performance and stagger beneath the blows of cheating and human catastrophe. It is not the aim of this book to chart the statistics of a volatile decade for goal-scoring and run-getting were overshadowed by 95 football spectators being crushed to death in a stadium and the most brilliant run in history dismissed as worthless because it was fuelled by drugs. Rather, by arbitrary selection of newspaper columns, it sets out to reflect its mood and style and significance through observing its giants, rogues, romantics, eccentrics, wise men and fools. Many of these pieces were written in admiration or affection, some in anger. Most of them, time being the eternal enemy of the reporter, were produced in a hurry.

Hacks are only too conscious of the perils of putting day-to-day journalism between hard covers but hopefully what follows will convey the perennial joy of writing about sport for a living. There are moments, ad-libbing shapeless sentences into some streetside telephone in California or Korea, when you would rather dig roads. But there is always the morrow when, from the best seats in the stadium, you witness the finest sporting talent of its generation, striving to push back the horizons of physical achievement. There are moments of shattering disillusion — none more so than Heysel, Hillsborough and Ben Johnson — when you feel like throwing the towel in. But the sun always rises and you are off again to Lord's or St Andrews or Las Vegas or Melbourne. I have never quite got over the fact that at the end of the month they send you a pay cheque.

All but one of these columns were written for the Daily Mail for whom, in the Eighties alone, I had the pleasure of travelling more than a million miles through 38 countries. Some are timeless in that, though written in the Eighties, they reflect what I hope is a consistent attitude to sport or merely attempt to capture for the reader the thrills and frustrations of a middle-aged somewhat overweight sportswriter trying his hand at what the stars accomplish with much skill and grace. I shall not attempt the Cresta Run again out of cowardice and it is unlikely that I shall be invited a second time to try to helm an America's Cup yacht in a straight line.

1980

1980 disabused forever the few remaining idealists who believed that sport could dissociate itself from politics. It was the year Muhammad Ali took the terrible punches that effectively finished him, the year John Arlott spoke the immortal last sentence of an incomparable career in the cricket commentary box: "And now over to Christopher Martin-Jenkins." There was marvellous frivolity when the old Test Cricketers of England and Australia got together for a drink or 200. And yet it was a year still damned from beginning to end by politics. For the first time in 84 years the Olympic Games were to be staged in a Communist country, moreover a Communist country that had just invaded Afghanistan. It can be tricky when a reporter holds views diametrically opposed to those of his newspaper. The Daily Mail strongly supported Margaret Thatcher's attempts to stop British athletes going to Moscow. I did not. They still permitted me to write what I pleased, pointing out in a leader column that that was the difference between Britain and the Soviet Union. Mrs Thatcher didn't hold any grudges either. One of Britain's rowing silver medallists at the Moscow Olympics was one, Colin Moynihan. Later in the decade she was to appoint him her Minister of Sport.

VIEWS ON THE MOSCOW GAMES

The Moscow Olympics were not due to start until July. But as early as January the controversy about whether Britain should attend them or not was already a bitter national issue.

LONDON: JANUARY 1980

MARGARET Thatcher's matriarchal concern for our country, you, me and the world, in roughly that order, is genuinely inspiring.

I fear, however, that her advisers have failed her badly over her stand on the Olympic Games.

No one would contest her public show of revulsion over the latest act of Soviet aggression. Most would applaud her courage in standing in the international arena to be counted.

Regrettably, her offer to house elements of the 1980 Olympic Games in Britain was based on spurious wishful thinking, impractical generosity and sheer ignorance.

No part of the 1980 Olympic Games will be staged in Britain. No part of the 1980 Olympic Games will be staged in any part of the world other than the Soviet Union, where they will open, absolutely on schedule, in the Lenin Stadium, Moscow, on July 19.

Apart from the impracticality of the British venues, the simple fact is that Mrs Thatcher's aides, in common with some commentators and many band-wagon politicians, have not even bothered to swot up the history and rules of the Olympic movement.

Had they done so, they would realise that however much Mrs Thatcher and President Carter may wish Moscow to be deprived of the Games, it could be achieved only by a violent act of war.

That, in turn, would probably ensure that posterity, for us all, would be mushroom-shaped.

There will be Moscow Olympics. They will be grotesquely hypocritical Olympics. They will be grim, tense and unpleasant Olympics. They will be Olympics dismembered by boycott and disfigured by understandable protest. They will, in all probability, be untelevised Olympics.

But they will go on because no amount of muscle-flexing in the White House or shrill condemnation from Downing Street can alter it.

The reason is that Mr Carter's and Mrs Thatcher's advisers are unaware of the quaint idealism on which the Olympics were revived at the turn of the century.

One stipulation was that any city awarded the Games willingly conceded its authority to the Olympic movement during the period of the Games. In short that for 15 days or so it actually became Olympia.

Romantically schoolboyish though this notion may seem, it has already survived one test-case every iota as beastly as the Soviet assault on Afghanistan.

In 1936, when Adolf Hitler was already well advanced in his plans to incinerate Jews and set fire to the world, he decided to decorate the Berlin Olympics with eye-catching anti-semitic messages.

These could hardly escape the eye of Henri de Baillet- Latour, the then Olympic president, who summoned Hitler into his presence. An historic conversation ensued.

Baillet-Latour said: 'Mr Chancellor, your signs are not in conformity with Olympic principles.'

Hitler replied: 'Mr President, when you are invited to a friend's home you don't tell him how to run it.'

Baillet-Latour countered: 'When the five-circled flag is raised over the stadium it is no longer Germany. It is Olympia and we are the masters there.' The signs were removed.

It is unlikely that Lord Killanin will persuade the Soviet Union to modify its militant foreign policy but it is quite certain he will reiterate that when the five-circled flag is raised over the Lenin Stadium it is no longer Moscow but Olympia.

Obviously there will be many athletes, spectators and officials who will not wish to go there but to imply that those who do are condoning Soviet military aggression is absurd.

If President Carter is really convinced the Soviet Union is on the march, why doesn't he drop a few professional parachutists into Kabul?

As alternatives go, pulling America's team out of the Olympics is as pathetic as shouting ya-boo through a keyhole and running away.

Mrs Thatcher's stand is no less bewildering. Only the other day she was defending the legal rights of British rugger players to tour South Africa. Now she wants to deny those same rights to British athletes bound for Moscow.

To write thus, of course, is to be branded a Trotskyite fellow-traveller and another bone-headed sportswriter who believes Afghanistan is a suburb of Sydney.

To write thus, in fact, is to know that there are dozens of mediocre politicians, from President Carter sideways, who are using the Olympics as a weapon because they are too scared to use anything else.

The Moscow Olympics will neither provoke war nor prevent it. They are now merely condemned to give us a hollow laugh of historic proportions when the Russians release the usual flurry of doves at the opening ceremony and sing us songs about eternal friendship and peace.

Far from staging a multi-million rouble propaganda exercise to the glory of Mother Russia, the Soviet Union has pledged to open its doors to the world at a time when its horrific ugliness has rarely been more exposed.

It is too good a chance to miss.

THE RELIGION OF RUGBY

Early in the decade Wales were the rugby power in the land. At Twickenham, England beat them in one of the most violent matches ever played. I spent the next few days in Wales, wondering if there was more to it than met the sporting eye.

TONYPANDY: FEBRUARY

THE FIERY rhetoric of hellfire evangelism still survives in the Rhondda Valley, but for all that the Good Lord and the Reverend Anthony Frost are fighting a grim rear-guard action down Tonypandy High Street. Eyes blazing, fist punching heavenwards, voice rising in passionate crescendo, Frost gave it to us for 35 minutes, 40 seconds, scarcely drawing breath. It was a bravura sermon in the great tradition of Welsh non-conformist preaching, but his congregation in the varnished pews of the Bethel Baptist Chapel numbered only 24. Nine children had been led out at half-time. By the time he clamped his eyes shut for the benediction the pubs were open and serving briskly. Three other Tonypandy chapels have been sold off to the property developers in the past six months. Frost leaves shortly for another mission. He drew on a thin, cheap raincoat to shake hands at the door with the quorum of worshippers he would meet again that evening. Back inside, alone with God and a reporter, he said: 'Wales has never been so spiritually desolate. We badly need to pray for the country and those who govern it. In hard times, it is no use pinning your faith in rugby.' Further west, the hard times have already struck. After 17 years, Taibach Rugby Club have cancelled their summer tour to Jersey. No one can afford the £110 a head.

A bar traditionally bulging with lunch-time drinkers echoes with the whispers of 11 unsmiling men. Its takings were down £1,000 a week.

Taibach is a satellite of Port Talbot and both are bleeding in the eighth week of the no-work no-pay steel strike. Some families are living on £9 a week and to flash around fivers and order concillatory drinks in an English accent is inadvisable.

The picket line on one entrance to the vast British Steel Corporation mills bore no resemblance to the ugly tussles you see on the TV news. It comprised three women standing by a brazier. Mrs. Pauline Letman wore green eye-shadow to match her coat, has a 20 year-old son at university and the articulacy of a Bloomsbury Fabian.

'They are trying to break us,' she said. 'If

they win this one, trades unionism in Britain will be dead.'

They meant Westminster and an English middle class indifferent to the spectre of recession that hangs over industrial Wales. She had an interesting theory.

'That's why that rugby international at Twickenham was so bitterly fought. It was about a great deal more than sport.'

In a pub back in the Rhondda, Robert White, who sells survival kit, to mountaineers, was even blunter.

'You English hate us,' he said dispassionately. 'Dave Allen got it right. He said that the English quite like the Scots, just tolerate the Irish, but hate the Welsh. No offence, mind you, but I reckon that's true. That Twickenham match proved it. It was brutal.'

It may have proved something far more simple: that collectively the Welsh don't like being beaten at their second religion.

The Cardiff-published Western Mail, which normally prints four readers' letters a day, cleared an entire broadsheet page to publish 22 letters on what even its rugby correspondent, the respected J.B.G. Thomas, described as 'an event resembling a Greek tragedy'.

Their tone was epitomised by a Ms Donna Lewan, writing as an expatriate despite the fact that she lives only a few leagues up the M4 from Wales at Slough in Buckinghamshire: 'Those of us from the Cymru who have been condemned to live among the English for many years ...'

She concluded: 'Since we scored two tries with only 14 men against 15, plus the referee, so far as I am concerned it was an overwhelming victory for our wonderful scarlet-shirted heroes. They were more truly magnificent than ever before.'

She may not have been alone in her assessment. Down at the Haverfordwest Golf Club, the England-Wales match was watched on television by a group of people who included a 35-year-old Englishman named Bill Ross.

They had a few drinks afterwards. Three hours later Mr Ross was found in some distress, a euphemism for unconscious with head and facial injuries and rushed to hospital.

The explanation was that he had walked into a door. Rugby men don't squeal.

There is no argument either side of the Severn that the England-Wales match was the most physically violent sporting encounter seen in Britain.

The Rev. Anthony Frost thought it 'filthy and disgusting.' Welsh rugby men themselves were disturbed by its ferocity.

Len James, ten years chairman of the Taibach Club, said: 'I've never felt such hostility. I was at Twickenham and there was this well-dressed Englishman behind me screaming blue murder for England to win. I turned round to him and said: "Is there something wrong with you man?"'

James is 63, a life-long Socialist who recalls his parents' shame at having to feed him at the communal soup kitchens in the workless Thirties. He dreads an economic slump in Wales, feels that the English middle-class couldn't care less, but insisted that this was wholly unconnected with the Twickenham violence.

He then said a curious thing. 'In rugby, a stand-up punch is O.K. because you can see it coming. Kicking a man on the ground is different.' In Wales, it seems, there are rules and Welsh rules.

Thirty years after Nye Bevan, South Wales has a better local road system than London. Front doors along the Rhondda are as colourful as those in Chelsea mews. There is a bar behind Tonypandy with brands of 70 different whiskies on sale. V- registration cars abound.

But there is deep Welsh suspicion that the good life is coming to an end, that what is happening in Port Talbot will creep along the valleys and plunge them back into their grandfathers' birthright, which was grim economic depression.

Whether or not this exploded the violence at Twickenham, a high temple of British privilege, remains a matter for fiercely polarised conjecture.

THE DANCING GYMNAST

The Olympics were played out in an atmosphere of suspicion and intrigue. They yielded many dramatic stories but, for me, it was an invitation to a late-night party that provided not only a nostalgic reunion with a legend but a sad insight into the pre-perestroika Soviet Union.

MOSCOW: JULY

WHEN she had exhausted the last of her flagging partners as dawn silhouetted the drab high-rises against the Moscow horizon, Mrs Leonid Bartkevich danced on alone.

She has always, of course, been a compulsive performer.

In the tiny seventh-floor apartment, before a small audience of three diplomats, two principals from the Bolshoi Ballet, a leading Soviet heart surgeon and a couple of reporters, she gave us the night club act that no roubles can buy.

To blaring music from the decadent West, there was first a slithering seductive send-up of Salome doing her thing and then a head-tossing, heel-kicking routine of sheer gypsy wildness.

She danced until the blue eye-shadow streaked her cheeks and was crestfallen only when the party was over.

The average Muscovite tends to be worthily dull. But Mrs Bartkevich, a visitor to the city, definitely doesn't hold with dawn bringing down the curtain on happiness.

It was that indefatigable vivacity that made her what she was in a more disciplined field altogether. Mrs Bartkevich is the former Miss Olga Korbut, the tiny bewitching elf who emerged, aged 14, at the 1972 Olympics and inspired a global gymnastics explosion.

There have certainly been greater women gymnasts in history: the austere Larissa Latynina, the serene Vera Caslavska, the ethereal Ludmilla Turischeva. But there has only ever been one Olga, who bounced on, beribboned and saucer-eyed, and simply turned the world's heart inside-out before bouncing out again.

If she infuriated the purists, which she did, they now concede that it was Olga who sold the gospel to an entire generation of sprites. Statistics confirm it. Before Olga there were 50,000 child gymnasts in Britain. There are now three million.

Multiply that by her impact on the world and it is probably quite reasonable to claim that no athlete in history has done more to propagate any sport.

Amazingly, it had never occurred to Olga herself.

Retired by two years, elevated to the title of Honoured Master of Soviet Sport but restricted now from travelling to the West, she said: 'I've never thought about it. If that is so, it makes me very happy.'

It was the guarded, party-line reply, but Olga — still only 22 but with the eyes of a woman of 40 — is well aware that had she been born in the West she could have turned her act into a travelling road show and now be a multi-millionairess.

What business entrepreneurs achieved for Sonja Henie and John Curry, after their skating successes at the Olympics, they could certainly have attained for Olga.

It was not to be.

Instead of a house with a swimming pool, two Cadillacs, an English butler and regular film contracts in California, Mrs Bartkevich has a three-roomed apartment in Minsk, a three-year old car which she is hoping to trade in fairly soon, one husband who is trying to change his job, a 15-month old son whom she adores to distraction and all the other problems familiar to 22- year-old housewives trying to make ends meet.

Rebellious to the end of her career, she married Leonid, a member of Russia's nearest equivalent to a Western pop group. Leonid promptly quit and is now trying to set up on his own with Olga in the act — a courageous ambition in a country where private enterprise is not exactly encouraged.

In a brief respite from dancing, standing drink in hand in a corridor where she could almost hear herself speak, Olga loyally explained that by Soviet standards she is pretty well-off. 'The kitchen,' she kept repeating, 'is 'very, very big.'

She recalled our first meeting eight years ago, outside the Soviet Olympic team headquarters in Munich. She was famous then by only 24 hours, and I had attempted to interview her in execrable Russian, failing to understand a single word she said in reply.

'You gave me scent,' she said. And so I had, a tiny bottle which she almost snatched and popped down the front of her shirt before it could be spotted by the large lady chaperone hovering in close attendance.

No-one hovers in attendance any more. Olga Bartkevich, née Korbut, has been summoned here to Moscow as a world-famous face at the Olympics. She undoubtedly enjoys certain privileges, but they do not extend to her husband accompanying her here by official invitation.

He is back home in Minsk minding their baby.

Olga has no particular ambition, she suddenly announced, to encourage her son to take up gymnastics.

It was an extraordinary remark from a woman whose example had launched millions of other people's children on to the beam. She said it with a look which I shall not forget.

It said more than all the words I have written here with considerable circumspection.

It may even have said that under the Soviet system you are as useful as your last gold medal. But, on the other hand, maybe she just wanted to dance again.

FINAL WORD

The night before John Arlott retired from cricket commentating I dined and stayed with him at his then home in Hampshire. He was quite emotional. Next day the old master showed us all how it should be done.

LORD'S: SEPTEMBER

FOR a man whose glorious imagery enthralled three decades of cricket listeners, John Arlott's valedictory sentence on Test match cricket was prosaic to the point of historic understatement.

There were no goodbyes, and no emotion tinged the deep rural voice that epitomised not only his game but the very English way of life.

All he said was: 'and now, after comment by Trevor Bailey, it will be Christopher Martin-Jenkins.' To the last the poet in him was ruled by sheer professionalism.

It was, of course, a desperately emotional moment, for Arlott has described every Test match played in England since the war, not to mention plenty overseas, to audiences who regarded him not only as a sports commentator but a national institution.

In the next few minutes he was to understand, at last, the esteem in which he has for so long been held. Behind him, in the tiny soundproof box high in the Lord's pavilion, his fellow commentators broke into spontaneous applause.

At the end of the over, Test cricket itself stood motionless in tribute. A loudspeaker announcement informed the crowd and cast of the Centenary Test that the great man had just uttered his last broadcast word on the international game.

The Australians were in the field. They turned to the pavilion and applauded. So did Geoffrey Boycott, an English batsman usually dedicated to turning a cold back on all distraction. And so did the crowd, for down the years, in sitting rooms and motor-cars and in dressing gowns on cold mornings, while listening to his voice home in from Sydney or Melbourne, they have hung on to his syllables, marvelling at the similes and metaphors, the humour and the humanity that he could manifest over a simple ball game.

As if to honour him, even the cruel summer relented on his final day. Lord's, the greatest ground of all, was bathed in sunshine as he came down the dark stairs from the pavilion and walked up six more flights of stairs to the press box bar.

'A glass of Beaujolais, I think,' he said and grinned. Mr. Arlott, purely in his other professional capacity as wine correspondent of The Guardian of course, has never been averse to a drink.

My fondest memory of his whole career, in fact, was of a single sentence he spoke in a hotel lounge in Cambridge in circumstances far removed from covering cricket matches for unseen audiences.

It was at the height of the huge controversy concerning whether or not England's cricketers were morally justified in touring South Africa and Arlott, a firm but restrained spokesman for those who were against it, faced the pro-politicians in a debate at the Cambridge Union.

'They tell me,' said Arlott very quietly, 'that I only have to keep sober to win this one.'

The politicians waved fists clutching sheaves of notes. In due course Arlott rose to speak. He was wearing what appeared to be a sports jacket that had seen its best days on the grouse moors, and into its left pocket he plunged a fist, leaving his right hand to gesticulate occasionally.

He won the day not only with sane persuasion, but a faultless flow of English so beautiful in its construction that you could almost hear the commas and semi-colons fall into place. He sat down to a standing ovation.

Arlott's genius over more than three decades, has been based on that mastery of the English language, allied to a wit epitomised by a pun he produced in his apprentice days at the microphone in 1947.

At Lord's, a crafty South African googly bowler named Tufty Mann was tying a Middlesex tail-end batsman named George Mann into such knots that the crowd was reduced to laughter.

When it occurred for the fourth time in a single over, John Arlott, apparently without a moment's thought, reported: 'So what we are watching here is a clear case of Mann's inhumanity to Mann.'

At 66, he says with a modesty that has never left him, the puns and epigrams are becoming harder in the invention.

The output, both spoken and written, has been prolific, the life harrowed by the two deep personal tragedies of the early death of a wife and a son killed in a road crash. But though still full of words and wisdom, his decision to retire reflects his respect for his profession.

'I wanted retirement to be my choice,' he said, 'not someone else's. Anyway, I've reached the point where I simply don't enjoy talking all day on the radio, writing my piece for The Guardian, driving 240 miles home and then getting up next morning to do it all over again.'

At the end of this month he will move from his rambling home in Alresford, Hampshire with its 10,000 books and autographed first editions of Thomas Hardy, and the personally inscribed early works of his close friend Dylan Thomas and its impressively stocked wine cellar, to the island of Alderney.

'I shall go for long walks and grow vines and stop drinking at lunchtime,' he forecast, without total conviction. 'Mind you, what I'm really up to is trying to extend this marvellous life by another 20 years.'

He will not, of course, stop talking. John Arlott only stops talking when he is writing, and the talk, if you had been privileged to be present at one of his 8 p.m. to 3 a.m. soirees round the bottle-laden refectory table at his home is surprisingly, only occasionally about cricket or John Arlott.

It is of Gladstone and bull fighting, and the adored mother who encouraged him to the local library, and the social development of the English working class, and politics and topography and the thousands of books which have been the constant friends of his life.

'Cricket,' he says 'has only been part of my life. It has never been an obsession.'

That, over the 35 years since his transfer from the BBC's Poetry Department for a trial in the commentary box, has been his ultimate strength.

The man who won a million friends for cricket always realised that war and poverty were reality and cricket, in the end, was only a glorious game and marvellous irrelevance.

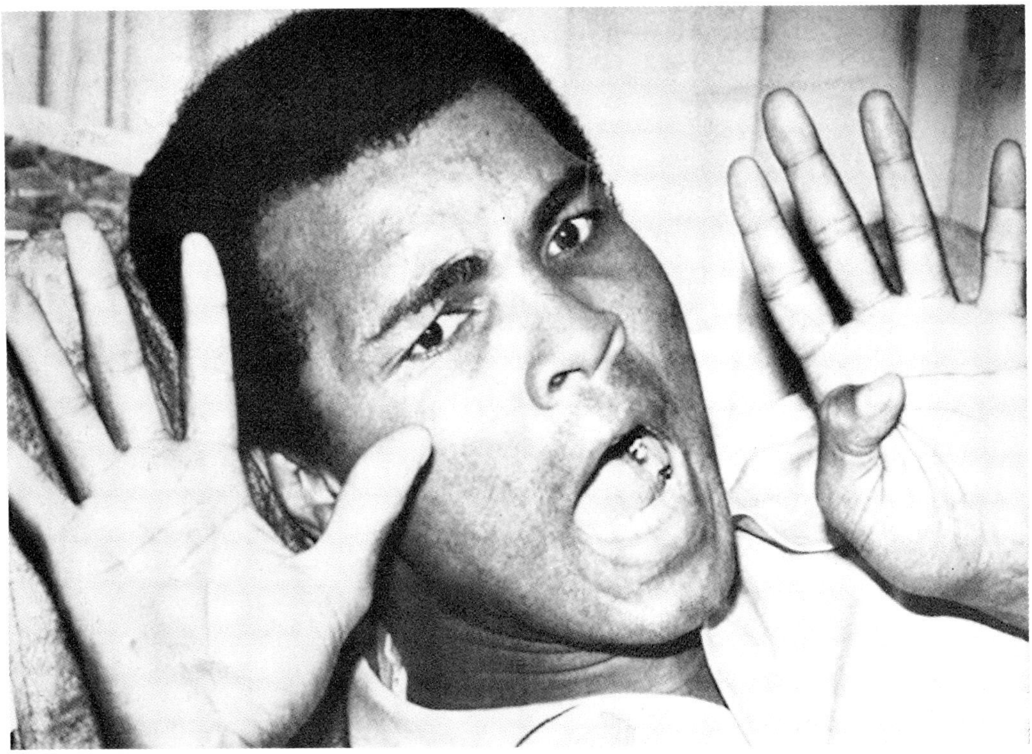

ALI AND THE VEGAS VULTURES

I first saw Muhammad Ali box at the Olympic Games in Rome in 1960. He was then called Cassius Clay. His rise and rise was easily predictable. Tragically, 20 years later, so was his downfall. This column was written on the eve of his fight with Larry Holmes in which, in the last three rounds, he took the most savage beating of his life. He fought on, briefly, to attempt to restore a bank account that had been systematically raided by the vultures who prey upon his game. He should now be a very rich man, basking in international affection. Instead he is a shuffling, frequently incoherent, shadow of a human being.

LAS VEGAS: OCTOBER

THE most legendary sportsman of our life-times will emerge here this evening and walk unwaveringly towards the precipice of self-destruction.

Whether Muhammad Ali can defy the betting odds, defeat Larry Holmes and delay the last chapter of a modern tragedy are now merely academic questions.

If he wins this one, there will be another and another and another until, some night, he is smashed to a pulp and carried feet first from our admiration.

There ought to be a law against it but isn't. The same democracy that allowed him to pile up debts defends his right to pay them as he will. That he is now, in boxing terms, past pensionable age is coincidental.

Whether the executioner is to be Larry

Holmes and the gallows a temporary ring erected in the bizarre environs of a hotel car park will be tomorrow's history. As of now, one can only hope that, if it is to happen here, it will at least be swift. It can't be painless.

Ali, of course, has made fools of us before, but he was younger then. Now, with hair dyed black, he is suffering from delusions of immortality. Here verbatim is what he told an American reporter last week.

'I might fight for three more years, defend the title seven more times, and then, I'll quit. To tell the truth, I'm not from this planet. I've come here from 25 billion light years away as prophet to the world.' It is not Ali's mental stability that is on trial here, or even the integrity of professional boxing. It is the morality of a small group of big businessmen who lured him back from two years of retirement. They are the only guaranteed non-losers.

Indeed, their morality is so questionable that in this gambling capital of the world — the only claim Las Vegas makes for itself which can't be challenged — there is precious little money being speculated on the outcome of the fight.

There is open talk of a 'fix', of some private arrangement by which the whole cast can be re-assembled in the not-too-distant future to stage another 15 million dollar killing.

I do not subscribe to this theory since it implies the compliance of either one fighter or both. For them intense pride as well as money is involved, and neither man, I believe, would enter into a predetermined deal.

The outcome is more likely to be decided by a single factor: the extent to which Ali's body can withstand the horrendous punching of a man nine years younger.

Had they met even four years ago, no boxing buff would have accorded Holmes an earthly chance. But four years is half a lifetime at these mountain peaks of boxing, and Ali's vulnerability has never been so glaring.

Whether Holmes can exploit it may depend as much on his personality as on his unquestioned strength. He fights from an invidious position, that of a former sparring partner against ageing ex-employer, that of prospective destroyer of a legend. Holmes is a nice man but, frankly, none too bright, and his ingenuousness has left him already wounded by Ali's scathing dismissal of him as an artisan privileged to be in the same ring as The Greatest.

Holmes's attempts to compete in the pre-fight ballyhoo have been as embarrassing as those of any introvert suddenly thrust into the limelight. Alone, he is a different man.

His respect for Ali, despite the insults, is genuine. But he is aware of the damage his own power could inflict. He has to steel himself to say: 'Why should I care about Ali when he doesn't care about himself?

'Ali's made more than 50 million dollars from boxing. I've made only 8 million, but I bet you I've got more money than he has now. What do they want from me, to stand there and get hit to pay his debts?'

And that is the crux of it. Our presence here as sports writers has less to do with sport than the complex domestic problems of a supreme athlete whose talent for making money is matched only by his phenomenal capacity for getting rid of it.

'If he had made a go of film acting as he planned to do,' said Barry Frank, the business manager called in to rescue him from bankruptcy, 'none of us would be here today.'

It would have solved his money problems and satisfied his ego. Unfortunately, he found that acting, like boxing, demands great skills that few people have. So here we are, back at the ringside.

If the ring were indoors, the betting odds might be fractionally more flattering to Ali. But it isn't. It is exposed outdoors to the unseasonable heatwave that has gripped Las Vegas for days. Last night, at the hour at which Ali will go into action, the temperature was still in the high 80's.

He will be fighting for the first time since September 1978 and said yesterday: 'I wouldn't be doing this if I thought I was going to lose.'

He's going to lose all right. Not here specifically, but sometime soon. By then, of course, the businessmen will be working on other expendable material.

CHINA'S SPORTING WINDS OF CHANGE

In 1980 China was still the sleeping giant of sport. It may be interesting to compare this column with another written from China in 1987.

CANTON: OCTOBER

ACROSS a battalion of dishes the Vice-Chairman for the Development of Sport among the 67 million inhabitants of China's Guangdong province belatedly attempted to stifle a belch of megaton dimensions.

It was neither successful nor mattered very much.

For the eight courses up to the snake soup and the three that followed, the Vice-Chairman's eating technique had drowned the official speeches and reduced casual conversation to shouting matches with one's immediate neighbours. Even then whole sentences were obliterated by what sounded like deep-silt dredging operations in the Yangtse. The Vice-Chairman is a lady. Equality is mandatory in China.

Sixtyish, built like Oddjob's mother, shovelling food as though she had just stepped in famished from Mao's Long March, she said nothing and ignored all questions.

Our gentle interpreter read my thoughts: 'She is not a sporting person,' he explained. 'She is a Civil Servant.'

They claim here, with justification that sport is awakening in Red China. In universities, specialist coaching centres and academies for the elite and promising, momentous advances, soon to be confirmed by the stop watches and tape measures of the West, are taking place.

Last week, for example, 200 tennis coaches were flown in over distances of up to 3,000 miles to learn from watching Jimmy Connors and 28 other foreign professionals playing in the first Grand Prix event to penetrate the Great Wall.

The previous week China's top gymnasts were competing in, and beaten by, the United States. Next week many of the world's leading athletes will be running in Peking.

Two years ago when I was here with West Bromwich Albion's footballers on their trail-blazing tour, you wondered whether it could ever happen. Well, it has but for all the wrong motives.

The Communist mania for using sport as a weapon of propaganda has gripped China just as back in the 1950s it consumed the Soviet Union and in the 1960s saw East Germany's phenomenal rise in the world's arenas.

We are all, through sport, as familiar now with the Russian and East German national anthems as we are with Greensleeves. But the exercise, of course, has been quite self-defeating. Having revisited all three countries in the past seven months, I can only report that nothing has changed. No one of sound mind would willingly live in any of them.

China, with its charm and self-deprecating humour, its deliverance from 50 centuries of maniac warlords and dynastic slaughters and Western opium traders, would I thought, be too old in the intellect to fall for the fallacy. But its politicians have.

The way you find out is very simple. You hire a car on a Sunday morning and drive out to the parks and playgrounds of an intensely populated city. Sunday here may have less religious significance than it does in the West but it is still a day of rest and relaxation.

I was fascinated to learn what Oddjob's mum, between mouthfuls, was doing for the locals in her capacity as Vice- Chairman for the development of sports around here. The answer was not very much.

Fewer people were playing anything in the whole of Canton than you will see any Sunday on Hackney Marshes or the open spaces of Manchester.

In one natural arena, 15 youths kicked a football around. The pitch was bare red earth, fringed at the corners with long grass. There

was no supervision.

The football pitch was surrounded by what once had been a hard surface six-lane running track. Some of the track lines were still visible between the weeds of disuse. There were seven high-rise apartment buildings in the immediate vicinity.

Each morning most of Canton's citizens perform their Mao instigated callisthenics before riding to work on bikes. They are lean and in little need of the Sport for All campaign of the fat, over-caloried cholesteroled West. It is just as well since there appeared to be no organised sport for anyone, let alone the young.

Afterwards I would have liked to ask Guangdong province's Vice-Chairman for sports development about all this but she was unavailable, probably eating.

When West Bromwich Albion were here China's stadiums were festooned with banners proclaiming the defensive slogan 'Friendship First. Competition Second.' They have all disappeared, as has the sentiment.

At the top, China's athletes are under training to take on the world. At rice-roots level, outside the ping-pong parlours, very little seems to be happening.

Peking has called for gold medals, just as Moscow and East Berlin did. Sport for fun remains the prerogative of the decadent West.

BRAKING AT BRANDS HATCH

One appears to have been still mildly hyped-up when one wrote this piece about one's first and only personal experience on the extreme periphery of motor racing.

BRANDS HATCH: NOVEMBER

IN FUTURE I shall leave it to the chauffeur, but just once in your life it is good for the soul to drive flat out for Paddock Corner on the Brands Hatch motor-racing circuit.

The Grand Prix gladiators do this with panache at around 180 mph, a manoeuvre I shall watch in future with even greater admiration.

At just half that speed, in the wake of James Hunt's fast-disappearing exhaust pipe, it evokes certain emotions all associated with sheer terror.

Suddenly you feel as lonely as a Concorde passenger watching the flight crew die out one by one of bubonic plague. At last you understand how those kamikaze pilots felt on their only mission.

'Don't try and steer the car,' they tell you. 'Just set it up on line and sort of drift through with your foot down.'

For goodness sake. Paddock Corner is a 90 degree right- hander where the ground falls away like Beachy Head and they tell you not to steer.

'Whatever you do,' they say, 'don't try and brake' — and they were dead right about that.

On lap five, with James Hunt now in the rear view mirror on lap six, we touched the brake in an involuntary spasm of vertigo.

The Talbot Sunbeam 1.6 TI instantly asserted a will of its own. Instead of heading up the short straight to the hairpin, it slewed sideways left in the general direction of Folkestone. An innocent family of five suddenly stared in through the nearside windows. They appeared to have reached 'Hallowed be Thy name'.

It was a bad moment, though hardly worse than waiting on the starting grid.

Getting in the cars, a metallic voice emerged from beneath a yellow crash-helmet that enveloped almost all of Mr W. Carson, the eminent jockey.

In essence, Mr Carson was inquiring into the incongruous circumstances that brought us together from many professions, some with car driving talent, others patently with none, on to the hallowed asphalt of one of the great homes of motor sport. In fact, Willie managed to condense that into seven succinct words which said it all and more.

There was the world backgammon champion. There was a disc jockey. There was an accountant.

There was also Miss Jean Rook, the columnist celebrated for her vitriolic attacks on such pre-eminent international personages as Amy Carter and Prince Philip.

Alongside me on the dunces' row of the grid, Miss Rook's famous jaw was set firm and her knuckles glowed incandescent white on the steering wheel. She looked as though she had just heard of the death of the Daily Express.

'I'm scared, lovey,' said Miss Rook, who normally drives an automatic transmission Rover 3.5 in a fur coat. 'Darling,' I said, using an endearment rarely directed at Miss Rook outside her own drawing room, 'I'm petrified.'

They advise you to get up to 5,000 revs on the starting grid and then let the clutch in fast. This catapults you towards Paddock Corner. Amazingly, Miss Rook and I both accomplished this and were still congratulating ourselves when we were suddenly enveloped by what seemed like a reconstruction of the Zero attack on Pearl Harbour.

Cars roared past on either flank. These were the Hunt brothers overtaking.

Amazing family, the Hunts. Apart from James, the only millionaire world champion who looks as though he's tailored by Oxfam, they are disarmingly studious looking men in spectacles.

In car 20 was Peter Hunt, a softly spoken accountant who only the previous weekend had run the 26 miles 385 yards of the New York marathon in 3hr 2min. In car 17 was David Hunt, aged 20, who drove one lap only one-tenth of a second slower than James. He also wants to be a Grand Prix driver, but James, who walked away alive, won't encourage him.

In the stands, fuming that he didn't get a drive, was Tim Hunt, last heard of jumping off the Clifton Suspension and Golden Gate bridges at the end of a strong piece of elastic.

The big snag about motor-racing is that you can't have a treble Scotch when you've never needed one more.

This may or may not have occurred to Mr Reggie Bosanquet when he arrived, secretary-driven in a Mercedes and wearing what appeared to be a pair of Cossack dancing boots, to announce that, in view of the new responsibilities invested in him as a candidate for the rectorship of Glasgow University, he had rescinded his decision to drive in the ten-lap race.

This required more strength of character than either Miss Rook or I possessed. We wished him good luck on his perilous climb up three flights of stairs in his new capacity as official starter.

James Hunt won the race by 6.5 seconds, as was to be expected. Happily, one car blew up which left Miss Rook and I to duel all alone at the back in a totally unrelated contest not to come second from last.

We both learned that it's hell at the bottom. Neither of us heard the roar of the crowd. We were too busy trying not to hit them. It was an afternoon of salutary lessons.

1981

1981 was a beautiful year. The odd years in sport so often are. It is the even years, with the Olympic Games or World Cup or Commonwealth Games, that attract the political blackmailers with their flat-toned dogma or the hooligans, a species that proliferated so malignantly through the decade that they left not only a trail of disillusion but dead bodies as well. But 1981 always seemed to be fun. It was the year of the birth of the London Marathon, which has since grown to be the biggest event of its kind in the world. At the front it may be a deadly serious sport. At the rear it remains an accessible challenge. A friend of mine, who would not wish to be named, ran in it. He had not long recovered from cancer and raised sufficient money through personal sponsorship to buy a scanning unit for a major London hospital. Many thousands have run similarly since: collecting fortunes for the less fortunate. Their names remain unknown to the world.

A LONG WAY TO LORD'S

The England cricket team flying out to West Indies included Roland Butcher, the Middlesex batsman. For a lovely lady in Barbados it was just reward.

BARBADOS: JANUARY

FAR from the fashionable beaches, on a headland with a toy-town lighthouse and a pink evangelical chapel and cottonwood trees that lean on their elbows under the trade winds and occasional hurricane, Mrs Marie Stuart heard the news on a crackling bulletin from the BBC World Service in London.

'I was joyous and I did cry and laugh at the same time and I thanked the kind Lord for being so good to an old lady,' she recalled in precisely those arresting half-Biblical phrases.

The idiom, part Devon-burred, part missionary-inspired, part Deep South in its syncopation, is pure plantation Barbadian and impossible to sustain in an English newspaper column.

But here, before I abandon it for good, is exactly what Marie Stuart went on to say about the one of her 19 grandchildren, a descendant as she herself is of the 20,000 African slaves shipped in during the 17th century to work the cane fields, who at last has brought celebrity to her family and the 184-soul East Point community where most ladies still carry the shopping on their heads:

'I taught he right,' said Mrs Stuart. 'I taught he that we'm all God's children, black and white. I taught he never to be disrespectful to nobody and then the Good Lord's blessings will shine on you.'

Last September they shone on her grandson, Roland Orlando Butcher, who was born 27 years ago in Mrs Stuart's Wendy House-sized cottage in the sloping pasture just down from the lighthouse. The fulfilment comes on Thursday when he flies back to the Caribbean with the unique status of being the first West Indian-born cricketer ever to be chosen to tour with an England team. And Mrs Stuart's pride, understandably, is sheer joy to witness.

If Butcher's success owes much to a hard six-year apprenticeship with Middlesex County Cricket Club, the strength of character that forced him on owes even more to the grandmother who alone schooled him in the simple humanities, table manners and the Ten Commandments between the ages of 2 and 13.

When Butcher was two his carpenter father carpet-bagged it to London in search of work.

When he was four his housemaid mother joined her husband in England. It left Grandma Marie Stuart in sole charge of the tiny boy who has grown into England's newest batsman.

During those critical formative years Butcher was, according to his gently prejudiced grandmother, 'a sweet, sweet boy who only came home from school in tears once. That was when they left him out of the school cricket team. Well, I went down to his master and said: "Why am you leaving our little boy out when you know he loves cricket?" So they picked him and he done real well.'

A determined sporting matriarch, Mrs Marie Stuart is a gracious, ebullient, affectionate lady as well who greets totally unknown reporters from London not with a boring sterile old handshake but a huge enveloping embrace and warm involuntary kisses on both cheeks.

East Point, in the parish of St Philip, does not have much to contribute to the Barbadian gross national product but such as it has is there for the visitor.

Marie Stuart instantly flew out of her back door and returned with a whole harvest festival of gifts: a huge pumpkin, tropical vegetables, a bowlful of eggs snatched from a flurry of indignant hens.

She dismissed our protests. 'You must,' she cried. 'Everybody was so kind to me when I was in London. White people and black people was all friendly and nice and nobody shouted at me in the streets like I'd been told they would. You are such good people for all that cold weather.' Mrs Stuart's brief visit had been to attend Roland's marriage to a West Indian girl in Stevenage.

She rushed into the tiny living room to produce the wedding pictures. They looked less like a nuptual group than some Martin Luther King memorial rally, but Mrs Stuart named nearly everyone, pointing them out with a gnarled, prominently-veined hand that still tends 13 sheep, nine black-belly goats, several squadrons of chicken, a large vegetable patch and profusions of tropical flowers.

She is 74 and doesn't have a single grey hair on her head. She looked gorgeous in the slim blue dress specially bought to be photographed in for the Barbadian newspaper that has just nominated her the island's Woman of the Week.

Alongside the shining, tiny living room with its mural of Buckingham Palace, Piccadilly Circus and a particularly harrowing Crucifixion, was the even tinier bedroom in which Roland Butcher had grown strong on the way to the age of 13 and his eventual departure to join his parents in London.

Outside was the pink telephone on which Roland had rung from Britain to confirm the news she had heard of his selection for England on the BBC. 'He telephoned me right away because he's a good boy and he's never changed even though he's now got famous in England,' she said. 'When he came back to Barbados last year he came out on the bus from Bridgetown and stayed in his old bedroom.'

Across two canefields there were goats tethered at backward shortleg and in the covers of the St Catherine ground where Butcher really came to prominence. It is a million miles from the piercing cacophony in which England are shortly to meet the ferocity of a West Indies pace attack powered by huge physical strength and fuelled by intense patriotism.

It is a patriotism Roland Butcher can no longer share. His allegiance is now to an England where he has a home, wife and son in Fulham. It is a patriotism, too, which has put his grandmother into something of a quandary.

She will catch the half-hourly bus on the 7p journey down the coast to Bridgetown's towering Test match ground and there watch her grandson playing for England. Well versed in the knowledge that the meek shall inherit the Earth, she will, she says, 'sit there just watchin' Roland make all them runs without cheerin' nor clappin' for no one.'

There is neither road nor even path to her cottage. She stood there, nuzzled by goats and sheep, in her field and waved until we disappeared over the horizon. The kind Lord had done a fine job.

MARTINI MARATHON

Christopher Brasher and John Disley invented the London Marathon. "Why don't you run in it?" invited Chris before the inaugural event. One replied that if he required publicity that badly, he'd better accept my way of getting from Greenwich to Westminster Bridge. A few days before the event, being Brasher, he did.

LONDON: MARCH

FOR the gruelling 26-mile 385-yard ordeal that lay ahead of us, Mr Christopher Brasher, the famous advocate of running-for-health, primed himself with two swift glasses of Mumm '74, lit the first of his 30 cigarettes of the day and inhaled like a man who'd only just grabbed the life-support system with seconds to spare.

'Go', he shouted beneath the statue of General Wolfe still staring at Canada. And we were off.

The Rolls Corniche moved noiselessly over the starting line. Mr Brasher settled back in the top people's upholstery and toyed with a little smoked salmon. 'We have just left the western hemisphere,' he announced enigmatically 'and are now proceeding to Woolwich.'

In his spectacles, woolly skiing hat and Alpine jump-suit he looked like a super-annuated Noddy but at 52 and 25 years after winning the steeplechase gold medal for Britain at the Melborne Olympics Mr Brasher is still game for anything.

He is shortly, in fact, to achieve what Hitler never managed. On the morning of Sunday, March 29, he will bring the metropolis to a standstill while 7,500 runners, many of them too old to know better, compete in the first London Marathon.

For upwards of five hours — even more if petulant stragglers cut up rough and insist on finishing — streets between the Meridian Line at Greenwich and Buckingham Palace will be successively closed while top athletes, gaunt clerks, crazy columnists, even one waiter who plans to balance a bottle on a tray along the winding length of the route, pass by on their way to fame, notoriety or premature death.

Being less than enthusiastic that the running cult has now spread to London from such neurotic battery-men communities as New York and Tokyo, we asked Mr Brasher to compete in an anti-marathon along the same course.

'Certainly', he replied, stubbing out a cigarette.

Exercising a gentleman's right to rise late, inconvenience the working class at every turn, drop in at Harrods for champagne and smoked salmon, phone our bookmaker and swear at a couple of lorry drivers, we were not more than an hour late linking up with our chauffeur, Mr Ted Law, whose jaws were working like an American baseball pitcher chewing tobacco. He said nothing.

Chris Brasher said a lot. Near the Greenwich start-line, he enthusiastically pointed out the innocent piece of parkland where on March 29 seventy-five portable loos for lady competitors and a 150-foot long one for men runners will probably gain it immortality in the Guinness Book of Records as the world's biggest lavatory. Runners are mad about records.

Our first feeding station, after passing a convenient hospital on the right and cemetery on the left at the two-mile point, was Booty's Bar, Limehouse, a Thames-side hostelry where trade has trebled for no other reason than it stands right next door to the converted warehouse from which Dr David Owen and the other Gangsters plan to save the world.

However, before we could get there, Brasher blew the gaff.

At the six-mile mark, the marathon route swings in a tight right-hand loop round two of our proudest maritime monuments: the imperious Cutty Sark, lately of the tea trade, and Gypsy Moth, which Sir Francis Chichester nursed round the globe. Between them stands a rather ugly domed building which the concentrated marathon runner is unlikely to accord even a second glance.

This, I can inform, would be a disastrous oversight. Erected in 1902 the domed building is the entrance to the little-known Greenwich Tunnel, a 600-yard pedestrian passageway under the Thames, reached either by 97 steps or a leisurely lift, which cuts 12 miles off the marathon route.

I read the bye-laws assiduously and see no legal reason to prevent runners using it on the big day. Brasher, using the lift, got across there in two minutes one second.

The world record marathon time is around two hours nine minutes. I see no reason why after some 2,000 years it should not be lowered by at least an hour.

At Booty's Bar, David Owen's nearby house was forgotten over several large gins when we discovered that the beautifully-spoken, immaculately-suited barman was none other than the son of Allan Hall, celebrated wine critic of Now! magazine.

Revived by Mr Hall Junior, we continued along the marathon route to this sort of grey building with moats and drawbridges and turrets and that. 'Ullo', we said, 'is this the Tower Hotel?'

'It is not', replied a gentleman who looked as though he would willingly conduct another beheading, 'the hotel is next door.'

Despite our lateness Mr Kenneth Hassall gave us the only window table which will overlook both the upper and lower routes of the marathon runners as they wind twice past his premises.

He also provided large dry martinis, some Burgundy, immense quantities of a Loire product and sufficient Grand Marnier to induce Mr Brasher to concede that whereas, so far, we had scrupulously followed the marathon route, a couple of deviations were in order.

So we directed the Rolls off the Embankment and spurted up to Mount Street where Mr Brasher's apparel and a two-hour 34.25 second lunch induced us to discuss with Mr Douglas Hayward, the tailor who dresses Michael Parkinson and other royalty, the chances of negotiating a mortgage on a suit.

Mr Hayward produced a bottle of chilled sherry and Mr Willis Hall, the famous Socialist playwright, and wished us well.

Definitely in the mood now we dropped off at Jack Barclay's place in Berkeley Square to trade in our modest Rolls for a coachbuilt Phantom 6 Landaulette which since they only build one every 15 months, costs £195,000.

We were plied with Scotch whisky in the panelled boardroom, ordered one each and were then driven to the finish line just short of Buckingham Palace.

It was rush-hour. We drank a celebration bottle of champagne and calculated our elapsed marathon time at eight hours 23 minutes, only 6 hours 14 outside the world record.

At a tactical debriefing in a Fleet Street ops room called Scribes, Mr Brasher, over the third reviving large gin and tonic, said that while he still believes running to be good for body and soul he did not think a man should become fanatical about it.

At this point he lowered his glass, threw his Alpine jacket on to a chair and took off to run the 11 miles home.

It is hard not to wish him a successful London Marathon. It was men like Brasher who won machine-gun outposts and half-continents single-handed.

THE BIG RACE MYSTERY

The 1981 Varsity Boat Race became a sensation when Oxford chose a woman cox. At enormous expense, America's CBS Television sent a vast team to cover the tumultuous occasion.

LONDON: APRIL

WITH a show of the drive that made America great Mr John Faratzis briefed his ace cameramen and sound recordists in the tones of General Patton psyching-up his infantry for a dawn assault on the Rhine.

'Okay, lessgo', cried Mr Faratzis and on the stroke of nine his CBS Television assault team, a kind of SAS of the arts, accelerated their crew cars south and west across quaint old London to film the thronging millions gathering for the start of the quaint old 127th University Boat Race.

The approach roads were dismayingly clear, Putney Bridge was deserted. The massing audience in front of the Tideway boat houses comprised three Special Constables, two boatmen and a rosette seller heavily wrapped against the bitter north-east wind.

'Crikey!' exclaimed Mr Faratzis, mocking an anglicism that had intrigued him during a fortnight's preliminary filming with the Oxford and Cambridge crews, 'where is everybody?'

At 10 o'clock the crowd almost doubled with the arrival of Mr Harry Carpenter, the BBC's distinguished commentator, who was carrying a clipboard and reminding himself that Magdalen is Maudlin and Caius is what you open doors with.

There were other palpably anxious TV crews from Italy, Germany and France, all of them equally lured by the unthinkable presence after one and a half centuries of a woman in the stern of the Oxford boat.

Eventually, Susan Brown arrived, looking very small, pale and nervous. Two people cheered. Mr Faratzis brightened visibly at the first evidence of British animation. 'If it moves, film it,' he commanded.

Just before midday, still rubbing sleep from their eyes, the great British public strolled

down to the winding Thames towpath in their twos and threes for a fleeting glimpse of two tiny shells flashing past in apparent desperate flight from a flotilla of gunboats.

At Mortlake, whence he had now moved his frozen cameramen in pursuit of clamourous crowd scenes and a dramatic blade-to-blade finish, Mr Fratzis cried: 'This is it', in the manner of the director who filmed the chariot race in Ben Hur.

Eventually Oxford came round the final bend. 'Where in chrissakes is Cambridge?' demanded Mr Faratzis reasonably, assuming that both crews rowed simultaneously just as they do in America.

Cambridge University, with a male helmsman, came into view some eight lengths later to elicit sympathetic applause from all but the CBS people who were starting to worry about how they were going to convince American audiences that this had indeed been a race, let alone one of the most historic since the Viking regattas.

'Is it usually like this?' demanded John Faratzis.

'Oh, by no means,' said an Old Blue at the finish, marvelling at Oxford's super row, 'some years it can really be quite boring.'

COMRADES IN TOP HATS

In certain respects Royal Ascot isn't entirely what it's cracked up to be. To make the point, 270 years after its inception, I assumed the identity of a Pravda correspondent reporting the event for his Soviet readership.

ASCOT: JUNE

WHILE the proletariat continued to slave under the satanic yoke of a four-day week plus luncheon vouchers in the northern industrial regions yesterday, others, affecting the dress of 18th century aristocrats, attended a sporting function on open ground some 40 kilometres from London.

At first sight Royal Ascot, for such it is called, is a competition between red-faced 50-year-old men, accompanied by 25-year-old women, to see who can throw the most £20 banknotes over a counter while shouting: 'Five bottles of Mumm and 17 Pimms very cold.'

Everywhere there are notices saying 'cameras forbidden', as in Moscow. The explanation here, however, is that the 50-year-old men are mostly married to 50-year-old women who have been left at home to till the fields.

Every half-hour the 50-year-old men rush away from their 25-year-old secretaries and return a few seconds later tearing up pieces of card in anger saying things like 'Lester got blocked'. This apparently is a reference to a famous cavalry officer called Piggott.

This Piggott is but one of several men who bring horses to run against one another in competition instead of pulling ploughs to improve the grain yield. These horses are called thoroughbreds and bear an amazing resemblance to some of the 25-year-old secretaries.

Unlike football, where the spectators now alleviate the boredom of the occasion by stabbing one another with kitchen knives, you do not just turn up at Royal Ascot and expect to get in.

To get into the Royal Enclosure you have to fill up a form in February giving the full name of your father, however long dead, and promising to turn up in the proper clothes. Only about one person in a million in Britain can now afford to own the proper clothes so the rest go to a place called Mozbroz where you can hire them for about £26 a day.

Practically no one who gets his Ascot clothes from Mozbroz owns braces to keep the trousers up. All over Britain 50-year-old men who are about to take their 25-year-old secretaries to Ascot are shouting to their 50-year-old wives: 'Where are my bloody braces?' To which the answer comes: 'Go and look in the attic.'

Then, all alone, they sneak off to the bathroom to see how they look in a top-hat.

Top-hats are obligatory in the Royal Enclosure. Last worn to keep the rain out by Comrade Gladstone, they are mostly ill-fitting and uncomfortable and used only to take off when the Queen arrives.

Meanwhile some wives and many 25-year-old secretaries who have spent £34 getting their hair done are covering it up with £80 hats decorated with fruit salad or birds' nests and shouting hysterically but with innate perception: 'What a bloody sight I look.'

To avoid traffic congestion most people who live within a 40-kilometre range of Ascot set off at about 5 a.m. This ensures their arrival at the track by 6 a.m.

Starving and nervous by opening time, they repair to hostelries in the vicinity. One immensely popular hostelry is The Hind's Head in Bray, a timbered building much photographed by American capitalist jackals and Third World diplomats spending relief funds on rossignol sauté washed down by Lafitte '26.

This is an error.

Ironically, comrades, when you get to Ascot you find it full of people just like us: salesmen on expense accounts, public relations men on bigger expense accounts, nasty journalists, colonials who will kid their relatives they have met the Queen and jockeys who are simply doing a job.

There is one thing I should warn you about. It concerns the relationship of all these people to their monarch who, while only a woman, commands a respect from her peoples unknown anywhere else in the world. She has merely to appear in an open carriage to set people cheering.

Ascot, in short, is not about sport at all. It is about something that makes men and women dress up to the tens in the sheer pride of being part of a family that exists nowhere else in the world.

Ascot is the only race meeting which could be held without horses. It is an institution, an occasion, a happening, a confirmation of loyalty which none but the British race could understand.

It is enough to make a Pravda man want to defect.

SEVENTH INNINGS SIT-IN

For hours I have sat in hotel bedrooms watching high-performance baseball without understanding it. I adore the subtle ballistics of the pitching and the incomparable throwing. So imagine arriving in America at the height of the season to discover there isn't any.

NEW YORK: JUNE

IT would be wildly inaccurate to claim that the art of good conversation is enjoying a golden renaissance in the bars of New York. But, at least, after decades of Neanderthal grunting and pretzel crunching, people are beginning to string actual words together again in a struggle to form things called sentences.

True they are mostly of a blasphemous and vituperative nature but anyway 'Gimme a bud enuh shat' (literal translation: kindly serve me a Budweiser beer and a measure of scotch whisky') no longer rates as a dazzling example of the American epigram.

The explanation of this struggle for articulacy regained is simple. The television sets over the gin bottles are silent and black.

It is not that the television people have gone on strike. It is that the baseballers have, thus plunging the United States of America into a crisis of a magnitude not easy to convey.

It is far greater than if Wimbledon had been summarily cancelled yesterday. It is rather Spain without wine, Italy without women, Australia without gambling or Germany without work. It is a disaster nowhere more so than in the nation's bars where omnipresent televised baseball rendered human speech redundant as long ago as the Roosevelts.

Yesterday, the 15th day of the blackout, brought no glimmer of an agreement between club owners and players. None of the 650 major league players, who just happen to earn an average £71,873 each season, was budging budging an inch. Nor were the icy-eyed gentlemen who employ them.

Up in Boston Richie Hebner, £170,000-a-year third baseman for the Detroit Tigers, was pictured helping his sexton father dig a grave. Over in Chicago Francisco Barrios, £200,000-a-year pitcher for the White Sox, was less gainfully employed. He was arrested for disorderly conduct in a bar and then hit with charges that may further interrupt his career when two packets of cocaine allegedly were found in his pockets.

The misery doesn't end there. As so often when disaster strikes elsewhere in the world, the shock waves hit the City of London. If the baseball strike goes on it could cost Lloyd's £25 million in insurance pay-outs between now and August 8 when the owners' policy runs out.

Poor Lloyd's. Their track record in sport reads like Ian Botham's in Test captaincy. In the early 60's they had to pay up when America's top golfers kept scoring holes-in-one for prodigious prize money in major tournaments. In 1980 they reportedly paid out £23 million to America's NBC television company when the United States pulled out of the Moscow Olympics.

Paradoxically the best hope Lloyd's have of getting away with the baseball disaster lies with American baseball umpires.

Yesterday, at the very hour that Lloyd's were due to start paying out at a rate that would soak up their one-million pound premium in a matter of minutes, the umpires filed a court injunction there to stop them paying out anything.

'If the baseball owners are getting their money anyway without any baseball happening,' they argued before Judge Stanley Greenberg, 'this strike could go on for ever.' Judge Greenberg thought this was all jolly logical and granted a temporary restraining order which at least stopped the Lutine Bell tolling another sports fiasco for a few hours.

None of which is of remote concern to the American baseball fan who reckons that Lloyd's is what Chrissie Evert married and doesn't give a damn who pays up, provided live baseball returns to the screen, thus ending the kind of cultural starvation that Britain would suffer if Coronation Street went off the air.

Practically no-one without honours degrees in contractual law, restrictive employment practices and advanced business studies has a clear idea of what the strike is about. What, amazingly, it is not about is an immediate demand by the players for more cash.

They are already fantastically paid. What they are now demanding is freedom to move to other clubs where they might be even more fantastically paid without the other club having to swap a star player in return.

In short they want roughly what British soccer players have had since Jimmy Hill won them their freedom. The American owners, may be glancing over their shoulders at the financial insanity of the British transfer system, are having none of it.

My hotel here, which happens to be the venue for daily meetings between rival negotiators, is besieged by reporters swapping unlikely rumours and TV front-men spraying their hair before stepping up to the camera to tell the nation coast-to-coast that nothing is happening in the sort of tones you would expect them to conserve for the outbreak of nuclear war.

Whole subsidiary industries, from hot-dog vending to TV commercial-making, are staggering under the strike but the most visible human misery of all is to be seen in the bars.

It's a whole new non-ball game which demands communication between people by a forgotten medium called human speech.

MINISTER OF SPORT

Throughout Europe it had become the rage for governments to appoint a Minister of Sport. An abruptly ended interview in Paris suggested that France could do worse than think again.

PARIS: SEPTEMBER

AT the risk of sounding less than gallant about Mme Edwige Avice, a French lady of style and conspicuously more than one outstanding physical attribute, I am forced to conclude that she is likely to contribute nothing to the improvement of sport.

Malheureusement, as they say in the 14th arrondissement of Paris which she represents in the new French Socialist government, she gave little impression of understanding her subject. Indeed, she confessed to being shocked by her own appointment, an admission which lends credence to rumours that it was a reward for unswerving loyalty to M Mitterrand during his long years of rejection.

Mistakenly claiming to be the world's first woman sports minister (Canada had an equally attractive one called Iona Campagnolo in 1978), she is nonetheless the current rage of France, being much pictured in the glossy photo-magazines wearing parachute harness and the triumphant beam of a fearless adventuress who has just hit earth after a baptismal fall from outer space.

Equally unfortunately, the photo is a phoney since Mme Avice, quite understandably, has yet to jump out of an aeroplane. She just happened to be wearing a parachute in case the wings fell off the glider she was travelling in at the time.

This emerged only after some heavy questioning about emotions engendered by falling thousands of feet when you have just made it to the top and led me to suspect that this celebrated champion of feminine equality is not averse to any old kind of publicity.

Not only that. The lady, despite a vast education, years of slogging advancement in M Mitterrand's research department and a 7 a.m. till 9 p.m. working capacity, is ingenuous to the point of not even pretending to have more than an academic interest in sport.

All this may appear to be a quite unprovoked and rather nasty assault on a wholly innocent woman with admirable ambition, a fine brain and the looks of a Francoise Sagan heroine.

It is nothing of the kind.

It is a weary sign of despair that yet another European Sports Minister will arrive at yet another European Sports Ministers' Conference at yet another congenial seaside resort with yet more advisers travelling on yet more taxpayers' money next year, to talk either nonsense or nothing about such desperate issues as proliferating hooliganism, political subversion in sport and tax evasion by the new professionals on a criminal scale.

Such views as Mme Avice imparted in her office under the noonday shadow of the Eiffel Tower amounted to platitudes of monumental ordinariness. She deplored the use of anabolic steroids and was very pleased with the flash of inspiration which produced the epigram: 'What is the good of high-fashion clothes if you don't have a healthy body to hang them on?'

At 36, with a husband, no children, rampant political ambition and the ear of M Mitterand, she is undoubtedly an engaging lady but under the gentlest of cross-examination her knowledge of many of the sporting subjects for which she is now responsible to a massive Republic remained lamentably naïve.

Asked to choose a sportsperson who epitomised the exemplary characteristics of sportsmanship she not only named a slightly-known French pole-vaulter but actually produced him. A member of her research staff, he came in and lit a cigarette.

Such views as she may hold about the now global crisis caused by the apartheid issue in sport must perforce, I fear, wait until some future interview. If any. Mid-question Mme Edwige Avice snatched up her handbag from her huge desk and fled.

POTTING WHITE

Early in the decade the snooker boom was at its height. But how could its stars cope with the great outdoors?

WENTWORTH: OCTOBER

BLINKING owlishly in the horrid sunlight of another perfect autumn day, Mr Alex 'Hurricane' Higgins arrived in time, but only just.

To be fair it was still only 10.53 a.m. and Mr Higgin's metabolism, geared to licensing hours, a cumulus of cigarette smoke and artifical light was in a state of considerable shock.

'Good *morning*', stressed his friend John Spencer. Mr Higgins silenced the awful rumour with a baleful glare from a face bearing uncanny resemblance to his dawn-vacated bed.

Giving every indication of having dressed hurriedly in a wind tunnel, the controversial Ulsterman, victim of a hundred headlines alleging non-conformist behaviour in public places, appeared to be rummaging around for his cue and small cubes of blue chalk.

'Its golf, not snooker', reminded Spencer. Mr Higgins brightened instantly. A quickening pulse brought colour to his cheeks.

The venue was appropriate. Wentworth's Burma Road, so named because if you hook or slice from its lawn-like fairways you are liable to stumble into a Japanese machine-gun nest still waiting for the war to end, is a course for champions.

It was here two weeks ago that Severiano Ballesteros made golf look child's play in the World Match Play Championship. It was here the Daily Mail brought together Higgins, Steve Davis, Cliff Thorburn, Ray Reardon, John Spencer and Kirk Stevens to strive to emulate Ballesteros. Five of them too, are world champions. The odd man out, Kirk Stevens, is still only 23 with lots of years to make it.

This week, of course, they are back with us on the box as more familiar faces than the BBC's latest team of news readers. Another 30 hours or so of TV exposure from the State

Express World Team Classic from Reading's Hexagon Theatre, added to their 231 hours, 25 minutes of screen time in the past 15 months, makes them seem like sons and brothers.

It is an image they like and preserve by dressing well, speaking courteously and containing their temper when the black stays out. But could that urbane and charming front, we wondered, survive the Burma Road?

Mercifully, in a number of cases, no microphones were in attendance. We are merely content to record that on a golf course, the giants of snooker are as schizoid as the rest of us.

Financially unrewarded beyond a crate of Mumm champagne for the outright winner, unwatched other than by passing greenkeepers and a clutch of caddies, they revealed unbridled ambition from the moment of arrival.

John Spencer, world champion 1969, 1971 and 1977 screeched to a halt from Radcliffe, near Bolton, in a Mercedes. Ray Reardon, six times world champion, displayed a modest reminder on his licence plates that he is PRO 1. Steve Davis, 24 years old with a golf handicap to match, brought along his manager as befits a current world champion. Kirk Stevens looked menacingly cool. Cliff Thorburn, Canadian and 1980 world champion, wore an exotic sweater and a air of modest confidence. Off handicap six, he was nominally the best golfer in the field.

Only Alex 'Hurricane' Higgins was out of character.

His nickname derives from his habit of running round snooker tables smashing down alternate colours and reds at a speed which suggests that all the world's bars are just about to shut. At golf, which he takes extremely seriously off an 18 handicap, his alter ego takes over.

He hovers, considers, addresses the ball, steps away, changes his club, disturbs small mice and much flora with a series of vicious practice swings, readdresses the ball and after a ritual of shuffles and waggles, eventually strikes it with a swing that reminds you of a lumberjack just about to shout timber.

This is not inappropriate. Fifty per cent of his tee shots scarred tree trunks, drilled small tunnels through bushes, made impressions on the lawns of adjacent desirable residences and even, on one occasion, threatened passing traffic on the A30.

For 17 holes his self-control was exemplary. On the 18th, with the side-bets now making a good approach-shot a matter of urgency, Mr Higgins engaged his caddie in a conversation of a nature rarely heard at Wentworth.

It concerned a matter of club selection, inspired a heated reply from the bag-carrier whose professional integrity had just been questioned and went on for a further 200 yards of expletive-deleted altercation.

'I never asked for a caddie anyway', explained Mr Higgins as he retired to the clubhouse, the Sporting Life, a TV set and a telephone to recover his losses. Later he shaved and set off for an exhibition against Mr Davis in some less well-heeled suburb of Surrey.

It was the only hell that broke out along the Burma Road all day.

If your golf is suspect, the course will eat you and Steve Davis, a devastating snooker opponent, stood not an earthly. John Spencer, off handicap 12, had the technique to play well but didn't rediscover it until his birdie two at the 10th.

Ray Reardon, off 14, has always trained himself to smile in adversity. He smiled in adversity. Kirk Stevens, as nice a man as he appears on the box, finished terrifically with two par fives but by then it was too late.

All that was eventually proved was that in golf, as in any sport or profession, only class or the nearest approximation to class, will tell. Four birdies in the first eight holes put Cliff Thorburn into unassailable dominance. Gary Player and Jack Nicklaus have gone out there and done worse than that, so the fact that Thorburn's adrenalin ran dry thereafter hardly mattered. He finished with 29 Stableford points and immediately poured champagne for his friends.

He is a large friendly man with a parable for the youth of our times: go after it. Aged 16, Thorburn quit golf to spend six years working at snooker. When he had mastered snooker he got his golf handicap down from 24 to 4 in five months.

Incidentally, it is amazing that snooker kings, with a pianist's touch on the cloth, have no more idea than the rest of us when it comes to potting white.

Not that it matters. They have made fortunes convincing the nation that blue equals five. They have wiped soccer out of the TV ratings and actually threaten Coronation Street as the most significant happening in British life.

CONFESSIONS OF A RESIDENT COACH

The 1980's saw the emancipation of the sporting wife. Frances Edmonds, married to Phil Edmonds, the England Test cricketer, was to match her husband's celebrity as author of three witty best-sellers. However, she was actually beaten into the literary field by the wife of a Southampton footballer.

SOUTHAMPTON: NOVEMBER

THE next time Mr Dave Watson, the distinguished England and Southampton central defender, is in possession of the ball in the penalty area, I shall listen intently for a shrill cry from the stands instructing him precisely where to kick it.

This, as I now discover, will not come from either Mr Ron Greenwood or Mr Lawrie McMenemy, who appear to have sufficient confidence in Mr Watson to assume he knows what he's doing, but from Mrs Penny Watson, his wife.

Penny was 16 when she first met 20-year-old Dave in The Beachcomber, Nottingham, but don't run away with the idea that it was love at first sight. Poor old Dave was painfully shy, had been on the dole, was bereft of O-levels and didn't even let on he was a professional footballer. It was a further three months before she granted him their first date.

Wedding bells chimed soon afterwards and in due course, along came Roger, delivered by vacuum extraction in the Kilton Maternity Hospital from which Penny discharged herself after a row.

'Never again,' swore Penny, but happily she relented and produced Heather in time for dinner one evening by the Erna Wright method which assists you in having babies without leaving the house.

Luckily Dave is good with kids. 'No task,' says Penny, with a side-long glance at one of England's great soccer heroes, 'is too menial for him.'

Mind you, being married to a football star is not all caviar and chips and big nights out in The Beachcomber. 'It is not drastically different,' Penny admits to her less fortunate friends back in Miss Tozer's Greek classical and tap-dance studios in Nottingham, 'from being married to anyone else. I still have to do the same dreary things all housewives have to do.'

Nor, I want you to know, girls, is there a lot of loose change to throw about.

'Contrary to public opinion,' warns Penny, 'footballers in general are not highly paid.' This is indeed substantiated by her later frank revelation that while with Manchester City in 1977 Dave was still only paying 83 per cent of his salary in income tax.

How, you will ask by now, do I know all these things?

Well, dear old Penny has written them all down in a book called *My Dear Watson: The*

Story of a Football Marriage. To say it is gripping is the understatement of the literary, let alone the soccer, season. I read it, at a sitting, mesmerised.

Would you ever have guessed, for example, that prudish, Victorian Tommy Docherty, when manager of Rotherham United, banned his players from sex after the Wednesday before a Saturday game?

Can you imagine that on returning from a spell in Germany poor Penny had to put her dog, Tina, into anti-rabies quarantine just like anyone else?

Would you believe it possible that on a soccer tour of the Far East a host club actually lined up an array of available ladies in case any of the visiting England players absent-mindedly felt like a spot of adultery?

Anthropologists 200 years hence, not to mention a few soccer wives right now, will be as grateful as we all are for Penny's truly original research.

There would appear no question that without Penny behind him, England's towering centre-half would not be half the man he is. Indeed, Penny herself is reluctantly forced to admit: 'Many people who know both of us say that if Dave had not married me he probably would not have become so successful. It is true he did need a push in the early days in almost everything he did, and I had to coax him quite a lot.'

Fortunately, Penny had diagnosed it right back there in The Beachcomber. 'The fact that he was born under the star Libra has, no doubt, something to do with his incessant procrastination and indecision.'

As early as page 18 Dave is diligently writing a transfer request 'after a little persuasion' from Penny. By page 22 he is doing it again. 'Even though we were happy with our life at that time I once again persuaded Dave to think about furthering his career.'

Dave's career was immediately furthered by a move to Sunderland where, after an unfortunate stay in the home of the manager — 'Mrs Brown, on her own admission, was not the world's best cook' — Penny joined Dave.

Unlike their previous home, a bungalow with 'paper thin walls and of poor building quality', Sunderland, sited as it unquestionably is in the north-east, was plagued by 'a perpetual cold breeze.'

This was nothing, however, compared with the ice-blast rejection she met from a bunch of false-eyelashed, painted harridans who turn out to be the wives of the other Sunderland players. This, combined with Penny's commendable struggle to understand the accents of the local shop assistants, may in some way have precipitated Dave Watson's transfer to Manchester City.

With Manchester City, as with Sunderland, Dave went to Wembley.

By coincidence, Penny stayed in the same London hotel which was not as good as she had remembered it. Also the reception after the game was 'to be frank, not up to much. I had expected much better from a club like Manchester City.'

In a chapter entitled 'Stormy Passage' Penny — luggage still at Heathrow, no welcoming committee to greet her at the airport, home not ready, children inhibited by having to stay in an hotel — recounts joining her husband for his brief playing career in Bremen.

This, I fear, was not a happy episode and, together with her description of some Scots and all Italians, brings an inspiring xenophobia to her prose.

Repatriated to Southampton on Hallowe'en Night, 1979, poor Penny 'cried tears of frustration, anger and tiredness' at arriving at a house which was 'absolutely filthy, with dirt and cobwebs hanging in every room.'

David Watson, meanwhile, was quite unreasonably required to go north to attempt to stop Manchester United scoring goals against Southampton. Penny was left behind 'cursing football.' She called in some industrial cleaners.

For sheer powerful descriptive writing, however, none of the foregoing begins to match Penny's total recall of Dave's nine days of bowel inactivity after refusing an enema.

Her extraordinary book, I must confess, did not have the same effect on me.

1982

1982 encompassed the World Soccer Cup in Spain, the Commonwealth Games in Australia and, after cloak-and-contract planning of le Carré dimensions, the rebel English cricket tour to South Africa which led to the international suspension of Graham Gooch and others. I have still to discover why I was held for seven hours at Johannesburg airport when arriving to cover the latter. South African cricket had made heroic strides toward multi-racialism but that most wretched of words, apartheid, still stained the constitutional statute book and was to remain there to shame its proponents and, by its repercussions, curse international sport throughout another entire decade. A year which began in the snow of the Austrian Alps ended for my wife and I with a 6,000-mile drive through the heat and dust of the Australian Outback where, among some of the most resilient people on earth, we were to make friendships that will last a lifetime.

A NATION'S LAST HOPE

The most dare-devil feat I have yet witnessed in sport was Franz Klammer's near suicidal descent at the 1976 Winter Olympics. In 1982 he was back on vertiginous home territory again at the World Ski Championships. Lightning did not strike twice.

SCHLADMING: FEBRUARY

MOOSWALD is Austria's answer to Nether Compton in Dorset. There is nothing to do there apart from milk cows, pick gentians and yodel for help. No one, even in Austria, would ever have heard of Mooswald but for one fortuitous happening: Franz Klammer was born to a farmer's wife there just before Christmas 1953.

Today, 28 years later, it is some kind of shrine and Klammer is slightly more important that Austria's president, parliament and armed services combined. He will be skiing to save his country's face at the one thing they always believed they had a head start on the world.

Austria, swept off their own backyard mountains here this past week by whooping Canadians and noisy Americans in the World Championships, have several men who could do it. There is Leonhard Stock, 23. There is Erwin Resch, 21. But above all there is Klammer.

'I ski,' says Klammer, clearly having read too many magazine profiles about himself, 'on the edges of fear.'

For all that, he remains a frank, open-faced farmer's boy, unspoiled by the enormous money he has made as an amateur.

Why Austria looks to him today is because his track record of calculated recklessness is probably without parallel outside the bullring or the Grand Prix circuit.

His most famous Houdini act on behalf of Austria was at the 1976 Winter Olympics in Innsbruck. Drawn 15th of the 15 seeded runners in the downhill his negligible chance bordered on the impossible when Bernard Russi went down second in a time so fast it was assumed the electronic timing device had fused.

Klammer, still at the top, turned to his coach, Tony Sailer, and said: 'What have I got to do?'

Sailer's reply matched Nelson's. 'Kill yourself,' he said.

Klammer lived and won. I watched it and will never forget it. Experts say it was the greatest ski descent ever seen. It is what Austria is looking for from Klammer today.

It will be a tremendous challenge even for a man of Klammer's courage, for he gave himself a headache and hurt a rib and foot in a training spill yesterday.

Innsbruck was a measure of the ferocity, let alone the technique, that Britain's Konrad Bartelski will be up against when he goes into the starting gate. He is very good. He is by so far the best that Britain has ever produced that I must repeat what I wrote before this race was postponed by bad weather six days ago: 'If he finishes 15th he will have done superbly well. If he finishes eighth it will be memorable. If he finishes one, two or three don't expect me home for a week.'

Merely to have a British contestant mentioned in anything more than minute print in an Austrian newspaper is on a par with reading the cricket results in Gothic.

THE OVERSEAS MEMBER

I have never been able to establish whether the following story is accurate. I include it because, if it is, one of its perpetrators may yet come forward to receive the acclaim he deserves.

AUSTRALIA: FEBRUARY

TALES from the Australian outback have room for embellishment by the time they reach the watering holes of Fleet Street but I am assured that the story of how the exclusive Marylebone Cricket Club — waiting list four years at least — recruited its latest member is true.

Last month a London banker and his MCC-member friend played a few club matches in Australia and then decided to hire a car and explore the vast expanses of silent nothingness that lie out there beyond Melbourne and Adelaide.

The vehicle had two unfamiliar steel bars above the front fender. 'These,' explained the car-hire man, 'are to prevent the bonnet being smashed in when those daft kangaroos leap out straight in front of you.'

Some days later with the banker touching 60 mph down a dirt road, a kangaroo seeking nothing more than companionship did precisely that. He was struck by the car and killed instantly.

The MCC member armed with a camera and a public school sense of humour, had a terrific idea. While his banker friend hauled the late mad marsupial to its feet the MCC member pulled his cricket bag from the car and proceeded to knot an MCC tie round it throat, place an MCC cap on its head and drag an MCC blazer over its front legs and shoulders.

The motive, of course, was to take a photograph which would raise a hell of a laugh back at Lord's and, if sufficiently good, even make the centre-page spread in a newspaper like the Daily Mail.

A jubilant thing then happened. The kangaroo, merely heavily stunned and not killed by the impact, shook its thick head a few times, broke from the banker's grasp and raced off.

It shook off the MCC cap but presumably is the only kangaroo now strolling around wearing an MCC tie and blazer. If so it is only poetic justice that the blazer still has the MCC member's passport in the left-hand inside pocket.

I was hoping to prove the veracity of this strange encounter by publishing a photograph. Unfortunately inquiries reveal that the MCC member is now in South Africa on a temporary passport, probably doing terrible things with a rhinoceros.

SPECTRE AT THE FEAST

It was by chance, strolling through the pavilion at Port Elizabeth, that I encountered Mr J.B. Vorster. He seemed less than ecstatic at meeting a British reporter.

PORT ELIZABETH: MARCH

OUTSIDE in the burning sunshine, 18,000 South Africans rose as one man to acclaim the brilliant century with which Graham Gooch at last set the rebel cricket tour ablaze.

Within, slumped in a dark recess of the bar, Johannes Balthazar Vorster did not move. The heavily-jowled face registered nothing more than perspiration. Then he scowled, furious at being recognised at this, of all moments, in the history of a sport he had done so much to destroy.

Vorster, 66-year-old disgraced ex-Prime Minister and President of South Africa — interned in wartime for his pro-Nazi proclivities and now pitched out of public life for complicity in the Muldergate political scandal — sagged in a plastic-covered chair.

The crested tie was slackened at the throat. The face was flushed. The low table in front of him was littered with empty beer bottles.

'Crrrricket?' he said rolling the 'r' with the wretched sound of the educated Afrikaaner speaking English. 'I have seen very little crrrricket in recent years.'

End of interview.

No sentence spoken in sport this decade could give greater ironic undertones.

It was, of course, the same J.B. Vorster, the hard-line apostle of apartheid, the unrelenting Broederbunde who detonated the D'Oliveira Affair, which ended with South Africa being expelled from world cricket and hastened its other sportsmen being barred from almost every major arena in the world.

That was in September 1968.

In the final Test at the Oval, London, Basil D'Oliveira had scored a glittering 158 to guarantee his selection for the England team imminently to tour South Africa. The trouble was that D'Oliveira, though a naturalised Englishman, was born a South African Cape Coloured.

His skin, though no darker than Colin Cowdrey's after two weeks in the sun, was unacceptable. In a passionate speech in Bloemfontein, the heartland of apartheid, Vorster described D'Oliveira as a political cricket ball and roared: 'Guests who have ulterior motives usually find they are not invited.'

In a motorway restaurant on the M1 in England, a mysterious South African big business contact offered D'Oliveira a £48,000 bribe to declare himself unavailable or unfit. He refused.

The England tour to South Africa was abandoned. South Africa's cricket isolation had begun.

No England team was to set foot on a South African Test match ground for the next 14 years. That sentence ended on Saturday when for fees of between £40,000 and £55,000 per man, England's defiant dogs of cricket emerged from their dressing-room to the kind of roar that greets Cup Final teams at Wembley.

Geoffrey Boycott, out to a stupendous catch for only five runs, received an ovation on his return that is usually reserved for a batsman who has made 200. Everyone knows here that Boycott was a major inspiration behind this freelance tour and if he stood for the South African Parliament tomorrow, he'd probably get in. Black Africans, of course, don't have a vote.

After a disastrous opening match in Pretoria, the entire success or failure of this venture probably hinged on what happened here in Port Elizabeth. To the discomfort of Lord's and the certain fury of the cricket authorities in the West Indies, India and Pakistan, I have to report that the one-day international between South Africa and the team blindly regarded here as England was what theatre writers call a smash hit.

More than 18,000 crammed into a ground that holds only 15,000. Half of them were in their seats at 8 a.m., two hours before the start of play. The cricket was scintillating. South Africa won, confirming the enormous talent that has lain fallow down all the years. Above all, Gooch's 114 — 97 of them before lunch — was so fine a piece of purist batting that it may be compared with Tom Graveney at his best. Apart from Dennis Amiss, who struggled for an hour before finding form, the English batting was average county standard for a damp day in Bradford, but at least they set a target of 240 for five off their 50 overs.

Then came Barry Richards and Graeme Pollock, all genius and arrogance, and a newcomer, Jimmy Cook, full of ambition, to knock off the runs for the loss of three wickets with 16 balls remaining.

No script writer could have arranged it better. The match was the opening item in every South African radio and television news and made the front page banner headlines in every South African newspaper.

Johannes Balthazar Vorster, having driven in 30 miles from his home near here, came out from the shadows later to witness the fun. He has the last word in this story.

The taxi I hailed to deliver his photograph for radio transmission to the Daily Mail in London would have been useless had I been Basil D'Oliveira or an Indian with a doctorate in English.

It had a 'whites only' sign on the roof.

SPORT'S DEADLIEST SIDESHOW

Alain Prost was the Grand Prix driver of the Eighties. But he didn't win at Monaco in 1982 and thousands didn't really care about who did.

MONACO: MAY

UNACCUSTOMED as I am to the proximity of enormous wealth, I discovered a new truth about sports watching at the weekend.

It was that a light snack of quail, lobster, wild strawberries and champagne is hardly the best gastronomic preparation to watch a Grand Prix driver hit the fence alongside Monte Carlo harbour in fifth gear at 130 miles per hour.

Alain Prost, of France, made an extremely photogenic job of it. He bounced laterally across the track, crashed into another guard rail, lost a wheel which went spinning away like a hula hoop and took some while to step out of a Formula One racing car reduced in three seconds to a crumpled heap of tin foil.

It is not exactly your heart which comes into your mouth on these occasions as you wait for the flash of flame and plume of smoke. Mercifully, this time, there was neither. Prost hobbled away, losing nothing more than a race which would have been his had he kept going for the remaining three of the 156 miles.

But everywhere there was evidence of the other option.

'Remember Gilles Villeneuve,' proclaimed a chalked valediction on the harbour wall, and how could you forget? Last year's Monaco Grand Prix winner was killed this month.

You glance back through the programme of previous winners and runners-up over the past 15 years and are stunned by a shocking fact. Seven of them, who might have been at home now with teenage children, are dead.

At intervals of 1½ minutes car No. 8, in the garish orange livery of Marlboro-McLaren, flashed past and you could only wonder what desperate financial pressures had dragged Niki Lauda back to this manic every-other-Sunday date with eternity. He got away with it once yet here he was, streaking through chicanes with barely six inch clearance, all over again.

Monaco, the slowest of all Grand Prix circuits, demands that you average only 89 miles per hour round the unreasonable hairpins, squares, escarpments, tunnels and short promenades of a tiny principality which stands straight up out of the Mediterranean. Its streets are so narrow that overtaking is a problem for taxis, let alone Grand Prix cars which have to be held on the ground by aerodynamic devices.

You wonder, as you watch it all from £40 seats — they are £80 each alongside the finishing straight — whether other people feel the same emotions. I suspect they don't. Wealth is a great insulation against the misfortunes of others and this, while less well dressed than Royal Ascot, is abundantly a richer event.

The top people at the Monaco Grand Prix don't merely have private yachts backed up against the harbour. They have yachts with personal helicopters on the stern.

They are here less to see than be seen. Some have their wives, many non-wives with tans to match their ambitions. The Monaco Grand Prix, the annual houseparty of the Grimaldi family, is also a major part of the Monegasque gross national product and may explain why Prince Rainer, despite all the efforts of his actress wife, continues to look like the president of the local Chamber of Commerce.

The lunch party I attended cost £20,000. The bill was paid without a bat of an eyelid because the business contracted over the damask table linen made that look like a teenager's pocket money.

Major hosts in Monte Carlo this year were Rothmans, the cigarette manufacturers. They were slighly embarrassed when Jochen Mass, the German who drives their patriotic red, white and blue car, didn't even qualify for a place on the starting grid.

They produced him at a party under a marquee behind a beautiful house in the country given to celebrate his survival in 100 Grands Prix.

He spoke briefly, apologised for not being in the position to entertain Rothmans' guests on Sunday and backed out of the limelight.

Rothmans, meanwhile, were debating whether the little matter of the £3½ million it will cost them realistically to contest the world Grand Prix championship next summer, is a viable business proposition.

Viable Monaco propositions, being interviewed by television displaying your wealth or latest amorata, hatching deals or even shaking hands with Her Serene Highness Grace Kelly or the soccer-addicted Prince Albert are what the Monaco Grand Prix is principally about.

It is not about the fate which could easily have befallen Alain Prost when he satisfied the blood lust by hitting the fence before an enormous crowd at very high speed.

Grand Prix drivers are accused of being the most trade union-minded of all the world's sporting industrial agitators.

They are, of course, absolutely right. Life is cheap when it belongs to someone else and to drive at Monaco requires a nerve which should be prohibitively expensive.

ALL-AUSSIE ACTION

You have to set aside about a week to enjoy an Australian Rules match but it's a great game as culture shocks go.

MELBOURNE: SEPTEMBER

TO the monumental disinterest of the outside world, Carlton beat Richmond by 103 points to 82 here at the weekend. What a waste. Not that Richmond lost, but that billions won't even recognise the game they were playing.

As indigenous to this country as the kangaroo and Edna Everage, Australian Rules football remains the game that hides its light under a bush fire. And that is a pity.

To see Australian Rules is to witness the ultimate in what some pompous wordsmith once labelled the body-contact sports. To watch its Grand Final is to step straight down from the time machine and into a XIV-dollar seat in the Rome Colosseum.

Actually to be present throughout the 36-hour build-up to the moment when 107,536 Australians stand and sing Waltzing Matilda in the towering edifice of Melbourne Cricket Ground is to go weak at the knees. One lady even died of it on Saturday.

Part rugby, part Gaelic football, with scores like basketball, played over huge tracts of land by men with no protective clothing and faces off wanted-for-murder posters, lasting 100 minutes of relentless aggression and resembling in its heroic climaxes a bare hands assault on the last enemy hillpost, no sport in the world so epitomises the uncompromising character of the nation which invented it to work up a thirst.

It is fair to say, I think, that the life expectancy of the average British soccer player caught up in it might be as long as eight minutes.

If defensive strategy exists, it is hardly noticeable to the newcomer. I had waited 20 years to see my first Rules match and wasn't kept hanging about when it started.

Inside one and a quarter minutes, Carlton had kicked two goals to go 12 points ahead. Inside three minutes, six fist fights had broken out on the field. Prisoners are not taken. Three men were subsequently dragged off, temporarily lifeless, and a fourth was stretchered off with a broken arm. He refused to have it set in hospital until he had seen the end of the game.

What will dismay the research scientists in Britain who relate crowd violence to aggression on the field is this: only six spectators were arrested for unseemly behaviour and one of those was Australia's first streaker, an 18-year-old lady with what are locally known as very large norks.

Far from closing the bars, the management stacked them all from floor to ceiling and flung the doors open, presumably fearing aggressive withdrawal symptoms.

It was particularly gratifying to know that Mr C.G.D. Butler was drinking in one of them, since he is officially listed, on an engraved plaque just outside, as having made the supreme sacrifice somewhere between 1939 and 1945. Charlie Butler thinks it is the funniest thing that has never happened to him, but you have to remember that this is Australia.

Up in Brisbane on Friday, they are going to play a demonstration game of Australian Rules for visitors to the Commonwealth Games. This, I fear, is a waste of time. The simple reason it would never catch on overseas is that it demands a pitch minimally 150 yards by 120. Even an umpire runs at least 12 miles during a match.

Here they can kick divots out of the Melbourne cricket wicket in the certain knowledge that it can be reseeded and rolled into a perfect batting pitch in time for Ian Botham to score 200 on it in the December Test match. You can't do that to Lord's or Trent Bridge.

It was actually Irish soldiers, garrisoned here in the 1850s, who invented the game by default. Unable to fathom the rules and finesse of rugby, they just kicked the ball anywhere and hit whoever caught it. This appealed immensely to Australia's youth, whose job opportunities at the time were largely limited to sheep shearing or robbing banks.

In 1858, they played a 40-a-side match on waste-land behind what is now Melbourne Cricket Ground between goals a mile apart. Now the game is 18-a-side, professional, scientific, highly coached, brilliant, brutal and still parochial.

It also remains very Australian in a remarkable way. Even if you kill an opponent, inadvertently or otherwise, you can't be sent off. You may be requested to attend a disciplinary hearing the following Monday when, in the event of justifiable provocation not being proved, you may suffer the disgrace of a three-match suspension.

This year's Grand Final was titanic, the toughest, they say, for nine years. But the biggest losers of all, as it happens, weren't Richmond. They were the Melbourne ladies who import Tatler, send embossed At Home cards to one another and try, with a corporate lack of success, to speak like the Queen.

For reasons only known to themselves, Melbourne's wealthier ladies suffer from the middle class delusion that they are hostessing the cultural capital of Down Under, an assumption as hilarious as it was cruelly exposed over Grand Final weekend.

This remains the male chauvinist capital of the universe. All week their husbands, who hadn't seen one another for anything up to 48 hours, were holding reunion breakfasts, brunches, lunches and dinners to discuss the respective qualities of the finalists, lay bets and listen to speakers imported from the Sydney nightclub beat.

I attended one of these lunches on the eve of the match. It lasted five hours. Each guest was introduced personally. One happened to be the locally-based manager of Japan Airlines. On hearing this surprising news, the chairman instantly sprang to his feet at the top table.

'Jesus Christ', he yelled. 'Stand up, you little yellow bastard. Who let *you* in? Where in ****** were you 30 years ago?

Actually, the chairman meant 40 but indignation left no time for precise subtraction. In the speeches that followed, in the cultural capital of Down Under, there were more fundamental four-letter words than probably at any other juncture in the history of public oratory.

To restore some semblance of propriety, Mr Harry Vallence, a legendary star of Australian Rules football, now 77, was invited to speak.

He revealed how on the eve of some Grand Final back in the Middle Ages, in which he kicked a record nine goals, he had prepared himself by getting very drunk, seducing one of Melbourne's socialite Rules groupies and falling asleep as early as half past three. 'I was,' explained Mr Vallence, 'very relaxed.'

Grand Final Day dawned chilly and damp. It made no difference. Breakfast and brunch parties were happening all over town. This time wives were permitted to attend before being packed off to the Ladies' Stand. At the one I went to, they served pumpkin soup and burgundy at 10 a.m. The speeches were suitably subdued, being only about adultery, sexual perversion and racism.

Mr Rolf Harris led 107,536 of his countrymen in the singing of Australia's national anthem. He was wearing what appeared to be an Hawaiian beach shirt and stamped his left foot like a weary middle-aged trendy. It was the only un-Australian thing that happened all day.

LOVE THE GREAT HEALER

During the Commonwealth Games I stumbled across a miracle. At the end of the decade, I am happy to say, its beneficiary was as fit as his marvellous wife.

BRISBANE: OCTOBER

THIS is the story of an old friend. It is not for the squeamish. I write it in tribute and gratitude. It is not often you dine with old friends who have come back from the dead.

Neil Hawke was more than a fine fast bowler who took 91 wickets in 27 Test matches for Australia in the 1960s. He epitomised uninhibited Australian manhood. He loved women, horseracing, sport and drink in strictly that order.

He radiated good health, self-confidence and optimism. He was so strong he also played Rules football at the highest level in Australia.

When his Test cricket days were over, he played on for seven years in league cricket in England, three of them with Nelson, four with

East Lancashire in Blackburn. He took up golf, got his handicap down to two and played in the British Amateur Championship.

He married an Australian girl and divorced. He then married an English girl and divorced again. He returned to Australia and fell in love with Beverley, a divorcee with two daughters. They became extremely devoted. Which was just as well.

On the afternoon of July 6, 1980, as they were dressing to go to the races, Neil Hawke was stricken by excruciating abdominal pains. Major surgery served only to expose a hopeless condition.

His body had collapsed. Kidneys, liver and bowel had failed. He was suffering from septicaemia and gangrene. His condition was such that his heart stopped beating on 12 occasions. In a single day 100 pints of blood were transfused into his body, only to pour out again from every orifice.

Doctors quietly advocated that the life support machine should be shut off.

Beverley said no.

For 14 weeks Neil Hawke hallucinated and raged in his semi-waking moments to the point where he had to be strapped to his bed. On October 24 that year he returned to sanity and also pain of such intensity that several times he, too, suggested it would be better for everyone if he quietly died.

Beverley said no. They injected him with carnitine, an Italian drug previously only used on animals. They injected hydrochloric acid directly into the areas of infection. They cut out infected ribs. They blatantly experimented on a man with no chance. In all he underwent 24 major operations.

For 9½ months he was in intensive care. For two years he was on a drip feed. For long periods he couldn't speak. Beverley brought a Scrabble set, pasted the letters on a board and Neil Hawke weakly used a finger to spell out simple messages.

Great cricketers like Sir Gary Sobers, Ian Chappell and Bobby Simpson came to his bedside and were so shocked that more than one left in tears.

Beverley decided he would be more comfortable at home. By now the doctors didn't argue. He went home and a priest arrived at the house and Neil and Beverley were married.

Two months ago the pain disappeared. For no scientific reason open wounds began to heal. His doctors said that what was happening was impossible.

Last weekend Neil Hawke was well enough to be flown from his Adelaide home to Surfers Paradise here in this Australian Costa del Sol. Beverley said Neil deserved the holiday. She had been at his bedside for 826 days out of the previous 827. He can now walk 100 yards unaided and he talked over dinner of a new business career in 1983.

He announced, laughing, that his days of womanising were over. Beverley laughed too and said 'Well, he's still a real man anyway.'

Neil Hawke, now 43, then broached a subject which rarely troubled him in the old days. 'Before one of the major operations a large group of people in Adelaide got together and prayed for me. I have learned that there is a super-human force called God.'

He did not, as they say, go on about it. It was mildly unnerving to be sitting there chronicling the facts of a miracle, New Testament fashion, but his doctors agree that no rational explanation is tenable.

It was good, anyway, to have had dinner with an old friend again.

1983

1983 evokes a vivid memory of an Australian journalist friend remonstrating with a slovenly hotel in Lancashire during the Open Golf Championship at Birkdale. It was extremely hot and the shower bath in his room wasn't working. After repeated requests for assistance had been ignored he went down in the lift, parked himself at the reception desk and announced he wasn't moving until repairs had been effected. Readers should remember the trick. He was stark naked. Elsewhere the first World Athletics Championships in Helsinki, bereft of political interference, reminded us how wonderful the Olympic Games used to be before white statesmen and black blackmailers determined they would use sport as an ideological or racial battlefield. I spent much of the second half of the year commuting to Newport, USA, to watch the unfolding of the greatest sports drama of the year: the storming of the America's Cup.

ON A SWING AND A PRAYER

Down the years I have watched many of the giants tackle the Old Course at the home of golf. On New Year's Day 1983 the scoring was mildly more erratic.

ST. ANDREWS: JANUARY

THE old grey city was still sleeping off its monumental annual bender when Anno Domini 1983 rode in on a pink translucent dawn and a stiff breeze from the west.

For that the Lord be praised, for it meant that there were but seven witnesses to this column's first of many acts of folly in another sporting year. The long history of humiliation on the first tee of the Old Course of the Royal and Ancient Golf Club is rarely as merciful as that.

Back in the 1920s more than 8,000 spectators were in attendance when Edward, Prince of Wales, as yet undistracted by the alluring Wallis Simpson, lashed out blindly and almost missed. The club heel just made contact and the ball trickled three yards back between his legs.

Another 6,000 were present when Earl Haig, lately of the Somme and other military debacles, proved that sport was hardly his metier either. His imperious swing produced a scuffed drive of almost 20 yards.

These noble personages, of course, were attempting to drive themselves in as Captains of the Royal and Ancient, a ceremony that started in 1754 and still daunts the many fine golfers who are called to office.

This column's aspirations were more demotic: merely to be the first of the 5,000 bad golfers who this year will make the pilgrimage at grotesque expense from places like New York and Nagasaki for the privilege of walking the 18 holes of Mecca.

There were a dozen other ways to greet another year of sport: the desperate Test match in Australia, the Round the Houses race in Sao Paulo, a sheep-skinned afternoon subsidising the bookmakers at Catterick or Newbury.

Instead, for reasons that will eventually bear a sponsored message, we chose St. Andrews and were much honoured when Ian Christie, the local postman, defied a bad bout of seasonal indisposition to partner us. 'I have', confessed the seven-handicap Mr. Christie, 'a hangover that would kill a horse.'

But that was his problem. Ours was an unashamed attack of nerves.

It must be worse waiting to bat in Sydney, but, even so, merely to walk down the steps from the austere clubhouse and stand there, engulfed by 229 years of unbroken history in the stud prints of Young Tom Morris and Bobby Jones and the immortal Nicklaus, is an intimidating way to start a year.

It is not at all like hitting off in some show-biz pro-am. On the first tee at the Home of Golf you are overwhelmed by a self-imposed desperation not to desecrate this place. One good drive, God, just short of, over, or even into the Swilcan Burn and I'll try to mend my ways. After prayer comes positive thinking: off an 18 handicap, with 25 years of rough-and-tumble golf behind you, the odds must be that eight times out of ten you'll hit it cleanly.

And then comes a sheerly pagan notion: maybe this shot will be an omen for the year ahead. You consider briefly, a cowardly four iron or even throwing it, but such sacrilege cannot survive the dread that unseen elders of the game are watching from the clubhouse windows.

So you hold your breath and take your driver, just like Arnold Palmer, and halfway up the backswing, commanding yourself to take it slowly and keep your head still, it bursts upon you that have waited half a lifetime to play this shot.

And your mind goes blank. Your brain clouds with octopus ink. Such powers of reason as you've ever had are lost on the wind: the downswing is someone else's altogether, but it's definitely not Palmer's.

You surge with relief at some kind of contact but from the seven witnesses there is no sound. You look up to see the ball scuttling across not much of Scotland and after 80 yards it stops. A new sporting year has started.

It could only improve and it did. Ian Christie felt sufficiently recovered to share the hip flask by the sixth and in the crisp and glorious morning the journey in along the back nine, a wakening St. Andrews shimmering on the skyline, was a badly needed reaffirmation that sport itself has not changed.

A RIGHT ROYAL RACKET

Few devotees of Wimbledon have ever heard of Tennis Lane. To walk down it is to meet the ghosts of British history.

HAMPTON COURT: MARCH

EXACTLY 447 years after a somewhat beastlier match, Mr. Christopher Ronaldson, a gaunt English craftsman of 32, will this evening almost certainly retain his world title before a restrained audience of precisely 127 people behind large wrought-iron gates and battlements on the outskirts of London.

There will be applause, a few handshakes, a little champagne and absolutely no shouting. Real tennis people take triumph in their stride and defeat with a stiff upper lip. They are very conscious that they are not Johnny-come-latelies in sport. They are also quite resigned to the fact that practically nobody writes about them.

This is surprising since their game is so rich with blood, scandal and politics that the Nigel Dempster of 1536, for example, would have picked up quite a ripe little diary item had he been lurking around the *dedans* on the afternoon Henry VIII popped in for a game on precisely the same stone floor that Ronaldson plays Australia's Wayne Davies in the final leg of their match tonight.

Small wonder if the monarch was looking faintly distracted. At that very moment his second wife, Anne Boleyn, was being beheaded for adultery just up the road. Infuriatingly, history does not record the score in his match so we just have to settle for the fact that then, as now, there's nothing like bashing a ball about to take your mind off a domestic tiff.

Small wonder, either, that as you walk through the massive gates of Hampton Court these days, with the dusk closing in over the lawns down to the Thames, you can see them all: Wolsey, in cardinal red, mumbling about injustice; Henry VIII, raving on about his latest divorce or the lack of it; Charles I fixing up tennis lessons for his son with John Webb, the professional, for 20 sovereigns a year.

You walk where they walked, down Tennis Lane, and then turn left, as they turned, along a high gloomy corridor and finally you arrive in a great chamber, cathedral cold, the grey stone alleviated only by the huge rich, gold entwined initials of King William III and Queen Mary II on a wall above the sagging net and a lurid portrait of Henry VIII across the grille.

There are sloping roofs called penthouses and a jutting buttress known as the *tambour* and netted gaps all down the left hand wall that resemble cloisters. This is hardly inappropriate. The whole is a replica of the French and Italian monastries where real tennis originated between 800 and 1,000 years ago with a few bored monks smashing handmade balls around with their hands.

Little has changed. They now use heavy, twisted rackets but the balls are still fashioned by hand from 14 yards of cotton webbing and every protrusion and architectural feature of the court is brought into play. It is a game of intense skill and bears no relation to its showbiz offspring, lawn tennis. Etiquette, impeccable manners and sportsmanship are absolute. John McEnroe, at the first murmur of dissent, would be removed from the court.

There are 17 courts in use in Great Britain, seven in the United States, two in France and three in Australia. The game is played by no more than a few thousand players aged from 10 to 85.

Its standards are such that when two bespectacled opponents went on to court there recently and one broke his glasses, the other immediately insisted on removing his spectacles to redress the balance.

There has been total silence throughout the world championship. It started last week, continued on Sunday and concludes this evening. Ronaldson will almost certainly win it because he leads 6-2 and requires only one of the remaining five sets to retain the title he took off the remarkable amateur, Howard Angus, in 1981.

There will be no gloating. Nor will there be excuses from his slender Australian opponent, Wayne Davies, despite every reason. On Sunday, in the fifth set of his challenge, he cruelly tore an upper thigh muscle. He didn't even limp until the eighth set and still said nothing when, in the 11th, he was clearly broken.

Both men are professionals. Davies, born in Geelong, makes £20,000 a year at the Ivy League Rackets Club in New York, where gentlemen members strive to be even more English than the English. Ronaldson, born in Cambridge, is professional at Hampton Court and lives in a seven-roomed, grace-and-favour-style apartment over the shop.

In a hip-bath lately used by King George V in a dressing room that may well have seen Nell Gwynne's undies, Davies's spirit was undaunted either by his injury or the extraordinary atmosphere in which he makes his living.

He's a hired hand, playing for money. No-one says how much. Cash is taboo.

The atmosphere is awesome to the newcomer. 'And,' says Christopher Ronaldson, 'it never wears off. I've lived here for 3½ years and I am conscious every day of the history that surrounds me.' Later this week, as plain Ronaldson, he will be back teaching the game and marking — scoring — for members he could beat left-handed.

LONG LIVE THE NATIONAL

There was a real danger that the 1983 Grand National would be the last. Happily it wasn't. But tragically our friend John Hughes, who did more than anyone to restore its glory, was to die soon after it was safely part of our heritage again.

AINTREE: APRIL

BETWEEN them they flew 30,000 miles to tell their children and their readers of how it was at the last great cavalry charge in British history.

They came, they saw and they were overwhelmed.

'My God,' demanded Pete Axthelm from New York. 'Are you telling me that you Brits are just going to stand there and let that die? You must be out of your minds.'

For a few moments David Lord, from Sydney, Australia, weighed his words against emotional hyperbole. Then he said: 'Never, *never* have I seen a spectacle to compare with that. That was why Britain used to win their wars.'

These, significantly, were not the impressions of tourists wishing to flatter or console. Between them Axthelm, NBC television commentator and acerbic Newsweek sports columnist, and Lord, Australian sports commentator, have logged 60 years of strictly professional sports-watching around the world.

Neither had seen a Grand National previously. Both were lured by the rumours that if they didn't come this year it would be too late.

Mutually they were staggered that the nation which gave the world Balaclava and the XXIst Lancers and a recent sharp reminder about who owns the Falkland Islands, should be seen wringing its hands about a paltry £1½ million to prolong the 146-year history of the world's undisputed greatest steeplechase.

'It's hardly any of my business,' said Lord, 'but it strikes me as pretty odd that a country which bets £30 million on a single horse race can't find a small fraction of that to save it.' He is not alone in his bewilderment.

On Friday, the wind at Aintree cut through you like a lance. Yesterday, it simply poured.

Yet on Saturday, a warm sun transformed the inevitable drama into breathtaking spectacle and conferred on the vast crowd an amiability rare these days at sports events where big betting is involved.

Alongside us atop the shabby County Stand a small, elderly lady with sandwiches and thermos and not even 50 pence each way on anything, had paid, like everyone else, £25 to watch from Aintree's super vantage point.

'It's an awful lot of money', she said, innocently implying that it was going to be sausages and mash until next pension day. 'But I've watched the Grand National for 20 years on television and I was determined to come here in case this is the last one.'

She hardly bothered to glance at the first two races but just after 3 o'clock, when Grittar came through from the paddock and led the long parade of brave horses and nervous riders below us, she stood up. Everyone around her shifted slightly to make sure she had a perfect view. It was that kind of day.

Strangely, you are not aware of noise during a Grand National. There is too much to watch. Down to your left there is an unseated jockey in vivid yellow, facing immolation astride a fence if he cannot hurl himself to safety from the hooves bearing down upon him. Simultaneously at the water-jump immediately below, a vast horse pitches on its head.

The metallic racecourse commentary switches like a relay baton from English public school to wild Irish rhetoric and classless comprehensive. It is wonderfully articulate but all the voices are two octaves up on dinner table conversation.

It gets less convoluted all the time as the casualties mount and you recall what Richard Pitman, not notably an ecclesiastic but the man who rode the hopelessly out-weighted Crisp round here in vain pursuit of Red Rum in probably the greatest National ever, used to do on his way to Aintree on the morning of the race.

He used to drop into a small church and say a word or two. It was for nothing so atrocious as to ask for victory. It was simply to hope that he'd still be in one piece for Sunday breakfast.

And so they come off the final turn. This year it was Greasepaint closing all the time on Corbière. For perhaps 30 seconds the world stands still upon its axis and what is happening down there is violent, heroic and unique.

It was certainly unique this year. When the glamorous Geraldine Rees and Midday Welcome went over at the first, and then the formidable Joy Carrier and King Spruce crashed at Becher's first time round, the chances of badly-needed distaff impact on the Grand National seemed remote.

But Corbière held on for Jenny Pitman, the first woman trainer to storm this masculine fortress. She is, of course, the ex-wife of the aforementioned Richard but let it be said that in what might have been embarrassing circumstances both parties conducted themselves with total dignity.

In the chaotic Press conference that followed, Richard stood on a table to ask civil questions and get civil answers. That Jenny Pitman shed tears and required a glass of water was not exceptional. Men have done that, too, when they've won the National.

Divine intervention did not end with the Riviera sunshine. Though only ten of the 41 runners ever saw the finish post, the casualty list was slight: one dead horse and one damaged human wrist.

'It was wonderful,' said the small, elderly lady with the empty thermos.

She was right. And so were Pete Axthelm of New York, and David Lord of Sydney, both strong defenders of a newborn faith.

I will punt a realistic guess on what will happen if we do not save the Grand National by the deadline date of May 1.

It is that those little Japanese will build an exact replica of Aintree somewhere on the fringe of Tokyo and start sending us satellite television pictures of our own sporting heritage within two years of now.

We don't need to build a replica of Aintree anywhere. We need to leave it precisely where it is, restore it with intelligent taste, develop it with vision, utilise its space during the 362 days of the year when it is currently laying idle and continue to run the Grand National there on a Saturday every early spring.

ADVANTAGE B. J.

By the end of the decade the age of 20 was beginning to look perilously old for a potential tennis champion. Where were the new prodigies coming from? It was humiliating to find out.

LONDON: JUNE

THE result not flashed up in Wimbledon lights yesterday was in the Generation Gap Singles where B.J. Stearns beat This Column 7-5, 6-2 in one hour 28 minutes. This oversight was not surprising since the match was played on something like Court 886, which is to say in Cadogan Square, London, S.W.3.

Let me first, however, recall B.J.'s stormy arrival in Britain on Sunday evening on Flight PA 106 from his native Florida. He was in a towering rage. 'Ridiculous, disgusting,' he said. The objects of his fury were the baggage-handlers at Heathrow who'd kept him hanging around that airport for nearly two hours.

B.J. didn't give a damn who heard him. Among those who did hear him, since he'd eventually been chauffeur-driven straight from the airport to a high-powered party in the West End were Sean Connery, Kiri Te Kanawa, Fred Stolle, the American writer Dan Jenkins and a lot of other people you'd also look up to.

B.J. certainly looked up to them. He had no choice. He stands 4ft. 2in., weighs 3 stone 13 pounds and is 7 years and two months old.

Those really in the know about tennis say he is, weight for age, the most brilliant young prospect America has ever produced. That makes him probably the best young player in the world. For reasons of crumpled pride, I do not dispute that.

One does not claim, of course, that 35 years of messing about on tennis courts produces anything resembling a competent player. But I would have risked the mortgage that native cunning and a weight advantage of 8 stones 8 pounds would overcome a seven-year-old who could hardly peer over the net.

Not yesterday. The early patronising shots, a strategic catastrophe, were put away with contempt. The long war of attrition then began. B.J. doesn't believe in mistakes. The little monster gets everything back. He gets you running until all you can hear in your ears are the imaginary sirens of onrushing ambulances. He doesn't actually beat you. He just sandpapers you into oblivion.

I had heard that B.J. was a juvenile graduate of the John McEnroe School of Delinquency. Indeed, even his parents admit that he can be quite as nasty with opponents as he is about baggage-handlers.

There was no evidence of it yesterday, but then B.J. was never on the retreat. There were plenty of soprano squeaks. There was some mild anguish when he double-faulted. There was a devastating hands-on-hips stare when I inadvertently attributed to myself a point I hadn't won. But otherwise B.J.'s demeanour was impeccable, though I suspect his dad had had a word with him.

B.J. stands for Billy Junior. He is the only child of Billy Senior and Rebecca Stearns who have on their hands an awesome parental responsibility.

Billy Senior, 27 and with a few years on the American tennis circuit behind him, is now coach to the Brazilian national team and personal coach to America's Betsy Nagelsen. There is no doubt that he wants B.J. to be the McEnroe of 1997, only much better mannered.

Billy and Rebecca married at college. They didn't set out to breed a tennis prodigy but they have one on their hands. B.J. was still only six when he demolished everyone in sight in the under-10 section of his first State tournament.

Tennis is on tap. He lives at the Seminole Racquet Club in Florida, plays two hours on schooldays, four hours a day at weekends.

Seeking revenge for what happened out there on Court 886, I tested his intellect. He read a few sentences out of a Harper-Queen magazine as though he had written them but his preferred reading is Paddington Bear. Anyway his favourite subject is maths.

THE AMAZING NUTS & BOLTS MAN

In the 1960's a young man walked into the Daily Mail office, squatted on my desk and announced he intended to become the motor-cycling champion of the world. I asked him his name, just in case he made it. 'Barry Sheene', he said. He survived it all and now, needing heat to ease the pain of his many shattered bones, lives in the Australian tropics.

NORTHAMPTON: JULY

THE INITIAL impulse is to describe the man as mad. Charming, amusing, honest, slightly deaf, rich, sensual, patriotic, male chauvinistic but, above everything, mad.

It was a year ago this week, cresting the blind rise that leads to Silverstone's Woodcote Corner at 175 mph with his chin on the tank, that he hit an abandoned motorbike lying directly in his path.

Not unnaturally he has no recollection of what happened between then and waking up, feeling rather less than well, in Northampton's General Hospital. But the most credible witness says that he flew 30ft. into the air, hit the ground 100 yards away and slithered for a further 200.

In itself this cannot be described as madness since no professional skill, no forked lightning reaction, could have avoided the collision.

Furthermore, if you reckon to gross something like £500,000 a year out of motor sport, you accept that the debit side can be sudden, violent death.

The madness argument is based on the evidence that seven years earlier the same man had come off at 180 mph at Daytona Beach and he has also fallen twice at Mallory Park, twice previously at Silverstone, at Brands Hatch, at Hengelo in Holland, at Quarter

Bridge in the Isle of Man, at Anderstown, Sweden, at the Jarama track in Spain, at Imola, Italy, the Paul Ricard circuit in France and at Sugo, Japan, to name but a few painful mishaps.

He has pins, bolts and nuts holding his slender frame together and has suffered the grief of seeing three good friends die in motorcycling accidents. Once to get the grit out of his ravaged back, some nuns used a small scrubbing brush with an iodine chaser.

You would have thought that would have taught him a lesson but all he did was fit himself with a strong plastic back protector.

You would certainly reckon that last year's Silverstone's pile-up, which almost smashed him to bits, might have warned him that the good Lord's patience was running out.

Not at all, Barry Sheene will be back at Silverstone again in Sunday's British Grand Prix and nothing said over a gastronomic masterpiece of a lunch this week could induce him to believe that it was anything other than the sanest possible way to relieve the boredom of another Sabbath.

No argument prevailed, not even the last-ditch reminder that his good friend James Hunt had the brains to get out of car racing the moment he made £1 million.

'Yes', countered Sheene, 'but James had come to hate driving. I still love it. When I don't, I'll quit.'

In all else the man is logical. He is, paradoxically, a safety fanatic refusing ever again to ride the lethal TT circuit in the Isle of Man, detesting Germany's long Nurburgring track because of the time-lag in getting an ambulance or a rescue helicopter to an injured rider.

He is scathing about motor cycling officials who have never ridden bikes at high speed but won't spend money on safety precautions. He has led riders' rebellions at circuits he regards as too dangerous. He is in fiery litigation with Silverstone over what he alleges to be the stewarding shortcomings that led to his horrific 1982 accident.

Materially, even emotionally at last, there is little more he could want.

He has a 33-roomed Elizabethan manor house standing in 22 acres in Sussex. He has his own helicopter and a Mercedes 500 SEL.

And after years of wild and indiscriminate wenching, high-lighted by a summer mostly spent in bed with two Finnish sisters, he has found Stephanie, who divorced to be with him. They have a stunning relationship that comes only from mutual adoration and will marry when they propose to have children. Lovemaking and a large English breakfast, he suggests, knowing that Stephanie will only laugh, is the ideal morning preparation for a big race.

Not bad, you reckon, for a Cockney boy whose only known scholastic achievement was the highest truancy rate on record. Too bad, you argue, that with all that to live for the ultimate thrill remains driving motorbikes at very high speeds.

But he refuses to listen. He is literally partially deaf, anyway, from his years alongside engines, but the ultimate deafness is in his soul.

He is a stubborn man.

On the eve of a French Grand Prix, when a hotel manager ignored his entreaties to stop the booming dance band playing so that the riders could get some sleep, he carried a 26-inch coloured television to a window and hurled it into the courtyard below.

In Finland, confronted by disgusting trackside lavatories for riders and their families, he poured ten gallons of 100 octane fuel into the loos, set light to it and blew the whole edifice sky high.

He refuses to go to restaurants which won't permit jeans or attend dinners where black ties are obligatory. The last time he wore a suit was in 1977 when he collected his MBE from the Queen at Buckingham Palace but even then, though both Tory and royalist, he would not wear tails and a top hat.

The Queen asked him then if he proposed to race on. He said he did. 'You be very careful then,' admonished the monarch.

There is no point at all in repeating the caution. Beneath the panache he is a careful rider. The madness is in not acknowledging that some day the surgeons might not be able to piece him together again.

THEN ALONG CAME CARL

Carl Lewis, for me the athlete of the decade, has won more races than friends. I once caught him autographing Bibles. I can't stand the man, but admire him for his single-mindedness and uncompromising stand against drugs.

HELSINKI: AUGUST

ULTIMATELY there was only one Man of the Great Helsinki Games. His name was Carl Lewis, a thoroughbred so rare that athletic class of such magnitude can miss whole generations.

To see him striding shoulder to gleaming shoulder with a thoroughbred of another genus altogether may seem like stretching the metaphor too far. Yet behind the sheer art of this beguiling picture there lies a desperate irony.

It echoes back 47 years into history when another black American dared to test his speed against a horse.

The great Jesse Owens, just home from raising the Star Spangled Banner almost permanently above the Swastika at the 1936 Berlin Olympics, won the race and instantly lost the respect of his nation.

He beat McCall, a famed horse of the day, by sprinting 100 yards in nine and a half seconds. He went on to race against greyhounds and midget cars for any promoter who'd pay. He had no job, and a wife and two kids to keep.

They got him, of course. To the rich Ivy League administrators of American sport, yesterday's hero was just another goddam nigger defiling the amateur credo. A year later he was caretaker at a children's playground in grubby industrial Cleveland, earning 18 dollars a week.

The double irony was that America was to wait almost half a century for another Jesse Owens — a man who could outsprint and outjump the world with such ease that he left the rest to quarrel about who came second.

They have found him.

Carl Lewis carried three gold medals and a new world record home from the World Athletics Championships in Helsinki. But the really awesome point of it was that no one even saw him break sweat.

He won the 100 metres with yards of daylight to spare. He won the long jump at his very first leap. And while the long jump was in progress he strolled to the far side of the stadium grabbed the baton for the home stretch of the 4 x 100 metres relay and was grinning broadly as he crossed the finish line with a world record.

Lewis is not a modest man. He paraded himself around the arena, arms on high, teeth flashing, like a Presidential candidate. He then addressed the American nation on live television on the subject of his next intention, which is to obliterate Bob Beamon's phenomenal 29ft. 2½ in. long jump from the record books.

Lewis, after a patronising little lecture on the geophysics of long jumping — apparently it requires nothing more than to reach the take-off board at a speed of 27 miles an hour after a 168-feet run covered in 23 strides, and then angling the upward thrust of the body at precisely 24 degrees — let it be understood that the record will probably be his inside a year. He's only four-and-a-quarter inches behind as it is.

America, dedicated to winners and winning, probably loves him more than his team-mates do. 'Some marketing man,' growls Ed Moses, America's champion hurdler. 'Yeah,' adds Larry Myricks, a rival sprinter and long jumper sardonically, 'there's going to be some serious celebrating going on around here when Carl gets beat.'

Lewis appears oblivious to all of it. A Houston University course in media techniques has drilled him carefully in the field of interview response.

Point number one is to remind the nation on every occasion that he's a practising Christian. Point number two is to lower the voice and the eyelids in homage to the memory of the great Jesse Owens.

'Yes', he always acknowledges exactly on cue, 'Mr Owens was my great inspiration.'

Fellow-athletes at this juncture tend to roll their eyes. 'Carl's only known inspiration,' says a colleague, 'is the dollar sign. Carl doesn't run against horses for money, you know. Carl runs against horses for the exposure that will bring him even more money.'

The envy is naked.

Just 22, Lewis has for a long while now been absolutely on course to become the first track millionaire — an ambition he cannot talk about openly in an era when athletics still maintains spurious pretences of amateurism.

It is no secret, however, that Lewis is unlikely to turn up at even the most insignificant meet for anything less than £3,000.

But that is the chicken-feed side of the account.

He is already as hot as any Hollywood star in the television commercial field, and he is the hottest property of all in the hush-hush business of major sports goods firms paying athletes to wear their products.

Already Lewis has a lifestyle unknown to previous black athletes: his own baroque home in Texas, where he lives alone, a uniformed man servant, much cut glass and silverware, a BMW car and Jeep run-about. A volume entitled 'Living Well' is probably the understatement of his small and not noticeably intellectual library.

He switches on the smile at the approach of a camera, charm at the sight of a TV unit and sincerity at the drop of an earnest reporter's question. In short he's almost as complete off the track as he is on it.

Jesse Owens has not lived to see it.

They eventually forgave him for running against horses and presented him with a government job touring the black American ghettoes lecturing on the subject of national patriotism. He died in harness.

MAGIC MATILDA

The night of September 26-27, 1983, was mildly hectic in the Daily Mail office. Against a five-hour time difference I was attempting to report from America the greatest-ever yacht race. Edition after edition was sent out to the country carrying stories of an uncompleted and still unpredictable duel. Eventually America lost the oldest trophy in international sport after 132 years. What follows is an appalling piece of dictation, yelled down the telephone as Australia II crossed the line. But it was live history and for the first time a yacht race made the front-page splash in our final edition.

NEWPORT, RHODE ISLAND: SEPTEMBER

IT happened and it happened in the manner of lurid fiction.

Australia II sailed back from the Dead Sea here last night to beat Liberty, win the America's Cup and leave this nation speechless.

Two-thirds of the way through the accurately billed Race of the Century you would not have risked tenpence on Australia's chances, at 100 to 1.

Outsteered by the brilliant Dennis Conner, outpaced by an American boat that had shed 1,000 lb of ballast to defend 132 years of unthreatened high-seas supremacy, Australia looked irrevocably doomed as the unluckiest also-rans in sports and Waltzing Matilda looked set to become a lament.

And then they won. They won a 4¼ hour race by precisely 41 seconds.

As America watched in helpless agony — and there is no greater frustration than urging a yacht to speed up in God's own good time — John Bertrand, Australia's self-effacing skipper, sailed right out of nowhere, straight past Liberty and unerringly into the pages of sporting history.

So the seemingly impossible was accomplished. The trophy won by America off the Isle of Wight in the presence of Queen Victoria in 1851 and never endangered in 24 challenges, finally fell.

It is due to be handed over by the New York Yacht Club — in whose premises it has been symbolically fastened to a plinth by bolts — within the next 48 hours.

To its autocratic members and to millions of Americans, it will be akin to surrendering the Crown Jewels, for it was the symbol of American human and technological superiority. How they lost it on the fringe of the Atlantic on a warm Indian-summer afternoon just stirred by sufficient breeze to avoid another agonising postponement will now become the plot for a dozen instant books.

The truth was that Conner, acknowledged by the yachting world as an unrivalled helmsman, gambled once too often.

The mild tragedy of the day was that the massive 2,000-vessel spectator fleet that had to turn back when Saturday's race was abandoned, did not reassemble to acclaim Bertrand's eventual triumph on behalf of the rest of the world.

There were probably only 250 spectator boats in attendance when, after one aborted start and an anguishing 55-minute delay, a single cannon boom announced that Race Seven, the decider, was actually on.

Ironically Bertrand, whose starting technique had been the one glaring weakness of the Australian campaign, scored his finest start of the series.

Unlike Conner, who had spent his Sunday rest day on a golf course with a laconic detachment first feigned on Plymouth Hoe, Bertrand had gone back to sea to rehearse start after start against two of his former rivals, Britain's Harold Cudmore and France's Bruno Trouble.

And with salutary effect. Although the official starting time placed America's Liberty eight seconds ahead, Bertrand went over on full acceleration and tactically dominated the first three miles of the 4½ mile first leg into the wind.

But such faint strains of Waltzing Matilda as may have been sounding in Australian ears were soon drowned.

Gambling with one of those genius strokes that have built the Conner legend, the American Skipper pulled Liberty over to the right of the course, collected a wind shift worthy of the term and hauled straight past Australia II to lead by 29 seconds at the first marker buoy.

A lead of that dimension, even at so early a stage, is generally a significant pointer. For Australia it pointed to defeat and there was worse to come.

She was 45 seconds behind at the second buoy, pulled back slightly to trail by 23 seconds at the third, but then slipped to a critical 57 seconds behind down the fourth leg. In yachting terms that is one foot in the grave.

The race defied all predictions. Australia, usually at her best beating into the wind, was floundering. Characteristically she is at her worst downwind yet yesterday it was on the fifth downwind leg that she achieved her miracle, with some help from Conner.

She turned into it 57 seconds behind and emerged from it 21 seconds ahead in the great race for home. That 78-second improvement in a swift down-wind run changed the history of the America's Cup. It may not have been so had Conner not moved out again to find a windshift that was not there.

Liberty counter-attacked but left it too late.

She tried to lure Bertrand towards the spectator fleet. Bertrand wouldn't play. Victory and the America's Cup was firmly in his sights and his wisdom was rewarded. He crossed the line to a fraction of the reception he deserved.

The one reception he valued above all others was from the plump, beaming man aboard the launch at the finish line.

Perhaps it is quite inappropriate at this moment to recall that the man who has financed probably Australia's greatest sporting achievement was born in Ealing, West London. I will certainly not dwell on it.

Alan Bond made his vast fortune in Australia and spent £12 million of it on four challenges for the America's Cup. Last week at 3-1 down, with America in a seemingly invincible position, he never lost faith. Nor did he yesterday when Australia II looked out for the count.

He was the man who had the courage to believe that Bertrand would stay cool under the ultimate pressure, and the ultimate pressure was certainly applied in the final shoot-out.

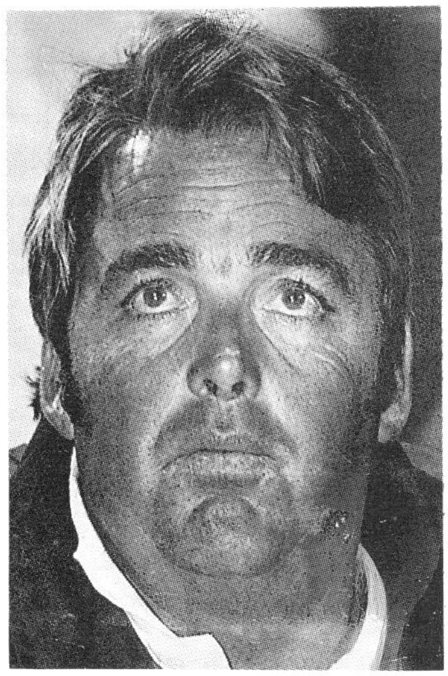

THE LOSS OF LIBERTY

While the Daily Mail was still printing the final report of the deciding America's Cup race, a shattered man was facing the Press. We were to meet again before the decade was out.

NEWPORT, RHODE ISLAND: SEPTEMBER

TO Dennis Conner, the man who lost the America's Cup, the homecoming was more like stepping through the very gates of the alternative hereafter.

The darkening sky was rent with flares and fireworks, the famous harbour filled with a cacophony of horns and sirens, the streets so jammed with the rejoicing and the stunned that police had to cut a path for him to Newport's National Armoury.

Champagne was sprayed all over him as he pressed through that gauntlet, face set in a waxen grin, to turn towards the inquisition of 63 TV cameras and the nation's predetermined verdict: 'Guilty.'

There was a white telephone beneath the table. It was the hotline on which President Reagan was to have followed up his good luck telegram with one of those personal calls in which he publicly thanks astronauts and generals and other heroes for their deeds to the glory of the American peoples.

It never rang.

There were to be no questions. Connor refused to duck the nightmare but was prepared merely to make a brief, personal statement.

He thanked the crew of Liberty for their unwavering support, then he said simply: 'Australia II was the better boat. They beat us and we have no excuses.'

There was bitter irony in that acknowledgement. Conner's recent autobiography, whose sales would have rocketed to the realms of a bestseller had Liberty won, is entitled *No Excuse to Lose.*

There were tears in his eyes as he turned away and walked, erect and with dignity, into the raving night.

It raved on till dawn and long after for Australian fans are not modest in their hours of triumph and the winning of the America's Cup is the greatest accomplishment of their century in the world sports arena.

There are many thousands, here, however, who will never wish to hear another rendering of Waltzing Matilda nor will forgive the manners of those who wore the hastily printed T-shirts that bore the words '*****The New York Yacht Club.'

In fact, in the bitterest hour of its 139-year history, the New York Yacht Club at least feigned a sporting attitude it has never been famous for. Most of its members did not witness the disaster, for its sixth storey Manhattan home does not contain a single TV set. But its committee men present on the finish line at least raised their hands and were much photographed in what appeared to be the act of clapping.

What's more, they did not have to be carried screaming to the handing-over ceremony of the longest held trophy in the world. They promised it within 48 hours and delivered it in 17.

In a scene more reminiscent of a world war surrender, at midday precisely, yesterday, in the great marble mansion of the Vanderbilts, right here in Newport, the America's Cup was transferred to the care of Alan Bond, the Australian who had spent £12 million to get his hands on it.

In contrast to their extrovert supporters the Australians who actually won the ugly 33½-inch tall silver cup for Australia, were impeccable in their behaviour. John Bertrand, the helmsman whose brilliant run down the fifth leg of the race turned history on its head, looked drained and exhausted.

He made a 'Right now I'm feeling very humble' kind of speech in a quiet voice. The ebullient Alan Bond is never quiet but his words won him many American friends at the end of a campaign which, behind the scenes even more than in public, had been waged with ruthlessness.

'We've won it and can change some rules,' he said. 'But one thing will never be changed. Out of respect for the people who held it for so long it will always be called the America's Cup.'

Bond made all the right noises about sport strengthening the ties between two great nations, but by birth and business methods, he is conspicuously not an Ivy League type. He well knew he had wrestled the autocratic New York club to the floor.

Australia's parting shot was brilliantly staged. With thousands crammed into their dock they at last lifted the heavy canvas skirts that, for months, had concealed their controversial secret weapon, the Lexcen-designed superkeel.

It brought gasps of surprise. It bore little resemblance to the many published artists' impressions. It was much less exotic than they had imagined.

To the uninformed, it seemed unthinkable that such a mild contraption could bring 1,300 journalists racing here to record the end of an era and the fulfilment of sport's wildest dream.

An America's Cup campaign will never be the same again. Winning it from Australia, if that is possible, cannot have the same impact as wrenching it from the club who swore that if they ever had to surrender it, it would be replaced by the losing skipper's head.

It will be up for grabs again, Alan Bond pledged, in the stormier waters off the coast of Perth, Western Australia, in 1987 or 1988.

But that's about five-billion renderings of Waltzing Matilda away.

FOR THE LOVE OF BRUNO

In 1989 Frank Bruno was to feature in one of the most intensely hyped sports promotions in history. Six years earlier he was still a thoroughly likeable young man grateful for the chance.

LONDON: DECEMBER

THE way it was going, Frank Bruno's future was pretty well mapped out: expulsion, street gangs, borstal, graduation to serious crime and prison.

That's not me guessing. It's Bruno being frank.

Without so much as an O-level to help him on the way to his first £1 million, his unsolicited testimonial to the fight game is almost an act of worship: 'Without boxing,' he said, 'I'd now almost certainly be in the nick. Boxing's saved me. Definitely.'

The downward path reached its lowest point with inevitable expulsion from Wandsworth's Swaffield Primary School, South London, the day Bruno registered the first knock-out of his career. It is not commemorated in the record books.

Black, aggressive, inarticulately sensitive and physically enormous for his age, Bruno stood up in class and punched a master flush on the jaw.

'He was being flash,' recalls Bruno. 'He used to stand there with his shirt undone half way down his chest, showing off to the girls at my expense. I didn't have any great problems about being black or that, but this guy just needled me all the time, so I hit him. And that was that.'

Frank Bruno was 11 at the time.

He struggled and kicked and appealed to his dying father to save him from the consequences but his mother, a strong Evangelical lady who used to drag him to church on Sunday mornings, was having no more of it.

So off he went to one of those boarding schools which don't celebrate Founder's Day.

'I cried for about a month when I got there,' said Bruno. 'I didn't believe my mother could do it to me. It took me six months to accept the routine, up early, make your bed, brush your teeth, sweep the drive, clean about five pairs of shoes for the older boys, stand up whenever you saw the headmaster. It was just like being in the army.'

He stayed at Oak Hall in Broad Oak, Sussex until he was 16 and his tribute to its headmaster, Allan Lawrence, and a curriculum designed to recycle excess teenage energy and sweep chips off shoulders is as gratifying as his acknowledgment of the remedial effects of boxing.

Last week he nudged his way into tenth place in the WBA's rankings of the world's leading heavyweights. Tonight in the Royal Albert Hall he will need another convincing victory if that sudden promotion of a London lad of 22 in the roughest of all games is to be endorsed.

There is careless talk that Bruno will finish up as Britain's first world heavyweight title holder since Bob Fitzsimmons knocked out James J. Corbett in the 14th round in Nevada in 1897.

For obvious commercial and psychological reasons Bruno himself has to subscribe to that opinion. 'I'm trying to be world champion two years from now,' he says, and then throws you a lightning glance, searching your face for scepticism. Interpreting whatever he sees there he adds: 'Well, in three years anyway.'

I do not understand the technicalities of boxing sufficiently to offer an intelligent opinion. But I can recognise a man who has worked his guts out to become a model citizen and an inspiration to loose-end, street-roaming kids when I see one and Frank Bruno fits the bill.

His wildest indulgence is a restaurant dinner with his manager, Terry Lawless, in Leytonstone.

Lawless, frequently accused of being overprotective to Bruno, can hardly be blamed for recognising a meal ticket for life. Bruno is on £1 million anyway, minimally £5 million if he reaches a shot at the world title and much more should he win it.

They have a strong, nearly telepathic relationship, so unorthodox that from time to time Lawless sits his fighter down in front of him and reads him notated passages from the Penguin paperback of Zen in the Art of Archery by Eugen Herrigel.

The selected Lawless reading this day concerned 'It', the X factor that separates the men from the boys.

'It', recited Lawless, 'takes the place of the ego, availing itself of a facility and a dexterity which the ego only acquires by conscious effort. 'It' is only a name for something which can neither be understood nor laid hold of and which only reveals itself to those who have experienced it.'

Does Frank Bruno have 'it'?

Leroy Dibbs, flown in from America to spar with Bruno in preparation for tonight's fight, maintains that Bruno not only has 'it' but everything. This was clearly a subjective view since Mr Dibbs, for the past three years not only sparring partner but bodyguard to Larry Holmes, the world champion, had just taken a terrible pasting from Bruno.

Bruno's own philosophy is refreshingly simpler. 'You can only succeed if you work very hard. I intend to work very hard until I'm 28 and then quit. After that I'd like to travel the world.'

I propose to write nothing more of Bruno's personal life than that he and his white girlfriend live at Chadwell Heath and have a daughter called Nicola.

'We met,' laughed Bruno, 'when she pinched my backside on the Battersea Park roller skating rink when I was 18. I love her very much and will marry her when we're both ready.'

There is further good news. Last summer Frank Bruno received an invitation to declare open the annual fair at Wandsworth's Swaffield Primary School. Driving away he took a long look at the prison just down the road.

1984

1984 was the year Mary Decker, Zola Budd and England's cricketers wished to forget. It was the year John McEnroe shocked everyone by playing Little Lord Fauntleroy at Wimbledon. He had to because if he acted up yet again they'd threatened to throw him out. It was also Olympic year again. At the Winter Games in Sarajevo, to the beat of Bolero, we held our breath as Torvill and Dean signed off with all the sixes that add up to perfection. But later, in Los Angeles, the Summer Games reeled beneath a steam-hammer act of revenge. The Soviet Union had no intention of forgiving America for boycotting Moscow four years earlier. With malevolent timing they withdrew, taking East Germany and most of the Communist hangers-on with them. The Olympics became a show-business production. America didn't seem to care. They made a profit and, with so many great athletes absent, the Star Spangled Banner rang out from morning till night.

THE £MILLION WAIF

This was the first major story to be published in Britain about Zola Budd. I deeply regret writing it. It led to an historic collision and intense unhappiness.

SOUTH AFRICA: JANUARY

THE last place on earth you are likely to hear a rendering of God Save the Queen is Bloemfontein, South Africa, the epicentre of unforgiving Afrikaanerdom.

Yet in a homestead ten miles out into the red dust beyond the city, there hangs a perversely unpatriotic picture.

It is an old nostalgic print of London Bridge and it provides a vital clue to an intriguing sports mystery of this Olympic year.

Who will win the diplomatic race for the almost anorexic 5 stone 4 pound body of Zola Budd, amazingly now the hottest property in world athletics?

Millions, understandably, will still ask who is Zola Budd and what — apart from an exotic name with undertones of French romantic literature and English opera — she has to offer. The answer is, minimally, £1 million-worth of sporting talent and possibly an Olympic gold medal in Los Angeles.

On January 4 this year, aged 17 but looking and behaving like a 12-year-old, she was virtually unknown. By the evening of January 5, still looking a bewildered 12, her name was causing eyebrows to be arched everywhere from Moscow to California.

Running barefoot on the university campus at Stellenbosch, near Cape Town, she had covered 5,000 metres in 15 minutes, 1.83 seconds, thus slashing by a monstrous six seconds the world record set by the greatest and probably most glamorous, woman middle-distance runner of all time, America's Mary Decker.

Confirmation from a disbelieving world was

immediately demanded. It came by return of Telex.

Thus the race for Zola Budd was on. A race that by yesterday involved nine American universities, the U.S. State Department, hot-shot business agents and, not least, the corridors of influence in Whitehall, London.

The reason, of course, is that so long as Zola Budd remains South African she will be banned from all international competition. South Africa has been expelled from the Olympic movement and from the International Amateur Athletics Federation and will remain so until it renounces its apartheid laws.

To run free she must change her nationality, which is why the picture of London Bridge, on the wall of her rambling home in the very heartland of the severe apartheid territory of the Orange Free State, is of such significance.

Her birthright ties, though tenuous, are British. Her paternal grandfather, Frank George Budd, was born in Hackney, London on February 4, 1886. He emigrated to South Africa early this century taking with him some heavy pieces of furniture which are regarded as heirlooms in the Budd household to this day.

But one grandfather and a few sticks of furniture are not enough. Which is why for the past nine days and possibly for weeks to come, remarkable diplomatic moves are happening to gain her a British passport and the right to run for Britain in the Olympics.

In the middle of this intense activity stands one totally bewildered figure. Zola Budd herself.

Off the running track, where her sheer speed makes her a commanding figure, she is a waif-like child of barely five feet who blinks nervously behind the steel-rimmed spectacles she discards when running, and is so acutely shy that her best friends are her pets.

The family isn't wealthy by white South African standards, but neither is it as poor as Zola's barefoot running has implied to many. She discarded spikes by choice.

They have ten acres of mealies and two black servants and her father still has a business interest in a small printing firm in town. But deaths in their family, the faint distant links with Britain and Zola's extraordinary talent have produced an unsettling effect.

Her family would like Zola to run for Britain. But unfortunately, it isn't quite as simple as that. Zola's inhibiting shyness, — she is a university student in Bloemfontein but her syllabus seems to start and end with running, is such that her family would not dream of letting her travel alone.

If she moves to Britain it will have to be on a package deal of naturalisation that involves five people: Zola, her parents, her coach, the Afrikaans-speaking Pieter Labuschagne and her coach's newly-married wife.

'Without all those people around her, to protect her from a world she knows nothing about, she wouldn't have a hope in athletic competition,' said one of the businessmen who is currently hoping to arrange for her arrival in Britain.

'We just hope that the British Government will be sympathetic.' Yesterday the British Government was being nothing other than discreet. 'Well', admitted a Home Office spokesman, 'there is a discretionary system, and exceptions can be made.' It seems likely that Neil Macfarlane, Britain's Minister of Sport, will be asked to explore those 'exceptions'.

Armed with a British passport, Zola Budd could run for Britain instantly. But once she has run for Britain she could never run in South Africa again, even in a club meeting.

It is not merely Olympic honours, of course, that the Budd family are considering.

A series of internationally televised head-to-head races between Budd and Mary Decker, either before or immediately after the Olympic Games, would yield a massive fortune.

There would seem to be no question about Zola's speed and talent. The questions are slightly more serious than that.

If Zola Budd burned her boats in South Africa, could she survive the so-far unknown pressures of celebrity? And, anyway, can Whitehall pull the strings that would bring the Budds back to Britain after two generations?

It is all bewildering to the tiny, 17-year-old, all-white victim of apartheid.

FOUR MINUTES OF MAGIC

There were few occasions in the 1980's when you could predict a British victory at the highest level with something approaching assurance. Miss Torvill and Mr. Dean were the exceptions at the Winter Olympics. I am still equivocal about whether ice-dancing is sport or showbiz, but how often do you watch sheer perfection?

SARAJEVO: FEBRUARY

THE fixed smiles could not mask the hopelessness. They came, two by two, condensed four years of training into four minutes on Mount Olympus and left.

Some hardly bothered to glance at the scoreboard for the sum total of their efforts was futility.

In ice dancing the stars skate last and the

very last couple on to the rink of the Zetra Stadium here last night were Jayne Torvill and Christopher Dean, the hallmark of whose genius is that they rendered all the 18 other couples impotent merely by turning up.

They won, of course. The sensation would have been if they hadn't.

But that was barely the half of it. You sat there, nervously at first, then with growing confidence, then simply spellbound, as they moved faultlessly to a victory that gave no other competitor the remotest chance.

You knew it was very, very good. But then came the moment that may well be the final acclamation of their amateur days — the row of nine sixes that declared that what they had just performed was, by the highest amd most Olympian standards, sheer perfection.

It had happened only once before in ice-dance history, and it was Torvill and Dean who had done it then, last year in Helsinki. They had no doubts themselves, skating down the rink to collect the flowers strewn on the ice by the 150 British spectators who had flown in for their performance and were flying straight out again.

But they were modest in their triumph, too, acknowledging with warm handshakes those who had come without a hope of beating them.

The audience, from across continents and ideologies, rose to acclaim them. On this night there was no argument, no controversy, only justice seen absolutely to be done.

That is the measure of the supremacy of the man and woman who for themselves, Nottingham and Britain, strictly in that order, took the solitary medal we shall celebrate at the XIV Winter Olympics.

I cannot prove that in those four minutes they became millionaires but I think it rather likely. When Miss Sonja Henie won the Olympic figure skating gold at Garmisch in 1936 she professionalised her talent so shrewdly that when she died of leukaemia, aged 57, she left £22 million.

Given inflation and the number of agents waving contracts in their faces last evening, I can hardly imagine Miss Torvill and Mr Dean underselling themselves.

Millions, not excluding the opposition, assumed they couldn't lose but, in fact, a fall or a bad blemish in style could have been very serious indeed because of the way ice dancing is adjudicated by that stone-faced jury of nine, not-necessarily-just, persons who sit there with a gravity more appropriate to Nuremberg than the Olympic Games.

The ice dance competition is fought out in three stages. The first, the compulsory dances in which Torvill and Dean visibly wiped the floor with the world, carries 30 per cent of the final marks. The second stage, in which they gave us their bull-fighting routine, yields only 20 per cent of the total.

But that left 50 per cent of the marks hanging on last night's free dance, a reward ratio cunningly devised to sustain the jitters and insomnia.

Those close to them say that Miss Torvill is the tough one during those awful waiting hours and this I quite believe. The Daily Mail gave a lunch a couple of years ago to Britain's reigning women world champions and, in the photo session afterwards, our cameraman asked Miss Torvill to sit, centre-group, on the floor.

The ice queen was outraged. 'I *never* sit on the floor,' she snapped, thus revealing a fraction of the character that made her unbeatable here last night.

Her partner, seemingly a perpetual study in blandness, proves at close range to be less cool than he looks. When he arrived here by train from Munich — they were taking no chances about being snowbound at some frozen airport — he was in a miserable tizzy about his baggage and the instant availability of ice to practise on.

The nerves were gone the moment he emerged with Jayne for the compulsory dances. It was here, so visibly a whole class superior to the rest of the world, that they demoralised the opposition.

European champions in 1981, 82 and 84; world champions in 1981, 82 and 83. What comes next for this transfixing couple?

I have not the remotest idea. Wait for the next book, for which the financial negotiations will undoubtedly be going on this morning.

JENNY'S DAY

They don't schedule a Ladies' Day for the Cheltenham National Hunt Festival. Between them Jenny Pitman and the Queen Mother shamed them into it.

CHELTENHAM: MARCH

ABSOLUTELY on cue, absolutely as Jenny predicted, Burrough Hill Lad broke clear from the pack in the middle distance mist and came up Cheltenham's last cruel hill as though it were a stretch of motorway.

The irony was that, brilliantly though The Lad ran, immaculately though Phil Tuck rode him throughout the 3¼-mile Blue Riband of steeple-chasing, it was entirely a feminine triumph.

Jenny Pitman, regarded in intimate racing circles as the distaff counterpart of the average marine commando, had nothing left to prove. The first woman trainer of a Grand National winner was, exactly 11 months later, the first woman trainer of the winner of a Cheltenham Gold Cup.

Fellow males, this one we have to take seriously!

Ms Germaine Greer and her fellow theorists of the so-called Women's Liberation Movement may well have irritated the hell out of us. This one doesn't. Mrs Jenny Pitman is as good as her word. She is tough. She is a winner.

The Gold Cup was won by Burrough Hill Lad precisely as Mrs Pitman told Daily Mail readers 24 hours earlier that it would be won. She had slagged off the book-makers for drifting The Lad's price out to the mediocrity ratings. She had castigated some of Britain's most eminent racing correspondents for believing and propagating the leaked rumours that he had suffered broken blood vessels in his legs.

'He's perfect,' she had said. 'He'll win.'

Mrs Pitman did not suffer an attack of the vapours when Burrough Hill Lad came over the line a full three lengths clear of the fiercely combative John Francome on Brown Chamberlin. Exactly seven minutes later she was behind the stands directing operations for the Gloucestershire Constabulary in the winner's enclosure.

Understandably, the photographers were pushing and shoving. 'Give us a break, lads,' cried Jenny. They didn't move. She turned on them a precise replica of the look I saw Muhammad Ali give George Foreman before he flattened him in that famous fight in Zaire.

'Get back,' she shouted. And the hard men of Fleet Street melted away.

She had, of course, looked to this day to justify everything: her aggressive response to the break-up of her marriage, her unforgiving autobiography published this week, her relationship with a new boyfriend, her talent as the stable girl with a genius for understanding such mental reasoning as horses have, her determination to prove her Aintree triumph was no fluke. It all happened in the moment Burrough Hill Lad came over the line. Her uncompromising, even brutal honesty, had been justified.

To be frank, since horse racing for many centuries has been a male domain, the reception she received was, by Cheltenham standards, restrained.

If there were some intentional slight it was repaired instantly the moment the Queen Mother arrived to hand out the trophies.

'Wonderful, wonderful,' murmured the Queen Mother before turning to Stan Riley, who was less at his ease than his trainer. Stan — who bred Burrough Hill Lad out of the small fortune he earned from buying railway sleepers, lives in a three-bedroomed bungalow outside Leicester and comes to race meetings in his mobile home — had been dreading this moment. He had no reason to be nervous.

The Queen Mother chatted him up, owner to owner, kept saying what a marvellous day it had been and handed over the Gold Cup which, for all the millions of column inches written about it, stands only eight inches high.

In the press of humanity poor Burrough Hill Lad had to be reversed out of the crush like a bread van caught in a cul de sac.

Despite loving the limelight he's a mild sort of chap. Anyway he was well aware that yesterday was Jenny Pitman's day.

THIRTY YEARS ON

For so many of the emerging stars of the 80's sport was to become an obsessive, consuming preoccupation. It wasn't always thus.

LONDON: MAY

THIRTY years on they are far and asunder. Roger is in Italy lecturing on nervous disorders, Chris is thrashing a typewriter on the outskirts of London and the other Chris is in Canada making money.

They wouldn't have indulged themselves in an orgy of nostalgia at some televised reunion anyway. That's not how the Right Stuff carry on. The Right Stuff plan, achieve and move on.

They are all in their 50s now, brilliant, fearless men at the zenith of their careers. That triumphant night at Oxford, when they beat the wind and the rain and the clock, was merely the end of an academic, physiological argument: could a human body sustain consciousness long enough to run a statute mile in under four minutes? Yes, it could. Okay, what's next?

For Roger Bannister it was damned nearly everything there was to be won. Doctorates, fellowships, a BA, three scientific degrees, the CBE, a knighthood and the international respect exclusive to men who can heal the dangerously ill. He is one of the world's most celebrated neurologists.

Naturally he's written a couple of books. They are called *First Four Minutes* and *Clinical Neurology*. He is as engagingly shy now as he ever was.

For Christopher Brasher it was a quick MA at Cambridge and then a dazzling assault on the media after picking up a gold medal at the Melbourne Olympics. He produced the sports pages of The Observer and a couple of BBC current affairs television shows before settling down as an abrasive commentator on everything from sport to Vietnam.

He is not shy at all. He smokes, drinks and shouts, has turned his lovely daughter, Kate, out on to the hard American professional tennis circuit and organises the London Marathon for business as well as pleasure.

For Christopher Chataway it was an honours degree in Philosophy, Politics and Economics and then a bewildering frontal attack on everything that life had to offer.

He tossed away an established career in TV current affairs for politics, became a Cabinet Minister and Privy Counsellor and then tossed politics away for banking. He is now vice-chairman of the Orion Royal Bank.

He smokes and drinks too, and over a late-night dinner table, gravel-voiced and mildly cynical, is one of London's most amusing conversationalists.

It was 30 years ago this Sunday evening that they lined up on the then primitive Iffley Road track at Oxford to do a little job for Britain. It was known that in Australia John Landy, and in America Wes Santee, were both in training to become the first man through the pain barrier to the unknown world of a sub-four minute mile.

There was, of course, collusion.

On a damp, chilly, unpropitious evening Brasher made the pace for the first two laps, ignoring Bannister's yells of 'faster' to bring his man to the half-mile mark absolutely on schedule in 1 minute 58 seconds.

On lap three Chataway charged to the front. Bannister slip-streamed him until it was time to go. And then, leaving Chataway and the charted territories of sport behind him, he ran.

'Amazingly,' Bannister says now, 'there was no pain. The world just stood still. The mind took over and somehow dragged the body after it.'

The altruism of two men left the glory with Bannister, home in 3 minutes 59.4 seconds.

It did not unduly concern them. The race was over. The next and bigger challenge was life itself. Sport was not the be-all, the end-all or even the half of it. It was a peripheral challenge. They knew, anyway, that once the bastion has been penetrated, the hordes would come storming through. They have. Almost 400 men have now run the mile in under four minutes.

Thirty years on it cannot be said that such grace and balanced living exists. Bannister, Brasher and Chataway were the back-markers of a golden age and all the more fortunate for it.

Their successors have lost the knack of combining sport and living. The athletes, even the amateurs, run for money now, aware that a record time can mean a lucrative contract, a dashed-off ghost-written autobiography, elevation to the instant world of TV personality, highly-paid TV commercials, professional assignments opening supermarkets.

And then there are the others who don't play games at all or play them so ordinarily that the impact of the blue-chip universities is either a myth or an embarrassment. The days when Oxbridge poured seven men into an England rugger XV and another four into a Test cricket team will never return.

In the ten opening days of the current cricket season Oxford conceded 1,929 runs while taking 25 wickets. It probably makes them favourites for the Varsity Match since Cambridge have taken just 27 wickets while being hit for 2,469.

'It isn't just cricket,' says Brasher without a hint of condescension. 'It's everything. There are very different rules now for getting into universities.

'The object of a university used to be to produce the accomplished all-rounder. It wasn't about books all day and it wasn't about sport all day. It was about producing a balanced man.

'Now it isn't producing the sportsmen and it isn't producing much else either. Get a couple of double firsts working for you and you'll find they're bloody useless. They cannot communicate with the public, you see.'

He doesn't claim to be an example of how it should be done. Nor do Sir Roger Bannister or Christopher Chataway. They don't theorise. They do things. They will go on doing things for the rest of their lives.

That is why there is no reunion on Sunday evening, the 30th anniversary of the night they stormed one of the last great frontiers of sport. Life, they agree, is too short.

ORDEAL AT WIMBLEDON

For years the public have been missing the best entertainment at Wimbledon. At the end of the decade it was still going on.

WIMBLEDON: JUNE

THE ORDEAL of the Wimbledon player does not end with the farewell courtesy bob to the Duty Royal. Next, out the back, comes the Press conference.

In wartime, Press conferences are essential so that Our Side can distort the truth into propaganda. In peacetime sport, Press conferences are of value only to the blind, disabled or illiterate. No reporter ever asks an intelligent question at a Press conference because if he gets an intelligent answer, everyone else hears it too.

Wimbledon is crazy about Press conferences. All day small petrified children from places like Wichita and Murumbra Creek are dragged in front of microphones to describe the high points of their latest 0-6, 0-6 defeat.

There is no escape. For the benefit of those who can't negotiate the stairs to these Press conferences, the proceedings are relayed by closed circuit to the room next to where those reporters who actually watch the tennis are trying to write about it.

They are such stunning entertainment that there is now probably a good case for screening them on the Centre Court while inviting players who aren't being interviewed to contest their actual matches in the Press room.

There are some fundamental differences in international approach.

American interviewers take Press conferences very seriously indeed, deliberately demonstrating to the British interviewers they despise their own deep understanding of such matters as racket angles just short of the zenith of the sliced backhand smash and asking such probing questions as: 'Really, Kathy, at 0-5 didn't you experience a certain psychological handicap?'

British reporters tend to be less esoteric. They confine their questions almost exclusively to such matters as transvestites, sex-change operations, broken romances and new friendships, particularly between players of similar gender.

While this makes me intensely proud to be British, I must say I am mildly surprised that the Wimbledon authorities, who have done everything else to accommodate the Press, do not relay the entire proceedings to the Albert Hall, thus alleviating the daily trek out to Wimbledon.

THE GREAT OLYMPIC HYPE

Once again the Olympic Games were broken by political boycott before they began. Los Angeles hardly noticed the difference.

LOS ANGELES: JULY

DEPENDING whether you quantify Los Angeles as one word or two, a former radio sports commentator named Ronald Reagan will be restricted to a speech of either 16 words or 17 when he declares the XXIII Olympic Games open here on Saturday to a global television audience of 2,000 million souls.

Savour, I implore you, the dignified simplicity of his strictly-scripted message.

From that moment onwards Olympic tradition, as we know and love it, will be swooped off this city's highest skyscraper by Superman himself.

Los Angeles, birthplace of a thing called hype, undisputed world capital of unbridled materialism, a city where the meek inherit duodenal ulcers and the modest crawl away to die, wishes it to be known that the boring old Olympics are at last to be staged with style.

Thus, in due course, 100 grand pianos will be trundled out into the great athletics stadium, known as the Memorial Coliseum, for a Guinness Book of Records rendering of Gershwin's Rhapsody in Blue.

Thus, laser lights will dazzle out from here to pierce the outer cosmos in the greatest orgy of self-congratulation the world has ever seen.

Maybe, in due course there will be some sporting contests but, for the moment, the world's greatest athlete could tramp the streets unrecognised. This is Tinseltown, home of the Oscar and the Emmy, epicentre of make-believe and real life dramas like Joan Collins.

Few, if any, have ever heard of Steve Ovett and none but the chief athletics correspondent of the Los Angeles Times would have even heard of Zola Budd. The corporate sporting knowledge around here is that the filthy, cheating Russians are too scared to turn up.

What Los Angeles is transparently in love with is the limelight generated by staging an Olympic Games.

There can be no other explanation for bringing in the Olympic flame from Ancient Greece fully seven days before it was needed unless, of course, it was that ABC Television, having paid £173 million for exclusive coast-to-coast broadcasting rights, required its attendance for emotive promotional purposes.

These, this past weekend, they have most certainly got, though of a nature so out of keeping with the Olympic movement's regard for protocol and the pursuit of excellence that had the grand old Baron Pierre de Coubertin still been alive he would have dropped dead.

As you, being British, will know already, the Olympic flame is normally relayed to a host city by fine athletes or at least runners who look like fine athletes.

Alas, the almighty dollar decreed that no such tradition survived here.

First on television, then live in the streets of Los Angeles itself, I watched speechless as it was borne to City Hall by wobbling geriatrics who could hardly walk, juddering ladies of haystack-hip dimensions, pot-bellied presidents of prosperous corporations, the sons, nieces and grandchildren of pot-bellied corporation presidents, local radio station disc jockeys who interviewed themselves along the way and one Hell's Angel motor-cyclist smothered in tattoos who kept saying 'Hey, man', into proferred microphones.

I am reliably informed that the Olympic flame went out minimally 70 times on its circuitous passage across America. It matters nought.

Conspicuous by their frigid absence when the flame finally arrived on the steps of City Hall were any members of the International Olympic Committee, whose oligarchic beliefs are that those involved in epic Olympic occasions should be beautifully dressed.

How right they were to stay away. Mayor Tom Bradley, in demotic vote-catching mood, chose to receive the flame in a two-dollar T-shirt and crumpled slacks.

The Olympic flame, incidentally, is now on its way down to the Mexican border and back to extract yet another million dollars from those willing to pay 3,000 dollars to carry it for one kilometre.

Next Saturday, when really needed, it will reappear again for the Olympic opening ceremony with its much publicised cast of 19,500 performers. Actually the cast at the opening ceremony at the 1980 Olympics in Moscow numbered 25,000 but to murmur that around here would be to be arraigned as a fellow traveller.

If I sound like a cynic it is because having witnessed Olympic Games since Rome in 1960, I have seen nothing to compare with the gross abuse of a movement which is happening here. We may well, despite the boycott of the Soviet Union, East Germany and all the other Warsaw Pact nations outside Romania, witness a very fine sports meeting. The simple fact is that gold medal winners cannot leave here in the knowledge that on the day they were the best in the world.

That said, six years ago Los Angeles was the only city brash enough to volunteer its acres for the 1984 Games. It gives it the right, I suppose, to treat the Olympic movement as a casting-couch supplicant.

At some juncture the Olympic movement had to run up against a city dedicated to the proposition that it could run the Games at a profit and here, believe me, it has certainly found it.

There is a price, mostly exorbitant, on everything, not least the sale of tickets.

While the local newspapers are full of protests from honest blueberry-pie eating Americans who say they still haven't received tickets paid for in advance — 'I sent 3,500 dollars exactly one year ago and am still waiting to receive tickets promised by the end of June,' writes an agitated New York businessman named George Lyons — thousands of black market tickets are openly on sale on the streets.

One British travel agent alone sold off 3,500 last Saturday because the dollar crisis had knocked the bottom out of the home market. He charged black market prices and could easily have flown home by Concorde showing a handsome profit. Other European and Japanese ticket-dealers have made such similar killings that I take an unaccustomed stance here.

It is that I would entirely support the athletes if they decided, next Sunday, to stay in bed until they were handsomely paid for competing in the 1984 amateur Olympics.

We are all being ripped off here by Los Angeles 1984 Inc. The sports-persons arriving here this week will be ripped off more than that, but it was always thus in Dream City.

THE BRITISH CONTINGENT

The British cavalry declared the horse redundant as a combat animal in the 1930's. Fifty years later it was a joy to discover equestrian attitudes remained utterly unimpaired.

SANTA ANITA: JULY

YOU will be proud to know there is a corner of this Olympic maelstrom that is as supremely and confidently English as Sloane Square and the Cotswolds.

True, in yesterday's sweltering 87 degrees, they had discarded their tweeds and twin-sets, but the mating calls of the British upper-middle classes and their sublime obliviousness to all matters foreign deserve a specially minted gold medal.

'Marxyear' cried one. 'Zannie-coming?' shrieked another. These, apparently, were references to the presence in the BBC TV commentary box of Captain Mark Phillips and the not unnatural request to know whether his wife, HRH the Princess Anne, was going to join him.

Of all the foreign tongues perplexing security guards, hotel waiters and even hot-shot American sports writers here, the most unfathomable is English as spoken by those who only read it in The Times, Horse and Hound and the novels of Dick Francis.

At four o'clock precisely I received quite the most civilised proposition I have yet heard in California.

'Dear boy', said this voice modulated by frequent school beatings and years in the hunting field. 'Come and have some tea'. Horsey people are probably the nicest at the whole Olympic Games.

They don't moan, bitch, make mountains out of molehills, muscle-strains or play the elusive personality game adopted by so many athletes. They just get in the saddle and get on with it.

Several years ago Virginia Holgate, who led off Britain's quest for the equestrian three-day event gold medal, fractured an arm so catastrophically in 15 places that amputation was advised. 'Leave it', commanded Virginia's mother, 'precisely where it is.'

That all this is going on at a Santa Anita race track in California which is normally populated by Spics, Micks and other demi-monde characters straight out of Damon Runyon, is particularly gratifying. The three-day event here is being spread over five days since today the whole entourage has to move out and hoof it 110 miles down to Del Mar for the second and most perilous of the triple disciplines, the endurance cross-country section.

Then they return here to Santa Anita for the show jumping finale. This opening round has been the dressage section.

It is quite true that to the incognescenti virtually nothing happens. A horse appears bearing a man dressed for a society wedding or a woman dressed like a man dressed for a society wedding. For ten minutes precisely the pair move about a rectangle the size of four tennis courts at a speed which reminds you of Bobby Fischer contemplating his next move in the world chess championships.

By the end of the first day Britain was sitting well placed with Miss Holgate on Priceless and Ian Stark on Oxford Blue in third and fourth places. Diana Clapham and the formidable Lucinda Green were still to come.

Ian Stark is a darker horse than his horse. A Scot from Selkirk, he was, two years ago, to international horsemanship what Lord Goodman is to the average mountain rescue team. Man and horse, first time out, performed beautifully.

They received from the 90 British equestrian supporters here the marvellously restrained applause reserved for a newcomer who has shown nerves of steel in his first day under a Hun bombardment.

'Lissen', asked a security guard observing such a cool reaction 'who are dese guys?'

'They are,' I was forced to tell him, 'a bunch of despicable Armenian horse thieves.'

'Goddit,' replied the guard. 'I guessed they was something like that.'

THE FALL OF ZOLA'S IDOL

The sense of doom that surrounded Zola Budd did not lift when she took to the Olympic track. It intensified. For she found herself centre stage in one of sport's most heated controversies.

LOS ANGELES: AUGUST

THREE times Zola Budd had to come past the scene of the accident and twice, filled with misery, she glanced backwards and downwards at her crumpled idol.

She seemed mesmerised by it, as we are mesmerised by mangled wreckage on a motorway hard-shoulder. The difference was that this small child could not murmur, as we murmur, 'There, but for the grace of God.'

Before an audience of 90,000 in the Memorial Coliseum, with half the world's population as television witnesses, she was deeply implicated in a whole new chapter of the controversy that seems to be her birthright. If she could hear at all, the sound was ugly. Thousands, cruelly prejudging a collision that was to be analysed in slow motion and then frame-by-frame more than 20 times before the night was out, were booing her.

On the last lap Zola Budd glanced nowhere. Her stride was faltering as the field streamed past her. It was almost as if she were postponing the moment when she had to run into the maelstrom that awaited her.

Let this much be understood. Zola, at these Games was never going to win a medal of any colour, in my opinion. She never claimed she could and her judicious caution was justified the moment she stepped on to Mount Olympus. The brilliantly gifted barefoot runner of South Africa's high veldt found herself, strategically, a tongue-tied school girl in a highly sophisticated and sharp-taloned society.

In the harshest conceivable way she has learned much about life and the intransigent personalities of those determined to claw their way to fame and enormous incomes through sport.

Zola Budd worshipped Mary Decker, she adored, idolised and imitated her. She slept for years with a near icon-like photograph of Mary Decker above her pillow. She read every word written about Mary Decker and dreamed of the day she would meet her. She achieved that dream after she left South Africa and, on April 6 this year, became a British citizen.

That made Zola a rival, and Mary Decker, all-American heroine, does not encourage rivals: particularly rivals who could steal the limelight and, with it, the international publicity that hooks the endorsement contracts, billboard advertising and public appearances that can bring in minimally one million dollars in an Olympic gold medal year.

Few in the largely ingenuous crowd that gathered in the Coliseum would have understood that. Few would have realised the tensions down there on the start-line of the first 3,000-metres race for women in Olympic history. Few would have known anything other than that this was Budd v. Decker, the media-promoted race of the Games.

What none could imagine was that exactly three laps into the race there should occur an incident which neither Greek mythologist nor 20th Century novelist would have dared weave into his plot. It will be screened and re-screened as long as the Olympics survive.

Sportswriters are normally undemonstrative but around me the 2,000 reporting the race rose as one and yelled 'She's down' in a dozen languages.

Zola with a startled glance over her left shoulder confirmed the source of the roar. Mary Decker was lying on the inside of the white-washed kerb thrashing her legs in frustration. She made no attempt to get up. She stopped thrashing and started crying. Zola ran on and around the top bend with three laps to go the booing began.

American TV hit the same instant conclusion as BBC. Budd, the novice from Bloemfontein and Guildford, Surrey, had stepped into the inside-lane path of the American goddess and sent her sprawling. Guilty. Nothing more to be said.

But there was. The first thing to be said was that, with Decker prostrate and Budd, beetle-browed with anxiety, trailing in seventh, the race had been won by a glamorous Rumanian named Maricica Puica, as heavily rumoured in the sports pages of this newspaper on the morning of this race.

The second thing to be said is that, in disqualifying Zola Budd before she could recapture her breath between sobs, the race judge disgracefully endorsed ignorant crowd reaction and instant TV commentary judgment.

Thirty minutes later, by the not insignificant margin of eight votes to nil, the jury of appeal declared Zola Budd innocent, rescinded her disqualification and reinstated her to seventh place. Even more significant was what occurred on America's ABC Television 19 hours later.

In one of the most handsome apologies ever delivered on that self-righteous screen, Marti Liquori, commentator and respected former American middle-distance runner, acknowledged that in the heat of the moment he had got it wrong.

Miss Decker formerly Mrs Ronald Tabb and shortly to be Mrs Richard Slaney, wife of a very large British discus thrower, will not go along with that at all.

Miss Decker's performance in the 24 hours from the moment she was carried from the arena in Mr Slaney's huge arms till she made her last tear-stained appearance on television trespassed on soap opera's territory.

Between hospital visits and consulting some of America's top medical experts over what, after all, was only a trivial and still unconfirmed injury in a foot-race against other human being she recovered sufficiently to appear on TV at the drop of an invitation and maintain that 'It was all Zola's fault.'

In the gushing obsequiousness of all these interviews, no interviewer stayed calm enough to ask her one question. It was this: If Miss Decker, world champion full-time professional and the intellectual guru of women's middle-distance running, was all that confident, what the hell was she doing in such close proximity to a nervous and unpredictable novice like Zola Budd anyway?

The truth is simply this. Twice over 40 yards Miss Decker collided with Zola who, unforgivably, was running without shoes. The second time Zola went two feet up in the air like a startled rabbit and, in recovering her balance splayed out her left leg in Miss Decker's path. Miss Decker fell over it.

Unkind though it is to say this, I do not believe Miss Decker is as dramatically upset as she appears. I believe she knew she was about to be beaten not by Miss Budd, but by the much more experienced and remorseless Puica.

But the greater significance is that in her ubiquitous interview appearances she was accompanied in one instance by her lawyer and in another by her chiropractor. Since when did Olympic athletes need to troop around with a household retinue?

Zola, as stunned as someone who had shot an albatross or slashed the Mona Lisa in some moment of nightmare madness, also withdrew in tears, shocked by her rejection. In the dressing room she cradled herself in the arms of Mary Peters, the British women's team manager, who knows there is more to life than sport. She is a declared atheist who won her gold medal at the 1972 Olympics not for Britain but for Belfast, where she lives. She raised more than £90,000 afterwards and gave it all to renovate a running track for Protestants and Catholics alike.

Miss Budd badly needs Miss Peters at the moment. Mary Decker could learn the odd trick also.

What we saw here was less a Greek tragedy than a modern morality play. Two great performers had been brought together before the world. Both of them lost.

JOLTING JORDAN

Frank Bruno met all manner of opponents along the path to his world heavyweight title fight with Mike Tyson at the end of the 1980s. Some were better than others. Jeffrey Jordan wasn't one of them.

LONDON: NOVEMBER

PROMINENT etymologists are in an understandable state of confusion about the use of the adjective 'Jolting' on a London boxing poster this week in front of the name of Jeffrey Jordan, an American medical student and pugilist.

The concern is centred on page 1,137 of the Shorter Oxford Dictionary whose definitions of the noun 'jolt', the infinitive 'to jolt' the adverb 'joltingly' and the adjective, as used above, all imply aggressive intent to dislodge, jerk or shake to bits.

Since the origin of the word can be traced back to 1599 it would seem that for 385 years authors, lecturers and intellectuals in many fields have been using it in entirely the wrong context.

Far from dislodging, jerking or shaking any bits off Frank Bruno in their Tuesday night fight, the only object jolted by Mr Jordan was the referee into stopping the contest in Mr Bruno's conspicuous favour long before the bell for the end of round three.

This is all very worring.

Are we to understand that a reference work with the reputation of the Oxford Dictionary has hopelessly botched it up? Or did Mr Jordan's parents actually chisten him Jolting Jeffrey back in Ohio simply because they liked the onomatopoeic ring of the word?

Alas, the extremely likeable Mr Jordan could shed no light on the matter. 'The fact is,' he said,' that I didn't even know I was called Jolting Jeff Jordan until I arrived in London and saw myself described like that on the poster.'

Are we then to infer that the addition of 'Jolting' to his name was the gratuitous inspiration of the poster's compiler? Was it

some arbitary alliterative device to attract the public eye?

Or, more sinisterly, was it intended to invest the ordinary name of a very ordinary boxer with a reputation for such unspeakable brutality that thousands more fans would buy tickets to see poor old Frank jolted apart?

There are, of course, precedents in tampering with boxers' names.

The great Jack 'Kid' Berg still a terrific advertisement for boxing at the age of 78, has the name of Judah Bergmann on his birth certificate. Ex-world heavyweight champion 'Jersey' Joe Walcott was actually christened Arnold Raymond Cream, which is as good a reason as I know for doing something fast by deed poll.

However, Jeffrey Jordan doesn't strike me as being a bad name at all for a young man who, however unsuited he may have been to fight Frank Bruno, probably has a shining future in medicine.

1985

1985 turned international golf on its head. At Royal St George's Scotland's Sandy Lyle won the Open Championship, at Augusta Germany's Bernhard Langer won the US Masters and at The Belfry a combined Great Britain-Europe team beat the United States in the Ryder Cup. The Americans weren't too pleased about the latter, claiming they had encountered some unsporting conduct among the normally impeccably behaved British spectator galleries. Thus they touched on the most sensitive wound of the entire decade: the galloping spread of an infection the Continental newspapers called The English Disease. Slowly, insidiously it was creeping into golf and cricket. Foreigners were watching for it. Understandably, for 1985 was the year of the Heysel Disaster when rioting Liverpool fans left a trail of death across a stadium in Brussels. I asked one on his return how it could have happened. "Ridiculous", he said. "There should have been at least 3,000 police on duty at that match." The absurdity of 3,000 police being required to control any sports gathering never occurred to him. English football teams were banned from Europe but the tragedies were to continue.

FROM FEAR TO ETERNITY

In January the Daily Mail took 12 young readers to the Cresta Run to prove that guts are not exclusive to any one generation. After a dozen runs most were flying down like veterans. Our in-house competition was won by Nick Ovett, young brother of Steve, the Olympic athlete. In the circumstances one had to have a go. The following was written, champagne at elbow, an hour after desecrating one of the supreme venues of sport.

ST. MORITZ: JANUARY

YESTERDAY we rode the Cresta Run. To be more accurate we bounced down it like a pinball. After careful thought I declare it to be the second greatest thrill that life has to offer.

Heroics are as entirely out of order as false modesty. I am proud to have got down it in 79.55 seconds, which is half as fast again as Errol Flynn. I am not proud at all to confess I was so enduringly terrified that I doubt I shall ever do it again.

Morally there was no ducking it. When your newspaper brings 12 young Britons here to brave the Cresta, you have to grit your teeth, ring your insurance broker and shove off from the vivid blue start line across the ice.

Many claim that the waiting is the worst. I can now authoritatively dismiss that as utter nonsense.

The worst is roughly 18 seconds into it on the mildly-banked bend named Battledore. It is here precisely that the novice is no longer boss.

It is here that the damned thing under you — a 60lb steel toboggan as aesthetically beautiful as a ripped-off oven door — takes over.

They kit you out with a pair of boots each with four metal teeth projecting from the toecaps. Till now you have been dragging these into the ice, just as they instructed you, arresting acceleration. You have done it so efficiently, despite one sledgehammer blow on the right hip when you hit the wall, that momentarily you enjoy it.

On Battledore that changes rapidly. Suddenly the Cresta falls away. It is not yet 9 a.m. It is minus 19 C. The Run is highly polished glass. And as its innocently beckoning camber hurls you violently to the right you are into a scenario roughly the equivalent of a thrashing nightmare.

Gravity grabs your 13 stone and your 60lb contraption with manic intensity. The toecap rakes are useless. You are out of control of your immediate health, let alone your destiny.

It is too late for discreet retirements, feigned muscle strains or the courageous withdrawals that are the privileges of the waiting minutes. Mayday calls will go unanswered. You are now heavily into this, brother, and the best thing you can do is keep your elbows tucked tight in and hang on. The dreaded Shuttlecock hairpin is down there somewhere and coming up to meet you very fast.

Somewhere to the right is a marker they told you to aim at to hit the line that gets you round Shuttlecock without flying off into the neighbouring forest.

Bloody hell, where is it? Gone. Missed it. Real trouble now. Blind panic. Jab a foot into the ice with a strength you never knew you had. Wrong foot. Slew madly to the right and smash the same hip against the wall again. Don't feel the pain. Swearing appallingly, out loud, far worse than can be reported here. Very frightened.

In his all-seeing glass eyrie high above the Cresta Run, Lt.-Col. Digby Willoughby, ex-Gurkha officer and now autocratic secretary of the St. Moritz Tobogganing Club, broadcasts a commentary on what's happening to the poor initiates trying to negotiate his fiendish ice-chute over a relay system which echoes over much of south-east Switzerland.

Sometimes he is extremely generous. Mostly he is heavily sardonic. 'Lord X', he is prone to say, 'has just negotiated Shuttlecock like a drunken crab.'

I am told he was kind to me. 'That,' he said, 'was an excellent execution of Shuttlecock for a beginner.'

I have news for Mr. Digby Willoughby. I have virtually no recollection of getting round Shuttlecock let alone executing it. It comes up so fast that there is no time for academic reflection about how the brilliant young James Sunley glides round this terrible curve like a horizontal ballet dancer.

By luck, or maybe as a reward for a blameless life, the toboggan flew through there coincidentally with me upon it.

You glance up and exuberantly realise that you're past it. From here, they all say, its plain sailing. They lie. In the very act of glancing up you wobble and smash the right hip into the wall again. This time it hurts a lot.

By now you are not thinking about wife, family, Queen, country or even Mr. Digby Willoughby. You are thinking about getting off this thing as soon as possible. You are still alive, soldiering on in the name of journalism, and beginning to feel a bit of a hero.

It is then, having flashed through the infinitesimal shadow thrown by the road bridge that traverses a station of this sporting cross called Scylla, that you top the Cresta Leap.

I grope for a description of this latest horror: racing towards the brink of Beachy Head, perhaps, in a car with faulty brakes.

You have leather knee and elbow pads, helmet and goggles and metal plates strapped to the outside of your gloves to stop the Cresta ripping off your fingers. You've also got three layers of clothing but nothing helps as you crest the Leap, exit line completely wrong again, and once more the right hip pounds into the wall.

You know it is slowly turning into raw steak but you don't care any more. Your eyes are shut. You have given up the toecap rakes. You acknowledge the ice-chute known as the Cresta as your unrelenting master.

And then, sublimely, you feel the ground rising under your chest. With no effort on your part the thing is slowing down. It stops. You lie there for a few seconds, gasping. And then a nice man with a hook comes down and secures your toboggan. You could embrace him, even though he has three days of facial stubble. But, of course, he's seen it all before.

He drags the primitive machine away and you stand there, reflecting on 79.55 seconds of curious life.

The Daily Mail team gather for champagne. Photographer Graham Wood is the hero. He half slid off his toboggan round Shuttlecock, regained it somehow, and made it in 70.33 seconds. Alwyn Robinson, just the oldest among us, was down in 86.57. Promotions manager, Desmond Nichols, flew off at Shuttlecock the first time, waited for a nervy hour and then negotiated it with intense concentration in 101.51 seconds.

The great Cresta runners watched us with quiet amusement. By their standards, we had just run a six minute mile. But they are kindly people. 'Well done,' they say.

The Cresta breeds a fraternity like that.

THE MASTERS' MAGIC CIRCLE

I have never met a more gracious sportsman than the late Bobby Jones. Visiting the course he designed for the US Masters Golf Championship I could only wonder whether he would have approved of the social grandeur it had assumed?

AUGUSTA: APRIL

TAKE the New Yacht Club and plant it in a landlocked pine forest in America's Deep South and there you have it : the Augusta National Golf Club, home of The Masters.

The voices are identical. So are the high complexions, the demeanour of inborn authority, the members' wives, the limousines in the parking lot, the lack of concern about the price of anything, the unspoken allegiance to Republicanism, and the completely unabashed determination to keep outsiders out.

Older members look like General Westmoreland, their wives like young Nancy Reagans. They are enormously charming to visiting firemen with English accents and are different to the New York Yacht Club in only three respects. They don't adorn themselves with self-invested gold braid, they wear green blazers instead of blue, and they don't cheat.

Golf, internationally, is not a cheating game, which is almost the only point of contact between the Augusta National Golf Club and, say, the No. 2 municipal course at Neasden.

From Thursday in America and Saturday in Britain, viewers will be able to tune in on television and witness most of the world's finest golfers paying homage to the great Bobby Jones, who in 1934 conjured this stunningly beautiful course out of an old Confederation plantation.

And that's precisely how they want it. They don't want you here with your fractious off-spring dropping chewing gum that may later cloy to the studs of members' shoes.

Try getting an admission ticket. Your chances, if you are not on the mailing list, waver between slim and nil. It is not that they are expensive. It is that their distribution is so carefully monitored that anyone traced flogging tickets outside the magic circle — a huge temptation since big business will pay ransom money to impress well-heeled clients — will be sent to a wilderness far chillier than Coventry.

It is much the same with the players.

Former winners, be they 29 or 92, may automatically compete and if some stubborn nonogenarian, crippled with arthritis and senile ambition, insists on turning up, that's how it will be and to hell with television. Some players do qualify by earlier deeds, but the rest are invited on such sheerly arbitrary qualifications as being thoroughly good chaps and knowing how to hold a knife and fork.

For years the Augusta National Golf Club was accused of being racist in that until 1977, and the arrival of Lee Elder, no black person's role at a Masters had exceeded that of caddie or clubhouse servant.

Disgusting though that will sound to millions, there is a rider which, while it won't placate the Left, will not exactly endear the golf club to many on the Right. For every black person excluded, minimally 50 white persons were also kept off the immaculately tailored premises. This, possibly, is the ultimate definition of exclusive.

Hord Hardin, chairman of everything that moves at Augusta National, lives by the English establishment credo that a gentlemen never apologises and never explains.

'Our membership,' states Hardin, 'is 350, many of them from overseas. Some play here, at most, twice a year. When they come here, they like to play unimpeded. That's the way we like it too. Most days of the year, outside Masters week, no more than 30 people play the course.'

End of statement.

Like it, or lump it, call in the United Nations or call out the National Guard. That is how life is the other 51 weeks of the year at the club at which the annual drama of The Masters will be enacted before a global audience of billions next weekend.

Most of the pictures arriving live by satellite in Britain will come via CBS, one of the three big American TV networks. If the Augusta National Golf Club tendered the TV rights for auction every year, it could probably double its income, thus reducing membership fees from comparatively small to nearly non-existent.

For the moment, it has no such thoughts. CBS plays the game because CBS does not wish to lose the contract. A CBS commentator who once described a running Masters gallery as 'a mob' — and, from past experience, I can assure you that American golf galleries are nothing like the dour, discriminating audiences who stalk the fairways of St. Andrews — was fired on the spot for reckless talk.

There is supposed to be no media reference to the size of the crowds or the money won by the players, statistics of this nature being too vulgar to divulge.

The latter point is nonsense since Sunday's 80-page broadsheet golf supplement of the Augusta Chronicle reveals every sum won by every player since way back: Jack Nicklaus, five times a Master, has won a total of $309,252 while Tom Watson is currently averaging $94 (total $265,617) for every stroke he has played in combat on the course.

The place is so beautiful that every lie lavished on it is absolutely true. The only professionals practising there when I walked the 18 holes on Sunday were David Graham and Bernhard Langer, striding out yardages with frowning intensity.

The other two dozen or so playing were members and their friends. I followed a fourball for half-a-dozen holes, one of three spectators. After a couple of holes, the other two spectators closed up and politely asked why I was interested in the game and could I furnish some proof of identity.

They were curiously dressed for Augusta National members, being in jeans, sneakers and loose jackets. They appeared to know nothing about golf, which was quite understandable since they were both carrying revolvers in holsters beneath their coats. 'State Department,' they explained. They requested I should not name the two prominent members of the US Government playing in the fourball.

That is how the Masters course strikes you before a ball has been hit in earnest. There is a soft wind from the South, the divot marks have been filled in with sand dyed green, the white clubhouse basks like some early colonial mansion up there on the hill and all the flowers, after a tardy spring, are coming to perfection in time for their annual TV appearance.

It is an exercise in elitism and the golf has still to come.

LANGUAGE BARRIERS

Bernhard Langer won the US Masters Championship. The irony was that back in Germany millions were unaware he'd ever been away.

LONDON: APRIL

IT is probably reasonable to assume that if Otto Bismarck, Kaiser William II and Adolf Hitler had been given sawn-off golf clubs instead of miniature duelling swords in their formative years, world history would have been far less depressing.

Alas the Germanic peoples were slow to recognise golf, with its inbuilt code of honour, as the most civilising outdoor activity there is.

Only Hitler, of the three, even acknowledged the game's existence by naming his retirement home The Bunker instead of Dunmurderin, though fat good that did him at eight down with nine to play.

Obviously building golf courses was not a huge priority in the autumn of 1945 but even so Germany's reluctance to take up the game when the going was good again was mildly surprising.

Since most of the world's commercial deals are now concluded on golf courses, it was astonishing to discover that Germany, at the end of last year, still had only 190 private golf clubs and precisely one municipal course.

What is more, Bernhard Langer, who in 1984 won the Spanish, French, Irish and Dutch Opens as well as finishing second in the British Open at St. Andrews, was for his pains and impact on the game internationally, rated only fifth in Germany's Sportsmen of the Year awards.

'Disappointing,' said Langer.

Well, it will take a 3½-minute mile or a 30-foot long-jump to deprive him of the title this year. His impact on the game in America is now such, after winning the Masters and a subsequent tournament, that American professional golfers are smiling their congratulations through tightly-clenched teeth.

Ballesteros was bad enough. To be upstaged and robbed blind by a German whom the TV commentators assured them putted worse than a two-stroke motorbike, could well inspire them to take matters up with the immigration authorities. Americans hate being beaten, even more so when the caviar is being snatched from their mouths.

The irony is that Langer is still more about profit than honour in his own country.

'The game has grown there in the past few years,' he asserts hopefully, 'but it is still not very popular.'

Certain documents have recently fallen into my hands which suggest that it is not so much German lethargy which holds the game's development back as the glossary of golfing terms which the newcomer must muster. Tautology half the not of it is. Hence:

CHIP-SHOT: Ein niedriger annaherungsschlag aus unmittelbarer nahe des gruns.

COCK (as in wrists): Anwinkein der handgelenke beim aufschwung.

BIRDIE: Ein schlag unter dem fur das loch vorgesschriebene par.

TROLLEY: Kleiner wagen zum transport der golftasche.

BACKSPIN: Ruckwarts drehung des balles un horizontale achse. Entsteht wenn der abwartsgehende schlagerkoof deb ball trifft.

On the other hand it is quite wrong to make any reference to the idiosyncrasies of the German language without recalling the intellectual exchange between an American golf writer and Herr Langer not long after the latter had pulled on the green blazer at Augusta.

'Where do you come from?' demanded the American.

Langer hesitated only for the split second in which it takes to translate Munchen into Munich.

The American wordsmith was visibly baffled. 'Spell it,' he cried.

ONE DAY OF HOPE

What the headlines fail to record is that thousands of friendly peace-loving people also live in Belfast.

BELFAST: MAY

PRAYER is not exactly up my street but I'd mend my ways if the brief vision I witnessed here yesterday could become a permanent condition. It was of Belfast at peace.

They stood shoulder to shoulder, Protestant and Catholic, militant, pacifist, middle-class and unemployed, along 26 miles of streets whose names are branded in the world's brain as synonymous with enmity and murder.

And all they did was cheer.

It was not a solution the 2,700 runners in the Belfast Marathon brought to this battered city but it was certainly a truce of the most extraordinary dimensions.

Among them down the six opening miles which covered New Lodge, the Divis and Unity Flats, the uncompromising graffiti of the Falls Road and the police fortresses of Andersonstown, ran more than 200 British soldiers.

Unidentified as such in the official programme — their haircuts tended to invite speculation and a couple had covered telltale tattoos with surgical plasters — they ran in vests and shorts through territory where they normally venture only with flak jacket and automatic rifle.

Yes, there was mild anxiety. Overnight two buses had been put to the torch in the Falls Road to commemorate the martydom of Bobby Sands. 'I shall be glad when I know they're all through Andersonstown,' admitted their officer-in-charge, 'but we had 280 running last year and nothing happened.'

It is true that four Saracen armoured cars suddenly burst on the course and weaved their way through the leading runners but their mission was unconnected with the Marathon.

The biggest danger any athlete faced this day was becoming engulfed in the exuberant crowds who said to hell with the pouring rain and so encroached upon the route that at times they were running through human avenues no more than four yards wide.

Draw no conclusions and look for no hidden meanings in what comes next. The stair-rod rain ceased and the sun broke through at the precise moment we arrived at our 16-mile vantage point to see Marty Deane take his commanding grip of the race.

We were standing directly in front of a prosperous red brick religious establishment bearing the name of the Martyrs Memorial Free Presbyterian Church which bore the reminder 'Time is Short' on its facade and advised prospective worshippers 'Authorised Version of Scriptures Used'. It was, so help me, Ian Paisley's church.

Marty Deane gave it not a second glance. He was concentrating on winning the race in a record time for the four Belfast Marathons run so far and proceeded, virtually unchallenged, to do both.

His two hours 15 minutes 51 seconds over a course with three hard inclines to master was almost two minutes faster than that of the second man home, John Griffin, who, appropriately on this day of ecumenical advancement, comes from County Kerry in the Irish Republic.

Deane is Belfast-born and bred and no-one in the field more richly deserved the modest £1,000 first prize. Married with a young son, he threw in a teaching career two years ago to return to university and study medicine. He is 32 and cash is short.

It was a marvellous time in tough conditions over terrain much more demanding than London's Marathon. Griffin's time was two hours 17 minutes 43 seconds and the third man home, Swansea's Trevor Hawes, recorded two hours 19 minutes 28 seconds. Belfast's Moira O'Boyle was the first woman home.

Statistics, however, fit strangely on the day's proceedings. Here was a sports event about much more than sport. It was about hope for an entire community and while I would not be as naive as to claim that we witnessed here the beginning of a new Belfast era, we assuredly saw sport, however briefly, draw a community together.

A NIGHT OF SHAME

I did not go to Brussels for the Liverpool-Juventus European Cup Final. A phone call alerted me to watch the proceedings on television and a 40-minute deadline imposed to write the following piece. Instant judgement, certainly, but I don't retract a word of it.

LONDON: MAY

THE shame is so great that it is beyond diplomatic discussion or conventional apology.

English soccer must today be seen to ban itself from further overseas engagements before the world — quite properly — shuts its frontiers in our faces.

We have heard ad nauseam the pathetic excuses: poor policing in foreign stadiums, frail barriers separating rival fans, small bands of anarchists who have hitched their wagons to star football teams, timid magistrates who ignore the powers at their command, inefficient Government control.

These are futile arguments and have been so for years. When dozens die because of a football match that hasn't even started, you stop playing football matches. That is not vindictive or punitive. It is sheer commonsense.

And English football — I hesitate to include the Scots and Welsh in this — must acknowledge this morning that it has no right to inflict the lice that have attached themselves to it on any other nation.

It must mean the withdrawal of every other English team that has won its way into European competition.

The usual authorities will this morning be putting forward their ideas or alternative solutions. There aren't any.

Last night in Brussels a brutal bunch of thugs chose to represent your name and mine as representatives of our country.

We must share the shame they have inflicted upon us. We must insist, before some foreign body takes the decision for us, that they do not do so again. For how long?

Until wiser men than are currently running football in this country come up with a solution to a problem that is conspicuously not of their making.

Maybe five years. Perhaps ten. Either sentence would be light.

Tragically the story of Brussels was of death. It seems inconceivable so soon after the Bradford disaster that human beings could actively precipitate another harrowing night, but they did so with determination and no remorse.

They went there for a fight. They got it. And, if it is any satisfaction to them, they have probably killed English soccer in the process.

The entire economics of English football at the highest level are geared to European competition. We are no longer acceptable. The case history is too long, the last act too serious to contemplate an alternative.

There will be screams from the soccer cognoscenti that England should not withdraw from the World Cup.

Why?

Should we desecrate yet another country? And, if so, in the name of what?

You and I are the scum of the world and if you do not believe that just read the newspapers in New York and Munich and Johannesburg and Tokyo and Melbourne and, particularly, Moscow.

They will have the measure of us by the time you read these words. They will judge us by association. And if you wish to be associated with what happened, then I don't.

I felt sorry for the poor football experts trying to explain it all away on television. They all had allegiance to the game they undoubtedly love which distorted their view of reality.

Bobby Charlton, the most honourable man ever to play the game, was, if I heard correctly, advocating the return of the birch, while Terry Venables, the street-smart genius of football management, was suggesting ten years inside for the troublemakers, and/or the reintroduction of national service.

No one in his right mind would reintroduce national service as a solution to the football hooligan problem. Anyone in his right mind would stop playing football where trouble was in sight.

And that, dismaying though it may be to millions, is what must be advocated today.

We just don't want any English soccer club to travel abroad again until wise minds have sat down together and determined that last night's horrors can never happen again in your name and mine.

LLOYD ON LLOYD

This was a review of Carol Thatcher's marvellous book, Lloyd on Lloyd. *The Ice Queen of Tennis wrote me a letter saying she thought it was disgusting. Both Mr and Mrs Lloyd subsequently divorced and married someone else. I am told they are blissfully happy, which is jolly good news.*

LONDON: JUNE

IT must be said of Carol Thatcher that she possesses much of her mother's determination to root out the facts.

Whether the subjects of her journalism appreciate this may be another matter.

Miss Thatcher's second book — her first was about the Prime Minister's last election campaign — vaults to the world of professional tennis which, as we all know, is a much more serious matter.

'Lloyd on Lloyd', a curious double entendre of a title, tells principally of the love affair between John Lloyd, a handsome, clean-cut young Englishman who will never play tennis at the highest world championship level, and Christine Evert-Lloyd, an American so groomed from birth that she will never do anything else.

Timed to catch the Wimbledon market, the book was launched in London yesterday at something called a 'finger lunch'. Finding fingers unappetising I failed to attend. Anyway, the only question I had in mind would have been unpopular.

It would have been directed at husband John and merely asked him why he had allowed the book to be published.

On page 14 the author informs us that by the age of 28 Mrs Evert-Lloyd was worth an estimated $10 million.

By page 54 she is breaking that down to show how the income is sustained and enhanced every year: $500,000 in tournament prize money, another $500,000 from exhibition matches and special events plus a little matter of a further $2 million in endorsement payments from the manufacture of virtually everything she wields, wears or eats.

This, by my rough calculations, adds up to around an annual £2½ million.

While it is hardly for me to lay down the law about where accumulation against a rainy day turns into avarice, it will strike many that the money the Lloyds get from this book may hardly be worth it. By the most merciful interpretation it portrays John Lloyd in a light which few husbands would tolerate, namely as a good-looking, well-meaning, hopeless dolt.

We all know he cannot hope to emulate his wife's remarkable achievements in tennis. Why should he?

But for what reason other than raking in money can he possibly have agreed to being presented to the world as a dumb scholar, a man too timid to approach his future father-in-law on the subject of marriage, a human being terrified of learning to drive a car and a chap so idle he sends his wife down to the video shop to pick up the latest horror-nasty?

Miss Thatcher can hardly be blamed for leaving her tape recorder running while the Lloyds bared their souls in the most embarrassing fashion. Indeed the brilliance of the book is that, either by innocence or design, it carries us deep into the one-track minds and egotistical megasphere of those who believe there is no life beyond Wimbledon.

Conducting their clandestine romance in London, Miss Evert and Mr Lloyd, determined to throw the despicable British Press off the trail, decide to dine not at the Inn on the Park but chat one another up in the foyer of the Hilton Hotel, fully 200 yards up the road. They decide on another occasion to eat at the unfashionable end of the King's Road in Chelsea, and are absolutely mortified when some fellow tennis players walk in.

The reader can only leap to one of two conclusions. Either they sincerely wanted to be discovered or else they were too dim to consult those who could have told them instantly where their anonymity would have been preserved for ever.

Turning page one of 'Lloyd on Lloyd' is entering a world of shattering egotism, populated by those who have no doubt that the future of the human race revolves around tennis. There is no curiosity about the wide world they travel, no humour, no comprehension that miners, taxi-drivers and midwives also, from time to time, have their problems.

It is a world of courtesy cars to the court and room service meals at the end of the day. The tennis reconstructions are thrilling. The rest is boredom.

At one juncture, however, Mrs Lloyd does raise a fascinating point for debate. She was too overcome on one occasion, she admits, to attend an obligatory press conference.

There she has my genuine sympathy. Obligatory press conferences, with questions either banal or deliberately provocative, are the bane of tennis. Players should play, writers should write and everyone should stop kidding themselves that press conferences are good for public relations.

TEE-TIME MEMORIES

Victory in the 1985 Ryder Cup detonated the great European revival in golf. But on the eve of the event my old friend Max Faulkner characteristically held different opinions.

THE BELFRY: SEPTEMBER

HARDLY celebrated for being averse to a drink in the halcyon days, Mr Max Faulkner's entrance into the cocktail bar of the Belfry Hotel understandably caused fleeting concern to the waiters.

Catching his right toecap into his left trouser-leg, Mr Faulkner, the Open golf champion of 1951, sprawled forward to a perilous angle before acrobatically straightening himself and emitting the famous laugh that endeared him to the crowds for 30 years.

'Good trick,' yelled Max. 'You all thought I was drunk, didn't you?' Quietly, he asked a waiter for a pot of tea, four tea-bags, army style. It came out the colour of riding boots. Max drank 14 cups between then and bedtime. He is 69.

Watching from the deep armchair always reserved for the emeritus was Mr Henry Cotton, Open champion of 1934, 1937 and 1948.

'He always was mad,' observed Henry benignly. 'I once saw Max play the greatest nine holes you've ever seen. He then decided to entertain the crowd by walking the 50 yards to the next tee on his hands. Never hit another shot. Pulled all his shoulder muscles, you see.' Henry was sipping champagne. He is 78.

Observing all this from a corner chair was Mr Fred Daly. He had just flown over from Northern Ireland and was worried that his wife might have seen the adjacent Birmingham riots on television. 'She'll want me to get back immediately to somewhere safe,' he said.

Fred, Open champion in 1947, was drinking gin-and-tonics. He is 73.

So dinner began. Max Faulkner said: 'Ryder Cup? It's nothing to do with the Ryder Cup any more. The Ryder Cup is between Britain and America. Now it's between America and Britain plus the Luftwaffe and the Spanish

Inquisition. There's no way that Britain plus the Luftwaffe and the Spanish Inquisition can lose it. Walkover.'

Fred Daly said: 'They should have scrapped the Ryder Cup as soon as Britain couldn't match the Americans any more.'

Henry Cotton diplomatically changed the subject. He said: 'Let's talk about cricket. You sportswriters have got it all wrong. I went to the last Test match at The Oval and I watched Ian Botham. Why do you chaps keep criticising him? I don't care if he does have long greasy hair and rows with the umpires. That man gives 110 per cent for England. He wants to bowl from both ends, bat all the time and stands in front of the other slips so that he can take all the catches. Is there anything wrong in that?'

Two beautifully-attired men, accompanied by their wives, then pass our table. It was late.

'Hello,' says Tony Jacklin, winner of the Open championship in 1969. 'Hello,' says Sandy Lyle, winner of the Open championship in 1985. There is hand-shaking, back-slapping, cheek-kissing and much other animation for ten minutes. The two young golfing millionaires then go to bed.

Henry Cotton recalled that he won £150 for his first Open championship in 1934. Fred Daly picked up 'something like £250' for his 1947 win.

'How much,' I asked Max Faulkner, 'did you win in 1951?'

'Bloody scandal,' Max announced to the startled restaurant survivors, '£350.'

Max now has a 27-acre homestead near Pulborough, Sussex, which he leaves in the charge of a man while he goes fishing every day off Littlehampton. He described, loudly, how you kill a conger eel.

Fred Daly, quietly, described how it is in Northern Ireland. You never report a man's views on Northern Ireland. Henry Cotton continued to talk cricket.

It was magic, laugh-a-minute talk, much of it unrepeatable. The years fell off them as they cheerfully slandered one another — and others — and infallibly recalled scores and individual shots struck back in the 1930s. It was the Last of the Summer Golf.

Next morning, with autumn in the air, they posed with Jacklin and Lyle for a unique photograph: all five surviving British winners of the Open championship together. They had never stood shoulder-to-shoulder before and never will again.

Max Faulkner will see to that. It was Henry Cotton, he acknowledges, whose glittering life-style and golfing genius established the social and financial status of the British professional golfer. But when a player like Sandy Lyle can gross £3 million for winning the Open, he believes it has gone too far.

Or maybe it was the familiar lament of the star born too early to reach Eldorado.

Max won't be there at The Belfry when Tony Jacklin's 1985 European team drive off in the Ryder Cup tomorrow morning. He'll be back on his boat, MF Jet II, searching for sea bass.

Faulkner played in five Ryder Cups, including the last victorious British team at Lindrick in 1957. Fred Daly played in four. Henry Cotton played in three, including the 1929 victory at Moortown. He was non-playing captain in 1953.

All three of them were there when Britain went through the mincer at Portland, Oregon, in 1947. We lost 11-1, a defeat which underlined America's surging advance in golf.

The recruitment of the top Continental stars, however ruefully Max Faulkner regrets the step, saved the match. 'The Americans weren't taking it seriously any longer,' says Tony Jacklin.

The revival has reached the point where many now see Great Britain and Europe as favourites for this weekend's battles over the 7,176 yards of The Belfry.

Four of the great quintet of Open champions toasted our hopes in champagne. Max Faulkner called for another pot of tea. It was mid-morning now and they all began to talk golf again.

'Every new morning,' said Henry Cotton quietly, 'I now regard as a bonus'. Suddenly it put the Ryder Cup, the rivalry, the money into sane perspective. The true wealth, they agreed, was their friendship through golf.

KEEP FIGHTING

I have long admired the excellent refereeing in British Rugby League. So it was somewhat disconcerting, then, to catch the game on an off day.

LEEDS: NOVEMBER

THE last thing Britain's Rugby League team saw as they filed out from the dressing room for the third and decisive Test match against New Zealand was a notice of uncompromising exhortation.

'Keep Fighting,' was all it said.

What transpired in the next 80 minutes proved two points simultaneously: Rugby League players can definitely read and, by God, they do obey instructions.

There were moments — I lie, there were whole extended instalments — when the third Test resembled nothing less than the house party the Campbells gave for the Macdonalds.

Certainly far more punches were thrown in it than in at least two of Joe Bugner's major fights.

At one juncture in the second half seven men were brawling bloodily in one sector of the field while four others were engaging in post-graduate gang warfare in another. It was at this point that two immensely brave members of the West Riding Constabulary dashed on the pitch.

No wonder. In a third area of the ground, well out of the crossfire, stood the referee, Australia's Barry Gomersall. He was flapping his arms about like an apprentice chaplain caught in a riot in the high security wing at Wormwood Scrubs.

I know nothing about Rugby League but I have seen a lot of referees at one sport or another and Mr Gomersall, on Saturday's performance, does not figure in the first 5,000. He lost control very early on despite his linesmen repeatedly imploring him to intervene, and never looked like regaining it.

Popularity, particularly in a confrontation as crackingly tense as an entire Test series in the balance, is something a referee should never aspire to. Mediation is pathetic. If judge Michael Argyle had been in charge, Great Britain would have finished with about eight players to New Zealand's five.

The irony about the 'Keep Fighting' notice over the dressing room portal is that its message wasn't even addressed to Great Britain's Rugby League men. It is a permanent fitting and since the Test was being played at Elland Road, Leeds — home of Leeds United *soccer* club — was presumably installed there to inspire another code of players altogether.

However, it was so literally interpreted that Dr Morton Novis, the British medico cheerfully attired in bow-tie and tweed trilby, was muttering words like Arnhem. 'Toughest match I've seen in 30 years,' he said, though his assessment must be questionable since he spent most of it in the bowels of the grandstand sewing players together again.

He treated one case of bad concussion and had to stitch up vast gashes in three other men. Significantly they were all facial wounds. In the rush local anaesthetic isn't used. 'They yelp a bit sometimes,' chuckled Dr Novis, 'but they're very tough.'

Since we can be heavily censorious around here about violence in soccer and rugby union there can be no condoning a five-star rough-house in Rugby League.

In the only two previous League games I had seen the refereeing was dogmatic and exemplary. This was not the case here.

With so much at stake — Britain hadn't won a Test series for 20 years — we were, of course, never likely to be charmed by a free-running spectacle. What we saw was Somme-like attrition and defences so tight that it needed less brutality than the ingenuity of Barnes Wallis to penetrate them.

New Zealand threw it away by conceding three penalties for incidents so horrendous that even Mr Gomersall couldn't ignore them. Lee Crooks saved it for Britain by nervelessly kicking all three. His third, to draw the match 6-6 and halve the series in the final minute, was hit right-footed from wide out on the right — the most challenging position of all.

It sailed high between the posts, thus determining that out of all the mayhem should come one truly classic moment of sport. It isn't true, by the way, that violence on the field induces violence on the terraces. The 22,000 crowd were impeccably behaved. The other phenomenon was the staggering absence of any acrimony between the two teams afterwards.

'Naw bluddy way', explained Jeff Grayshon a 36-year-old, 16-stone Yorkshire bricklayer. 'We'll goan an' 'ave drink wi' boogers in minnit.'

In my innocence I asked Mr Grayshon, the areas of whose face that hadn't been stitched looking as though they'd received ten minutes' intensive treatment from a cheese grater, whether the third Test was the toughest match in which he had ever played.

Grayshon looked at me as though I was just starting second year in some effete preparatory school. 'Naw, lad,' he said pleasantly, 'they're all bluddy like that.'

That was 4.30 p.m. Saturday. Yesterday he was playing again for Leeds.

1986

1986 seemed to be spent in airplanes. It was probably the happiest year of my working life to date, full of laughter with colleagues and a long stay in Australia with my family. It was not quite such fun for some of the people we were writing about: England's cricketers under extreme pressure in West Indies, England's footballers only slowly acclimatising themselves to the World Cup in Mexico, Australia seemingly investing half its gross national product in its first defence of the America's Cup only to lose everything early in the following year. But there was another incident. In New Orleans, after a very late night following the Super Bowl, I awoke mid-morning and I switched on the television to watch the live transmissions of the Challenger blast-off into space. It was not the year to watch. A sudden ball of fire put matters like courage in sport into their true perspective.

SUPER BOWL FRENZY

The rising cult of American football in Britain prompted a trip to watch the game in its natural habitat. The hype for Super Bowl XX was hilarious. The match was dreadful and it was soon to emerge that several of the players had been fuelled by drugs.

NEW ORLEANS: JANUARY

THE art of the interview reached the ultimate in intellectual attainment here yesterday when a young reporter from an American mid-West newspaper thrust a tape-recorder beneath the granite jaw of a Chicago Bears defence man.

'Hey,' he yelled, 'what question ain't you been asked yet?'

While hardly the style of Panorama's school of interrogation it was, in the circumstances, both valid and witty. One has never, in one's fragile attempts to elicit information from professional sportsmen, witnessed such amazing scenes. Press Conference II, upleading matchwise to Super Bowl XX, was a hoot.

The Chicago and New England players, having given everything but their fingerprints to the media barely XIV hours earlier, had nothing original to say. The press had nothing else to ask. The true measure of how absurd it was is that, as the possessor of something akin to an English accent, I was continually being interviewed by two-man television teams from Wichita Falls and Medicine Hat.

Since I would have extreme difficulty in distinguishing a loose tackle from a London telephone kiosk — and the difference, I have to tell you, is slight — I am expecting scant fan mail from these regions. Anyway, I gave my name as Rupert Brooke and no-one raised an eyebrow.

Though intensified here by America's fawning attitude to the press, this is a classic situation in sport the world over: two charged-up opponents kicking their heels in their training camps while reporters are reduced to

interviewing one another. Heaven knows what's appearing in the Boston Globe. They have 23 writers on the spot, but then the New England Patriots have never previously experienced the sheer frenzy of a Super Bowl.

I use the description 'training camps' figuratively. The days of monastic pre-match isolation in log cabins up in the Catskill mountains are over. The patriots are enduring the five-star rigours of the New Orleans Inter-Continental while the Bears are just down the road in the Hilton. Both are hostelries appropriate to their astonishing financial stations.

Vulgar though it may be to discuss money in public, I can inform you precisely what each player in both teams earned last year. This required no investigative initiative on my part whatever since, at a press breakfast of coagulated egg and something called grits, a frantic publicist thrust all the information into my hand.

I must advise British soccer players not to read on.

Before bonuses and commercial enterprises outside the game, Walter Payton, the celebrated running back of the Chicago Bears, received £482,394. His quarter-back, Jim McMahon, earned £422,535. John S Hannah, said to be the greatest left guard in history and currently in the employ of the New England Patriots, appears to be relatively underpaid at a meagre £352,112.

After what's happening here, Chicago's total wage bill will rocket next season from its current £3,481,866 and New England's will show a considerable advance on its present £3,907,746. Real talent in this violent game means you can almost name your own price.

The bonus for each player in the winning team on Sunday is a modest £25,352 but this has to be weighed against the fact that as a Super Bowl victor, unless you are senselessly profligate, you virtually have a meal ticket for life.

'Winning just one Super Bowl,' admits Joe Namath, the nationally-lionised ex-quarter back with the New York Jets, 'bought me a life-style that I don't hesitate to describe as fantastic.'

Mind you, Broadway Joe certainly worked on his image. He claimed to have trained for most matches on Johnnie Walker Red Label Scotch and calmly announced in an infamous Playboy interview that he had scored his 1,000th field goal in the distaff stakes long before the end of his playing career.

American football equally has no reticence about revealing the source of all these amazing sums. It is, of course, television, the pace-maker that keeps the whole American sporting show on the road.

The actual fee that the National Broadcasting Corporation is paying for rights to screen a show that will keep Americans glued to their chairs for well over four hours is not disclosed. However, a single 30-second commercial for this prime prime-time re-enactment of World War Two costs a little matter of £387,323.

Just count the occasions when your screens are blanked out if you are watching the match in Britain — that is when the advertisements are appearing here — and you will get some idea of how the cascade of money comes in. It will total, by the end of the game, somewhere in the region of £36 million.

It is hardly extortion. Major corporations and business houses fight like wolves to get a Super Bowl commercial slot. Timex, for example, is launching a new style of watch, the Atlantis 100, on the back of Super Bowl.

It cost £700,000 to make the film of the watch submerged, for some reason, in the Red Sea, and they will pay a further £774,646 to show it on the screen during a stoppage late in the match.

It is banking, obviously, on a nail-biting finish but this is something of a gamble. The Chicago Bears are the shortest odds Super Bowl favourites for years.

But that is reckoning without the X-factor of all sport: adrenalin. No-one quits in the Super Bowl for here, in a single afternoon, life styles are forged. It is why Sunday's match will be played in the spirit of premeditated homicide.

By then the talking will be over and the only significant question answered.

TEST OF BRAVERY

The two pieces that follow were filed on successive days from the Caribbean. They reflect first the apprehension, then the outcome, of standing yet again in the firing line of a merciless West Indian pace attack. Supplication is not for the professional sportsman but occasionally a sportswriter is entitled to question the morality of playing games in a certain manner.

TRINIDAD: MARCH

JUST occasionally a sports event generates a tension that makes the waiting a physical agony. You only had to watch England's cricketers at the nets yesterday to know that this Trinidad Test is such a landmark in many young lives.

There was no skylarking. There was neither leg-pulling nor laughter. The intensity of it was epitomised by Ian Botham, normally a lax rehearser who just slogs a few sixes to loosen the muscles. Yesterday, heavily padded from right shoulder to knee, he batted as though his family's lives were at stake.

They are aware that England's eyes are upon them, ready to heap scorn upon ridicule, imply cowardice or leap on the bandwagon in the unlikely event that they beat the West Indies in a proper cricket match.

Their one-day victory here on Tuesday did more to set the Caribbean alight than restore their own confidence. Five-day cricket against the most relentlessly hostile attack in history, played before a crowd which in the past I have heard literally bay for blood, is a very different ball game.

If I were 20 years younger and an experienced Test batsman, my heart would still miss a beat on the way to the ground. Indeed, I might even feel that a minor injury sustained in a small traffic accident before we got there would be no inconvenience.

It will not happen, and I shall be hooted down here even for suggesting it, but the batsman I would like to see in the England team is the highly paid commentator, Geoffrey Boycott.

He is such a raving egocentric, so battle-hardened in situations like this, that he is capable of throwing off the years and writing a new chapter to his own glory, coincidentally helping England along the way.

It is not only Boycott's accumulative obsession that England needs at the moment, it is his meanness of spirit. You simply cannot take what the West Indies are currently hurling at you and still play to the Queensberry Rules.

At the height of the body-line fracas 54 years ago Bill Woodfull, the Australian captain, uttered one of the frequently quoted remarks in sport: 'There are two teams out there and only one of them is playing cricket'. The wheel has turned the full circle. The West Indies aren't playing cricket at all. They are waging war.

Under no circumstances must England squeal and to their immense credit no England player has attempted to do so. Four potentially lethal bouncers an over is no way to play the game, but while I can write that since I don't care about the repercussions, David Gower would be pilloried here even for hinting it.

This is an extremely volatile part of the world. The most innocent remark is analysed for racialist undertones.

Gower, happily an intelligent and perceptive man, is performing a superhuman job on the diplomatic front and deserves a few dazzling innings out there in the middle as a reward. However, the attack he will face here these next five days is from a different planet to the Australians he emasculated at the Oval last year.

That said, England should not be napalmed out of it in three days, as they were in the first Test in Jamaica.

Compared with the murderous ice-rink pitch at Sabina Park, the wicket here is a drawing room carpet. Based on clay, as in tennis, it takes the venomous speed out of the half-volley and restricts the bounce. By the fourth day, and pray God there is a fourth day, we may actually see some intellect restored in the shape of spin bowling.

Inconceivable though it may seem, the two teams get on very well off the field. On it they can be quite remorseless.

I do not believe cricket should be played in this fashion but I am clearly out of date. Television appears to have decreed that vicarious audiences want the thrill of Grand Prix motor-racing and bull-fighting introduced to cricket. It will, of course, destroy the game if the violence continues.

Men will make or break reputations here in the next few days. Unashamedly I take the unusual course of wishing England well.

They are up against it. The disparity between West Indies and any other team in the world is now such that you almost regard losing on the fifth day as a triumph. We sleep uneasily here to see how it will work out.

IT must be hard to imagine that merely watching Test cricket can be nearly as nerve-racking as playing it, but that's how it was yesterday as England gave every indication of vanishing on another funeral pyre.

Their dressing room balcony affords no privacy so the grief was cruelly evident. Graham Gooch was slumped deep in a chair, staring at a magazine whose pages never turned. Wilf Slack's eyes were fixed on something somewhere in the middle-distance. Peter Willey looked pale. He was entitled to. The 24th ball he received could have killed him.

All three were out. The Test was ten overs old. England were 30 for three. Even watching it, from the cowardly comfort of the Press box, provoked nausea. The sight of England's remaining batsmen, padded up against protracted collapse, did nothing to suggest the day would improve. They looked like men on Death Row.

It was the ball from Patrick Patterson to Willey that did it. It rose like a deflected rifle bullet from only fractionally short of a conventional length and screamed straight for his face. He had no hope of avoiding or playing it. By the grace of God and self-protective reaction, he got part of his bat in its path. But, of course, he was out.

While cricket like that is in progress, you tend to forget what made you fall in love with the game in the first place: the skill, the unspoken code of honour, the beauty of the grounds.

David Gower's battle for form and Allan Lamb's courageous batting did provide an hour's respite in which to enjoy, in the dragging intervals between balls, the stunning setting of this Trinidad arena with its mountain backdrop.

We deserved that for the doom-laden mood was soon to descend again. A colleague bet me five dollars to ten that Ian Botham wouldn't survive it for half an hour. He won with a luxurious 18 minutes to spare. Inevitability had set in again.

For the retreating batsmen the agony of dismissal is compounded by the cacophony of hearing the manner of it vividly described over hundreds of transistor radios tuned to ghetto-blasting levels. Even the mellifluous Etonian tones of Henry Blofeld do nothing to alleviate the misery of the moment.

But, outgunned, out-firepowered and out-classed, England, by contract and fixture list, are stuck with this tour. It is hard not to feel sympathy for them.

THE MONKS OF MONTERREY

England's footballers began their World Cup campaign in Mexico in hardly better shape than England's cricketers had completed theirs in the West Indies. It raised a fascinating question.

MONTERREY: JUNE

SOME years ago in a television interview I asked Joan Collins what she thought about celibacy as a cause. She considered the question gravely. 'Not,' she replied, 'much.'

Maybe England should take heed of Miss Collins.

Frankly I am flummoxed. Two months ago in the West Indies I was watching England's cricketers, surrounded by wives and never banned from the bar, lose five Tests in a row.

Here I find myself with the most teetotal and monastic England football team ever to leave our shores and they can't score a goal.

There is much debate about this peripheral matter here at the moment since England, who arrived with a glittering 11-match unbeaten credential, are playing like Yeovil Reserves, and that is hardly flattering Yeovil Reserves.

Indeed, when you see the most experienced man in the team, the 82-cap Ray Wilkins, throw a ball at a Paraguyan referee in dissent, you despair. Of course, he should have been sent off. For stupidity. This isn't the Saint and Greavesie Show. This is the wily old World Cup, where the South Americans have a vested interest in England falling flat on their faces.

But that apart, how is it that an undoubted fine collection of footballers can disintegrate so totally that it seems they are flicking through the index of Teach Yourself Football to find an idea about what to do next?

Bobby Charlton, a hero of England's 1966 World Cup triumph, looks genuinely distressed, which is not always the case with yesterday's superstars. 'Knackered,' he diagnoses. He believes they have sweated their chances into the scorching training grounds here.

Ron Greenwood, England's manager at the last World Cup, looks thoroughly relieved to be out of it all. He knows the lonely torture Bobby Robson is going through and gently ventures: 'All the travel, 120 miles there and back to the training sessions, may have something to do with it.'

The earthier come straight out with it and say that squatting up there on Men-Only Mountain, sipping purified aerated water with only a Gideon's Bible for company and the sound of cicadas to send you to sleep, is as conducive to bravura performance in the arena as a strawberry yoghurt would have been to the immortal Keith Miller before he went out to bat.

One cannot say that the English Football Association officials — though when you see them en masse you wonder who jogged their memories — were oblivious to the problem. While the England team were in a pre-World Cup training camp in Colorado, their wives were flown in for ten days of what the American forces euphemistically call rest and recuperation.

However, since their departure, England have played like Subbuteo pieces to lose 0-1 to Portugal and achieved the unthinkable by sharing a goal-less afternoon with some gentlemen from Morocco. Pundits around here keep raving on about how swiftly the Third World soccer nations are advancing to which one can only reply that the day we can't beat Morocco at *anything* amounts to early national redundancy.

The Danes, who are setting the World Cup alight at their first appearance have their wives with them. So have the Spaniards, who have come right back to form.

On the other hand, there is the contradictory evidence of Argentina who, in 1978, periodically emerged wild-eyed and raging from their female-proof redoubt and carried off the World Cup almost like that. Four years later, in defence of it, they were allowed to have their wives and children with them and promptly lost it.

'Ah, yes,' whispered a shrewd observer from the back of the group, 'but who said anything about children?'

I anticipate a number of heavily sponsored academic units will now find this a suitable subject for long-term research and come up with a 26,000 word evaluation circa 1998. I doubt that it will add very much to what Miss Joan Collins hit on in two words after a pause of three seconds.

Meanwhile it transpires that mathematically by beating Poland by an adequate margin and assuming that neither Portugal nor Morocco concedes a goal in their simultaneous match, England could not only still qualify for the next stage of the World Cup but actually finish top of their labouring group.

It only confirms how contrived this World Cup, by stretching its finalist teams from 16 to 24 for the sake of vast additional television revenue, has become.

Let us hope England benefit by it. But if they are world champions on current form, Yeovil Reserves really will have something to be elated about.

MILLION DOLLAR LEGS

This column was to prove more prophetic than I had remotely imagined. England's form improved to bring them into conflict with Argentina and a man named Maradona. We all knew about Maradona's feet. But it was to be the famous Hand of God match when the little man punched England out of the World Cup.

MEXICO CITY: JUNE

FOR a gasping and unworthy moment here yesterday I felt that England's footballers might storm on towards the World Cup Final on the strength of a tragic act of fate.

As the little bull-like figure came bustling round a corner — pursued by a running horde of reporters and about to be ambushed by an encircling wall of cameramen — he trapped his right leg in a heavy metal spool used for storing hoses.

For an eye's blink he began to fall. But then the phenomenal balance that is the secret of his artistry saved him. He recovered and strode on, the swarthy face darkened by fury at the fool who'd left it there.

Never mind a broken leg. A ripped ankle would have made blazing headlines around the world and plunged Argentina into national mourning. It may well have transformed the entire destiny of this World Cup.

The leg's owner, of course, was Diego Maradona, whom England's defenders have the monumental assignment from high noon here tomorrow of attempting to reduce to mortal stature.

Stop Maradona and they can surge on to win the World Cup. Lose him and they will look like blundering artisans condemned to the next plane home.

There are great stars here of the brilliance of France's Michel Platini and Mexico's Hugo Sanchez but of none but Maradona is it said that on his day — and such days are so frequent that his market value is now £7 million — he can win the World Cup alone.

He *can* be stopped, of course. The Italians stopped him dead in his tracks in the last World Cup in Spain by cynically kicking him from groin to ankle whenever they could lay a boot on his passing figure.

I hope, pray even, that England have no similar thoughts in the darkest recesses of their minds. Such tactics would be interpreted here as nothing short of a flare-up of the Falklands war and, amid a passionate short-fused Latin crowd, no Briton would be safe.

Maradona will not be drawn into admitting there has ever even been a tiff to ruffle the long history of friendship between Argentina and Britain. 'I am here,' he repeated in a hundred interviews yesterday, 'to play football.'

Carlo Bilardo, Argentina's coach says: 'Among his team friends he is a very humble man who wishes only for the team to win.'

Argentinian journalists smile at this diplomatic evaluation of a star whose postures and temperaments they know so well and, when out of earshot, they confide that there was not universal dismay when Maradona packed his bags, rounded up his coterie of hangers-on, his rude and bloated business manager, and headed off for Europe.

Europe was where the money was. Barcelona, where he arrived in 1982, is also where the culture is and where the fans expect their idols to act with style. Maradona and clique roared around the gracious city as though they were cowboys in downtown Buenos Aires.

The favourite trick with money to burn, was to hire out an entire restaurant for an evening and have the public excluded. This out-raged the proud and formal Catalans and Maradona's star was soon in the descendancy. For a while his football talents followed it.

Two years later he was to meet his match: a London Cockney quite as street-smart as he was. For a while when he took over as manager of Barcelona, Terry Venables quietly assessed the character and lifestyle, the habits and the roistering friends of the world's greatest footballer.

He then decided that Barcelona was not big enough for both of them and performed the unthinkable: he sold Maradona to the Naples club in Italy.

There was scarely a whisper of protest in Barcelona for what turned out to be not only a stroke of great perception but an act of salvation. Barcelona won the Spanish League championship. Maradona fired his business agent and began to recapture the football form that, at its height, has the bewitching quality that transforms mere spectatorship into a trance-like experience.

Now a mature 25, he has brought that peak of form to this World Cup. You find yourself holding your breath and not blinking as he bullets himself and ball into a labyrinth defence, weaves through non-existent spaces and then emerges, still with ball, running clear from a scene of carnage.

When the Argentines opened their training camp to the world's press, Maradona displayed none of the churlishness which for so long has come so naturally.

He wasn't charming, for it's hard to be charming with milling media men shoving microphones, tape recorders and cameras into your face. But he was patient, compliant and polite — and very wary.

He is always wary of crowds, for twice in his career he has been seriously kicked by hostile fans hoping to injure him before a vital game.

The biggest fortune ever yet amassed from football is still invested in those legs, which accounted for the murderous look which crossed his countenance when he collided with that very heavy lump of metal yesterday.

Thus Maradona: the man who could well stand between England and the World Cup.

If England lose, the lone consolation may be that they lose to a bravura performance by a little man whose artistry can transcend even patriotism and partisanship. It's hardly one to sleep through.

KEEPING CALM IN A CRISIS

Turnberry is one of my favourite places on earth. But when the wind blows there at an Open Championship fortitude is the only name of the game.

TURNBERRY: JULY

ON a day when the seagulls flew backwards and men blasphemed through clenched teeth and the scores exploded like an innings by Bradman, one man survived on serenity.

After 2½ hours, by which time he was still only playing the 8th, Mr Ho Ming Chung, in his first British Open, had explored areas of Turnberry never even visited by the most erratic high handicap member.

He had played most of his second shots out of the kind of rough that snapped shafts and on the greens had revealed a delicacy of touch normally associated with Frank Bruno's sparring partners. He was seven over par and clearly headed for the check-in desk at Prestwick airport on his way back to Taiwan.

He had waited 40 years — 19 of them as a golf pro — for his big chance and had even brought his wife, Daughter of Spring, to witness him take it. Daughter of Spring, cocooned in anorak, head scarf and what appeared to be heavy WRAC-surplus slacks, looked more like the Mother of Winter when Ho dutifully three-putted the 8th.

'No he played good. He like tree' explained Daughter of Spring enigmatically. It was a reference, apparently, to the pitiless Turnberry terrain where there is hardly a bush to break the cutting-edge of the Westerlies that scream in off the Atlantic.

The fantastic spectacle amid all this carnage, however, was Ho Ming Chung's face.

While others winced, grimaced, shook heads in despair and from time to time even bashed clubs into the ground in frustration, Mr Ho brought a whole new meaning to oriental inscrutability by never remotely changing his expression.

Well, he did just once. When his hat blew off and cartwheeled back down the 7th fairway.

Nor did it change when he stood on the 9th tee and hit the perfect drive that prefaced one of the most resolute passages of golf played by anyone on a day so horrendous that par scoring was virtually impossible.

From there to the club house, a further three hours away, he parred every hole except one, picked up a birdie on the 17th and came in with the eminently respectable 77 that keeps him well in contention. Then, and only when Daughter of Spring hugged him tightly, did he reveal an emotion. He laughed.

There was a lesson there somewhere. 'Do you always keep as calm as that in a crisis?' I asked Mr Ho. 'Yes.' he replied.

'Did you ever feel like quitting?' I asked. 'Yes,' he replied.

'Do you draw inner strength from your religion?' I asked 'Yes' he replied.

'What is your religion?' I asked. 'Yes,' he answered. Anyway he's a very good golfer and greatly rewarded the small gallery that followed him yesterday.

Poor Andrew Broadway couldn't quite match that Eastern equanimity. A part-time labourer on a Brighton building site until he turned pro only this year, he crashed to a 10 at the 7th hole, found himself 18 over par at the 10th and, discovering a pain in his back, withdrew on medical grounds.

'Actually,' he said graciously, 'it wasn't fair to my playing partners to carry on. I was ruining their concentration.'

Andrew will be back in Brighton this morning and won't be reading the newspapers. Ho Ming Chung and Daughter of Spring can at least look at the pictures.

DRIVING ON THE BURMA ROAD

Severiano Ballesteros has the reputation of being extremely testy. But when he turns the charm on, playing against him is no worse than having a nervous breakdown.

WENTWORTH: SEPTEMBER

IT was like tackling the Times crossword in front of Einstein. Or driving James Hunt to the airport. Or writing a letter to Graham Greene.

You know the true giants are invariably tolerant, yet lunch — in this column's case two stiff gins and a bowl of soup — rested in the stomach like suet pudding. One is old enough to recognise the symptoms of a bad attack of nerves.

At 2.42 p.m. precisely the starter at Wentworth's Burma Road calls this column's name with all the enthusiasm of an auctioneer selling off a job lot of back copies of Farmers' Weekly. One steps forward, waxen-smiled, armed with a four iron.

As anyone who knows anything about golf will tell you, a four iron is probably the most stupid club a man can carry on to what the critics have called the most intimidating first tee in Britain. Even if stupendously struck, it will hardly get you into competitive play on this switch-back par four.

Why, then, take a four iron? Because it is the only club with which your correspondent, an occasional golfer, can make contact with the ball on a reasonably regular basis.

Shrewd thinking, though I say it myself. The usual purple mists cloud the brain at the top of the back swing but somehow the ball flies 170 yards straight as an arrow into a fearful lie in some transverse rough.

Like every amateur who has ever played in a pro-am we thank Our Maker for sparing us an air swing.

Proceeding down the fairway, an arm falls lightly round my shoulder.

'Why you hit four iron?' he say.

'Because,' I say, lapsing into the pidgin-speech we British use instead of foreign languages, 'I no good with any other club,'

'Rubbish', says Severiano Ballesteros, the best golfer in the world.

'You just stand up there and hit the ball with any bloody club you please. We all friends here, unnerstand?

This you are not going to believe. Our foursome, also involving Dennis Hart, a Scottish travel agent and Ian Chubb, a Bell's Whisky man, all got down in five at the first hole. So did Sevvy, who may well deliberately have punched his second shot left of the green to make the rest of us feel better.

At the short fifth, we halve another in par. 'Estupendo', he cry. We are feeling better now. The knees have stopped quivering and mists are clearing. This was Sevvy's being-nice day to the public.

Ballesteros flew in to Wentworth by helicopter. Since he's staying in a not distant hotel for this week-end's European event at Sunningdale, he could, possibly more swiftly and certainly at one-tenth of the price, have come by car.

But it was a day for style, not economy. When the rotor blades stopped he stepped out to devote an entire day to publicising the La Manga Club, a sports resort in South East Spain, to whom he is attached as travelling professional.

True, La Manga rarely sees him. His brother, Manuel, runs the place. But Sevvy is the flagship. Eight days a year he dedicates himself to promoting its activities with all the intensity he gives to winning championships. It involves playing golf with the likes of me.

This he tolerated with a smile and no semblance of impatience. Understandably. It is not possible under the terms of his La Manga contract to state precisely how much he earned for his day among the golfing lower classes but had it been a one-off job the price would have been minimally £25,000.

He chats amiably along the fairway. 'No,' he says, 'I no learn a single word of English until I 17. Then I began to travel and picked up a few words.' He now speaks English engagingly. 'No problem' is his favourite phrase.

'No problem,' he laughs as you hook another tee shot into foliage. 'Funny game is golf. It's the only sport which the professionals practise all the time and the amateurs never practise at all. Do you practise?'

'Never,' I admit.

'Yes, I can see that,' he says.

'Me, I am like a pianist. When I am not playing in tournaments I still practise six, seven hours every day. It is the only way I know to stay where I am.' The great man demonstrated the controlled draw and slice, issued a few tips, signed autographs and dispenses bonhomie all day, earning in the process slightly more than Max Faulkner won in prize money during his entire career.

SAIL OF A LIFETIME

We were to spend five months in Australia covering Dennis Conner's campaign to win back the America's Cup. It was an idyllic period blighted in only one respect. The apprehension in this column about jumping off a 12-metre yacht in heavy seas was justified. I slipped a spinal disc and take this opportunity of thanking Dr Ken Kennedy, the ex-Irish rugger international, for giving me hell but getting it back.

FREMANTLE: OCTOBER

VIEWED from a helicopter yesterday the passage of KA8, the glorious royal blue, gold and scarlet-hulled South Australian 12-metre, must have given considerable cause for alarm.

So erratic was its progress into 15 knots of Indian Ocean headwind that it may well have been assumed that its helmsman was off his rocker , hopelessly drunk or simply working his ticket.

In fact, he was none of these things.

Firstly, since he can't even swim, he was petrified about falling off the bloody thing. Secondly, having got on it, he was constantly in a panic about how he was ever going to get off again out there in a high-pitching sea.

Well here we are back on dry land, probably for ever, to offer sincere thanks to the captain and crew of South Australia for permitting a landlubber Pom reporter to have 20 minutes at the helm of their 26 ton, 65 foot, £400,000 toy and thus get a closer glimpse at this America's

Cup game.

Boy, that's some sport out there. The horizon spends all the time disappearing up its own axis, the deck is never there when you feel like putting your foot on it and driving it is like coming very fast down a motorway on a 300 horse-power eiderdown.

When all the canvas is up the noise is amazing. There are two distinct sounds, a constant groaning which reminds you of about 2,000 mortally wounded men on a battlefield, and sharp cracks that sound like small-arms fire in films about the American Civil War.

'See that tall building,' commanded Phil Thompson, pointing out a Perth skyscraper that was swaying around on the distant shore like a metronome, 'try steering for that.'

Phil was in charge for the day while John Savage, South Australia's resident skipper, was having a 10,000-mile service in a local clinic in preparation for the start of Australia's four-syndicate battle to find the one yacht that will defend the Cup.

Behind us, in what appeared to be a 2 ft 6 in high broom cupboard, navigator Steven Kemp and tatician Gary Simmonds, were hammering away at a computer which would probably win the World Chess Championship on its own. If I could have understood what they were saying I would have assuredly complied, but merely steering South Australia at that skyscraper was like wrestling with Geoff Capes.

'Keep her at 7.9,' yelled Phil.

The problem was 7.9 of what? There were three computer dials and nine switches immediately behind the wheel. One of the dials was registering 8.6. 'That's the one,' shouted Phil. 'Get the boat speed down to 7.9.'

But how? More significantly, why? What's the point of coming out here to make Dennis Conner look an idiot and then slow the boat down?

Phil had no time to explain. Instead of heading for the Perth skyscraper we now appeared to be en route for Durban, South Africa, with only a few sandwiches on board. Phil jerked the wheel with his left hand and there, dead ahead, as we slalomed down a waves, was the skyscraper again.

The answer, apparently, is that when you're beating to windward — which is say sailing directly into a headwind whose natural instinct is to blow you back to where you've just come from — you close-haul the yacht to 25 degrees to the wind at an optimum speed which gets you to the turning buoy considerably quicker than going much faster at an angle of 35 degrees.

That achieved, the sense of power when you've got her going is like being Prime Minister or piloting Concorde.

While you are striving to retain the foregoing, there is one further thing to remember. Lurking at your shoulder is a metal branch which sticks out from the mast down to the back end of the boat and scythes across the deck every time you tack. This is called the boom. It weighs about 240lb and if it hits you in the head you'll probably get washed up in the Falkland Islands.

Meanwhile, there is the nagging terror about disembarking. South Australia will be out here all day, rehearsing hard. One has to leave them to it. This means jumping from the swaying 12-metre in to a bobbing chase craft about the size of a Serpentine rowing boat.

It's only a five foot drop but what concerns the layman, I can authoritatively report, is the gap of water that keeps yawning between the two hulls. You close your eyes and go for it. Back on shore John Savage, returned from the clinic, laughs.

These guys walk on water every day. 'It's just like ball games,' he said. 'If you're born with a ball sense you don't think about anything. You just do it. It's the same with the sea. If you don't have an affinity with it, you'll find it hard.'

I found it hard.

South Australia's 11-man crew never laughed once. They were as impeccably mannered as the wardroom of the QE2.

Meanwhile, a mile or two down the ocean, 12 of the challenging yachts were fighting it out to take on Australia at the end of next January.

The America's Cup is an extraordinary business. Yesterday our education into it was marginally widened.

DENNIS CONNER SPEAKS OUT

Dennis Conner was eventually to win back the America's Cup in piratical fashion. He is an outrageous character who drinks more alcohol than any sportsman I have ever met. Our evening of reconciliation won't easily be forgotten.

FREMANTLE: DECEMBER

AT shortly after 1.15 here the other morning a few passers-by were treated to the unorthodox spectacle of Mr Dennis Conner, the distinguished yachtsman, playing golf down Fremantle's main shopping street.

Actually he struck only one shot which, in the circumstances, was rather a good one. His three-iron off a tight Tarmacadam lie faded only fractionally, thus obviating manslaughter or carnage to property.

Mr Conner tossed the club back into the boot of his car with a laugh, resumed his seat outside Papa Luigi's coffee house and picked up the theme of his raving evening-long monologue: the iniquitous mendacity of the world's Press.

Plum-complexioned from the months at sea,

with the slightly stammering diction of a light sub-machine gun on the blink, he demanded: 'How the hell can I be sure Jesus Christ wasn't a Hindu? How can I be positive the Vietnam war even happened? I mean, all that's history now but at the time it was news and news is written by reporters and reporters lie. They lie.'

Across the table Judy, the first and only Mrs Conner, grinned and shook her head. One formed the impression she may have heard all this irrefutable logic before. She has much in common with Mother Teresa and is better looking.

Mr Conner, whose dismissive opinion of contemporary journalism is based on what he sees as the scurrilously inaccurate reporting of his races in the America's Cup, then proceeded to another of his favourite subjects.

This turned out to be whether or not he is the most famous man in the world.

Someone suggested the Pope might also be in with a chance. Dennis considered this unlikely possibility in brooding silence. His expression cleared when it was conceded that while there are plenty of religious leaders around, there is only one America's Cup and Conner is the best known helmsman.

Over dinner Dennis Conner had occasionally punctuated his assault on the Press with a few philosophical and autobiographical observations. 'I am', he yelled at one stage, 'the happiest man in the world. I can't wait to get up in the mornings. I've got no money but what the hell, I'm the son of a fisherman, you know.'

Whether this last disclosure was meant to elicit sympathy for the happiest man in the world was rather difficult to determine. Few get close enough to question him deeply. His crewmen, though, would die for him and apparently have to be prepared to daily.

'There's no thrill in the world', he suddenly cried, 'like crossing over another boat with all the crew hanging out waiting to jump overboard in case there's a collision.' His eyes indicated that he was still out there, tacking sheer fear into another opponent.

He has made such a stunning comeback in this America's Cup that there's much money here now that says this extraordinary man is going to win it back. He reckons, through certain terms in his contract with the Stars and Stripes syndicate of California, that it will be worth 25 million dollars to him if he does.

Three times during dinner he announced to anyone who happened to be listening at distant tables that he proposed to do just that. Once, he even walked the length of the restaurant to confirm his objective to Alan Bond, who was quietly dining there with business associates. As a precaution against being stricken by thirst on his walkabout he carried his glass and a bottle of Californian red with him.

Despite his aversion to reporters our dinner, in the true spirit of Christmas, was in the nature of a reconciliation. Apparently I had written on some occasion that he rates C-minus for charm, a grading Mr Conner was graciously prepared to submit for reassessment.

Well, let's put it this way. Under full sail Dennis Conner makes Muhammad Ali seem reticent, John McEnroe shy, Ian Botham domesticated, Ron Atkinson bashful, Greg Norman unambitious and Hurricane Higgins an exemplar of the conventional lifestyle.

That may not add up to charm exactly, but it makes him monumentally unforgettable. And, anyway, his genius at the helm of a yacht, was never in dispute.

There was evidence to imply we may even have finished up pals. With Dennis it's hard to tell. But after ranting that never again would he attend one of those nightly vituperative exchanges with the world's press, he changed his mind and came up with a suggestion.

'Let you and me go down to one of those Press conferences together', he said. 'I'll sit with all you reporters and we'll give 'em hell up there on the platform and then we'll all go away and I'll learn how them lies are written.'

And he laughed a laugh that must have struck terror into the hearts of dozens of small creatures out there in the Outback. It wouldn't have done much for his yachting opponents either. He's going to be a very hard man to beat.

1987

1987 took us back to China and a frightening moment: standing on the first tee of the Chinese Open Golf Championship at Chung Shan, not to report it but play in it. Heavy veils must be drawn over your correspondent's performance but it may be disclosed that he missed the half-way cut by a total many of England's middle order Test batsmen would have considered almost respectable. Rome hosted romantic World Athletics Championships — romantic, that is, until it became known that the Italians had cheated their way to a long-jump medal. It was to be almost two years before we also discovered that Ben Johnson had cheated his way to a new world record in the 100 metres. The year ended on a sour note of cynical and bad behaviour, but there had been compensations: meeting the brave Mike Nemesvary, a champion among disabled sporting champions, and lending a hand to stop the developers chipping another chunk off our green and pleasant land.

TIMELESS TWICKERS

It was reassuring to return from abroad and visit a corner of a home field that will forever be our England.

TWICKENHAM: FEBRUARY

TWICKENHAM is the Tory party at play, and the proof of it on Saturday lay in its expedient interpretation of 'bulk supplies' and the wonderful singing of God Save Our Queen. Not just any old Queen, please note, but Our Queen: Elizabeth II, Defender of the Faith.

Hats came off, thumbs brushed trouser seams and the sound that arose was not so much a hymn of patriotism as a reproof to the yobs. This was Twickers. Interrupt here with any of that 'Ere we go' nonsense and you'll get a thick ear.

Yet the spectre of yobbishness was present and could be found as early as page three in the England-France programme where, for the benefit of any old shire Tories who usually depute such details to the butler, the following amazing paragraph appeared:

'The description of cans is self-explanatory, but by bottles is meant any bottle-shaped container, whether it be of glass, polythene, plastic or any other material.'

Anxious to co-operate with Government and police, Twickers announced, they would deny entry to anyone bearing 'bulk supplies' of any receptacle containing alcohol.

But how bulky is a bulk supply? Two cases of Nuit St Georges '74? A mere half-dozen bottles of Rioja? A BMW bootful of champagne, whisky, gin and vodka?

Clearly, at Twickers, such supplies are regarded as a mere post-breakfast apertif. If there is anything more enjoyable than a big international at Twickers, it is the two hours in the freezing North car park anticipating a big international in the high cathedral of rugger.

And even on medicinal grounds it requires stocks which, in other hands, would result in the wrecking and probable sinking of cross-Channel ferries and the demolition of entire European cities.

There was probably more booze in the Twickenham car park on Saturday — not counting the emergency supplies for impromptu toasts at half-time carried in non-bottle shaped hip flasks — than has ever been dispensed before a European Cup soccer match.

Old friends met after years, old internationals stood under old hedges and said they'd never bothered to train, old school ties were everywhere, old sheepskins kept the cold at bay and a glass or two of old brandy settled the stomach before the big game.

In five hours on the premises I witnessed not one hint of trouble even though England played their guts out and were beaten.

The first half was mostly spent watching Marcus Rose rehearsing the quadrille in slow motion: six measured steps backwards, two sideways, one obliquely forward and then freezing, a still-life in concentration, before he kicked England in with a chance.

The second half, sacre bleu, was illuminated by the sort of try you'd cross half the world to see. A devastating, chest-out, jinking, dazzling 70-yard run by Monsieur Sella which was about as effective as the guillotine. To a man, woman and children with names like Charles, and Angus, the Tory party, present and future, rose and politely applauded.

But, then, one had travelled half the world to see it. Home from five months exile at the America's Cup, reading daily that the old country had gone to the dogs, Twickenham, in truth a multiplicity of voters, was less a rugger match than a matter of welcome reassurance.

BRAVERY AND BRAVADO

A few days after this column was written Mike Nemesvary made his attempt on the world toboggan record. At high speed his machine slewed sideways, then cartwheeled down one of the most dangerous pistes in Europe. When his rescuers reached him Mike was lying on his side, laughing. He told them he was unhurt.

LES ARCS: MARCH

THE subtle distinction between bravery and bravado is graphically defined by a young man closely acquainted with both.

'Bravery,' said Mike Nemesvary without modesty, 'is what I and hundreds like me are doing right now. Bravado is what I shall be getting up to in the Alps in the next few weeks.'

What Mike was doing right then may hardly strike you as requiring physical courage. He was eating rare fillet steak in an excellent restaurant in Hindhead, Surrey, and telling stories that got randier by the glass as we abandoned the afternoon to the second bottle of claret.

Regrettably he could only grab his glass after a series of convulsive jerks and then hold it in precarious finger tips as he drank through a straw. To manhandle the meat, when cut up on a board on his lap, he jammed a fork into a tightly laced half-glove and negotiated it between first finger and thumb.

With the expert help of his full-time nurse it had taken him only two hours to get bathed, shaved and dressed. So it is and forever will be, every hour, every day, every month, every year for the rest of Mike Nemesvary's life. He had his 26th birthday last week.

Calmly and logically he has contemplated suicide — 'doing myself in' as he casually puts it — but each time he has struggled back from the beckoning darkness by committing himself to a new outrageous project.

That is why in the coming days, high in the Alps, he will have what remains of his body and his very sharp brain strapped into a contraption that looks like a chromium bullet and be cast loose off a holding rein to career down a hypotenuse of packed snow in pursuit of the world speed record in a toboggan.

Electronic chronometers 25 metres apart at the steepest point of his run will record his optimum speed which, if the air is clear and the piste fast, should broach 100 kilometres an hour.

His greater problem, since he is paralysed from the chest downwards apart from some flickering response in his fingers, will be how to stop himself.

Much engineering ingenuity in Leon Smith's cluttered back-street garage in Shepherd's Bush, London, has been concentrated on coming up with what hopefully could prove a failsafe escape: an arrester tail parachute activated by Mike smashing the left side of his head against a survival button.

It was only into the second bottle of wine that one could brace oneself to confront him with the terrible question: 'Mike, are you trying to kill yourself?'

'Good God, no,' laughed the young man hunched in the wheelchair that wouldn't even fit under the restaurant table. 'I know plenty of ways that are more efficient and economical to do that.'

It was then, with an insight beyond the comprehension of the etymologists who compile dictionaries, mow lawns and make love, that Mike Nemesvary talked about the difference between bravery and bravado.

'Bravado,' he said, 'is what's keeping me alive.

Every day the thought of it gives me a reason to live. It presents me with something to shoot at.'

Bravery?

'Bravery,' said Mike very carefully, 'is waking up sweltering under a duvet in the middle of the night knowing that you can't move a single muscle to kick the thing off.'

'Bravery is watching guys dash off to work in the mornings knowing that it's going to take two hours of agony to do what they have just done in 20 minutes to get out of the house.

'Bravery is putting up with all the bloody trouble you have with your bowels and your bladder.

'Bravery is not giving in to the thought that strikes you first in the morning: 'Christ, I simply can't face all the fuss and the mess and the turmoil and the wheelchairs and the lifting and the stares of people who really would prefer you to be institutionalised out of their sight and their conscience.'

Mike Nemesvary, like many others, has sustained that kind of bravery since a glittering world fell in on him in a tragic instant on the afternoon of May 18, 1985, on the lawn of his temporary home in Bentley, Hampshire.

A self-confessed showman, Mike postponed lunch to dazzle his new ash blonde girlfriend Suzy, with artistry on the trampoline.

Nemesvary — the tongue-tripping surname comes from his father who escaped from Hungary in the 1956 uprising, married a Scottish girl and emigrated to Canada with his four-year-old son in 1965 — started skiing, trampolining and gymnastics at the age of seven and by 13 had so skilfully merged all three sporting disciplines that he was the hottest free-style skiing property in the world.

Free-style skiing, loosely known as hot-dogging, is the sport in which skiers perform spectacular feats in mid-air as they zoom off high ledges.

Mike was so good at it that he won four Canadian national titles, came to Europe to win the British title in 1982-3-4, turned professional and eventually earned some real cash performing his parabolas for the opening sequences of the James Bond film, A View To Kill.

So everything was going for him that May afternoon as he sprang on the trampoline: radiant health, good looks, good-looking girls, a career in films and the revamped Olympics, the go-getting drive that guaranteed money would never be a problem so long as he kept his head.

Unaccountably he lost it mid-air going for a double-twist, double-back somersault which normally would have been as testing to him as tying a shoelace would be to us.

He became disorientated, crashed down on his neck and broke it.

He woke up in the Royal Orthopaedic Hospital in Stanmore the following evening. The sun was setting. 'God,' he said to himself 'it can't be true. I've just got to wait here until the feeling comes back.'

But it never did. And more than 600 days later he is now as reconciled as he ever will be to the living nightmare that it never will.

Today he lives only for the challenges he piles up before him: to pass his driving test on the specially-converted Audi outside his ground-floor flat, to lend his name and experience to Back-Up, the British Ski Federation's programme to take other paralysis victims to the mountains and, more immediately, to win a three-line small-print entry in the next Guinness Book of Records as the fastest-ever man down a mountain in a toboggan.

For the moment, great secrecy surrounds the engineering skills that will get him down the mountain in a blur of speed. 'I've still got great strength in the biceps,' he reveals, 'and everything is being converted mechanically to make use of that. All, hopefully, will be revealed in due course.'

His face shines at the prospect.

'Some mornings, driving up through the outskirts of London,' he said, 'I look at all the grey faces and actually think that I'm luckier than all of them. Life isn't worth living if there isn't a quality to it and, for a while at least, there is a real quality to mine.'

The indomitable spirit survives. 'Now,' grinned Mike, 'for a bit of bravado.'

LORD HAWKE CALLING

Lord Hawke, captain of Yorkshire 1883-1910, later president and treasurer of MCC, was seen by many as the game's most autocratic martinet. He died in 1938 but when, almost 50 years later, Lord's auctioned off 844 items of cricket memorabilia — Lord Hawke's blazer among them — one had to try to contact him.

LONDON: MARCH

CAN'T hear you very well. Got some backguard of a German bandsman called Beethoven up here who plays the trumpet all day. Deaf as a post, he is. Hold on while I shut him up.

Ah, that's better. Blazer, you say? Yes, know all about it. Get the London papers by satellite.

Damned sad day, I can tell you, when they've got to sell a chap's coat. Young Cowdrey's going to have a bit to answer for when he arrives. Wants the money to titivate the fillies' thunder-box in the Long Room, I suppose.

I presume it will be brought by one of them johnny-come-lately property developers who've wheedled their way into sport. Damned shame. Rather it went to Oxfam as a bedspread for three Ethiopian families.

Best of all I'd like to see it go to that Botham fellow. Hits the ball just like Jessop, y'know. We simply had to drag Florence Nightingale away from the telly for lunch the day he played that fantastic innings at Leeds. Even C.B. Fry admired it and, Boss knows, he's hard to please.

What's happening with Boycott? Is he a millionaire yet? If he'd been playing when I was Yorkshire captain he would have had half the average and been twice as popular. Yorkshire won eight County Championships under my captaincy, you know, and I'm proud to say I did a lot for the professionals. Stopped them getting drunk every night, made sure they got paid through the winter. Come to think of it, I probably did more for Yorkshire cricketers than that Scargill man did for Yorkshire miners.

Must make a note to take that up with Trotsky over dinner. They let anyone in here these days, you know.

I know, you're going to ask me about that 'Pray God no professional shall ever captain England' remark, aren't you? First thing Bernard Shaw asked me when he arrived. Got so heated he was immediately transferred to Gandhi Wing.

Yes, I *did* say it but, as usual, it was taken out of context by you Fleet Street wallahs. What I meant, and what I still believe, is sport will destroy itself if it's left in the hands of those who see it only as a vehicle for making money.

Look at boxing. Fitzsimmons and Corbett fought toe to toe for the world title and the better man won. Both got paid and that was it.

What happens now? Businessmen who never get hit keep setting up new versions of world boxing authorities until you've got half a dozen champions at the same weight.

Do you know what Rocky Marciano said about that fight the other night between Tyson and that chap who calls himself Bonecrusher Smith? He said it was fixed so that American television could squeeze in all the commercials between rounds. Television was only a magic lantern at Savoy Hill when I made the move up here so I'm no expert, but Rocky is called a street-smart guy by the younger inmates and I must say that his view makes sense. It was the worst fight I've ever seen and we video most of them.

Take tennis. Do you think McEnroe gives a toss about what happens to the game when he and his father have wrung the last penny they can out of it? Admittedly, we're some way from the scene up here, but that twosome should be written up by Arthur Conan Doyle.

And what about the Olympic Games?

I was a mere lad of 36 when that French cove, de Coubertin, relaunched the Olympics but one had to admit, for all we felt about the Froggies, that they were a damned good idea. Get the kids involved, give them something to aspire to.

What's happened? The professionals have taken over. Now the kids have to fight out their finals at breakfast-time to fit in with east coast peak viewing TV times in America so that a bunch of sweaty, nervous businessmen can entertain one another to lunch for the next four years.

We see it all up here, you see. We have time without end.

Have I made my point about the damage that professionals can do to sport? Have I made my point that I wasn't attempting to be snobbish when I said I hope no professional would ever captain England?

I hope so. My fellow Yorkshireman, Mr Michael Parkinson, has from time to time most wittily implied that I am some reactionary figure, wing-collared and stiff with prejudice against the working classes. It wasn't my fault that I inherited a lot of land. That was my cross as much as Scargill's.

Anyway, they're selling my blazer. I shall watch the bidding with interest. Thank you for ringing. Reverse charge call I hope. They're very hot on that up here.

IN LIVING MEMORY

As a young reporter I had covered many First Division football matches at Burnley. None was as passionately fought as this Fourth Division game there in 1987.

BURNLEY: MAY

WE gathered like predatory undertakers and professional mourners, lured by the death throes of a stricken giant.

Reporters who'd forgotten where Burnley was, spilled out over the Press seats which had gathered the dust of disinterest. Some had their obituaries already written.

There was coruscating criticism of the club that became too big for its boots, posthumous debunking of Bob Lord, the small-town butcher who'd built himself a grandiose memorial and there was lyrical lament for one of the 12 founder clubs of English, and thus, world football.

We noted that the sun shone down on the old dying mill town with ironic brilliance. We recalled that for years it had the highest suicide rate in Britain. We looked at the beautiful appointed ground with a pitch barely scarred at the end of the season and agreed how sad it all was.

We'd done our homework, too. Burnley, founded March 1888 as a League club; the smallest town in Britain to sustain a First Division team for years on end; the first club in

England to establish a training ground elsewhere to work on brilliant tactical moves; the club which had a crowd of 49,734 for a match in 1914 and a record gate of 54,775 for a cup game against Huddersfield in 1924.

Now, poverty-stricken on attendances of fewer than 3,000 they were about to fall through the floor of the Fourth Division. They had to beat Orient and rely on miracles elsewhere. It wasn't going to happen so let's get it over with and catch the 5.47 back to London.

But it was, of course, the day that Burnley made fools of the ghouls.

The script started going wrong when Burnley and Orient came out for the 3 p.m. kick-off and were immediately shooed off again by police. Thousands were still outside the ground clamouring to get in, yell their encouragement and join in the singing of 'You'll Never Walk Alone.'

Burnley would never have been in this plight had they not been abandoned to walk alone several seasons ago but their players were too panic-stricken for cynicism when they finally kicked off in front of 15,781 spectators. They were playing for their own careers, let alone Burnley's survival and the sporting term 'sudden death' takes on new shades of meaning when the last pay cheque is only 90 minutes away.

I shall never quite determine who won that match: the Burnley team or the crowd.

The Burnley team were fuelled by 45 per cent talent — which means they played above themselves — and 180 per cent adrenalin. The crowd, in this recently echoing concrete mausoleum at the foot of a damp Lancashire valley, was as passionate, pro rata, as I have ever heard.

They came from everywhere. Cliff Knights, who left Burnley in 1960 to become a prosperous chartered engineer near Bristol, had driven up that morning with his wife Betty, for what he was convinced would be a wake. John Ratcliffe, who cut his teeth on Burnley football until he went to London University and started teaching geography in Catford, spent £100 simply to go back and stand on the terrace and roar.

There were hundreds in the crowd who were on similar pilgrimages back home, thousands who had actually stirred themselves from TV just down the road now that Armageddon was near.

They were immaculately behaved, as were the visiting Orient fans from London, and I have to report that if I could see matches of such passion and intensity even three times a season I would cease being one of the soccer's missing millions tomorrow.

It was a classic sporting occasion, if not a classic exhibition of football, superbly refereed and ferociously contested by an Orient team themselves in contention for promotion.

The roar that greeted the goal that put Burnley 2-0 ahead was probably heard in Blackpool. The silence that met Orient's goal was such that many couldn't believed it was scored until play restarted in the centre circle.

A draw was no good to Burnley. So began the 35 minutes that were to determine whether Burnley died, aged 99 without so much as a formal telegram from the Queen. The spectator immediately in front of me, a local businessman with a tartan scarf wrapped into an extremely expensive mackintosh, had assured me earlier that if Burnley lost the match Burnley, as a town, would die. Hyperbole to the visiting undertakers but in his case a personal understatement.

I thought he was going to have a heart attack every time Orient fired a shot at goal during those leaden minutes to survival. He turned round and almost strangled me when it was over.

Burnley made it at the expense of Lincoln City. The recriminations of lunchtime were forgotten in the tea-time euphoria.

But have the lessons been learned? Did Burnley really deserve to live? Is reprieve merely the prelude to more complacency? And is 'You'll Never Walk Alone' the anthem of ultimate hypocrisy?

The answers, I suppose, are that if you want a League football club locally, go and support it. Burnley did, with only a few minutes of almost a century to spare.

RACING ON THE GLORY TRAIL

A famous marque was to make its mark again at Le Mans towards the end of the Eighties.

LE MANS: MAY

WE waited in the sort of meadow to which Parisian madames used to bring their girls for hard-earned picnics on warm Sundays in spring. Larks ascended above a profusion of flowers. It was as quiet as 1908.

Suddenly it was not. Two miles to the right the idyll was shattered by a tiny speck that fast grew into a monster of screaming aggression.

The noise, as it passed, buckled the eardrums. The meadow faced the Mulsanne Straight on the far side of the Le Mans circuit south-west of Paris. It is 3 miles long and the fastest motor-racing stretch in the world. At the wheel of the new Jaguar XJR-8 LM the Brazilian driver, Raul Boesel, passed us, radar-timed, at 230 miles per hour.

Next time round he played an audacious trick. Two of my watching colleagues were wearing the purple-and-white anoraks of Silk Cut, the company sponsoring the Jaguar renaissance in sports car racing. Boesel flashed his headlights.

'How in God's name could you recognise them at 230 mph?' one asked. 'No problem,' said Boesel, 'it's the most boring part of the track.'

Like most racing drivers, he is deeply and heroically mad. Last year a colleague was instantly killed when he struck a telegraph post 150 yards from where Boesel flashed his lights. There have been many fatalities at Le Mans. In 1955 a French driver and 82 spectators were killed when his car ploughed into a grandstand and exploded.

But it is re-birth and not death of which we write here, for Jaguar, a name once synonymous with supreme British workmanship and daring, have returned to the track after a downbeat era and are really putting it across the Porsches of Germany and the Nissans and Toyotas of Japan.

There have been four major sports car races this year so far. Jaguar, with scant recognition, have won all of them. The big one, starting at 4 p.m. on June 13 and ending 24 hours later, is Le Mans. It was for this they were practising.

'It is like no other race in the world,' says John Watson, contracted in from the Grand Prix circuit as one of Jaguar's six drivers. He has raced Le Mans three times previously and never finished yet. 'It's sheer endurance for both man and car,' he says. 'You get through the night and the sun comes up and it's approaching midday and you're jubilant and think "We've cracked it" but there's a hell of a lot that can still go wrong.'

Watson, who will share one of Jaguar's three entries with Jan Lammers, heads next week not to a track but to a clinic outside Vienna to prepare.

'You get your heart-rate checked out. You go on a very strict diet which retains the water content in the body. Dehydration under all the anti-fire clobber we wear is a terrible problem. Everyone talks about the Mulsanne Straight but all the other straights at Le Mans are 200 mph-plus. You have to be super-fit.'

Times have changed at Le Mans since a British driver pulled unexpectedly into the pits at nightfall during the inter-war years.

'What's wrong?' demanded an agitated mechanic. 'Tyres? Fuel? Overheating?'

'None of them, dear boy,' replied the driver. 'I've come in to change my clothes. No Englishman should be seen anywhere abroad after 8 p.m. unless he's wearing a dinner jacket.'

The first Le Mans, in 1923, was won by drivers covering 1,372 miles in 24 hours at an average speed of 57.205 mph. By 1971 those figures had risen to 3,315 miles at 138.133 mph.

The authorities then subtly altered the shape of the circuit to reduce speeds. Last winter they introduced a new chicane to cut them yet again.

On Sunday Jaguars were the first and third fastest cars on the track, averaging 149.005 and 147.855 mph respectively. Porsche's Hans Stuck averaged 148.526 mph over the full 8 mile circuit.

More than 300,000 spectators will watch the race, among them Sir John Egan, who in 1980 picked up an exhausted Jaguar company by the scruff of its neck and shook it back into life. He got the factory floor behind him and then hurled his cars back into motor-racing.

'It's what is expected of us,' he said. 'Car racing is an essential part of our heritage. Image is money in the bank. Brilliant cars on the racing track are far more cost effective than conventional advertising.'

Jaguar are already selling as many cars as they can make but he admits he will be edgy for 24 hours at Le Mans. It is an old, shabby circuit, with weeds growing out of its spectator terracing, but victory there — a fifth victory in succession — will restore Jaguar to the world supremacy of the 50s when it won five Le Mans in succession.

LEST WE FORGET

It was the year we indulged in a small personal campaign. One month separated the following two pieces and I include both here to encourage others to fight the good fight.

NEW MILTON: AUGUST

SHORTLY after dawn on July 1, 1916, my father Private Edmund Wooldridge endured a great stroke of luck. He was shot through the legs by a German machine-gunner. On that insane morning on the Somme more than half the 120 men of his unit were killed. My father was hauled off the battlefield after nightfall and lived for a further 56 years.

Thus by a matter of inches he avoided becoming the 66th name on the simple war memorial that on summer evening casts a poignant shadow across the football pitch on the town-centre Recreation Ground at New Milton in Hampshire.

Among the 65 men it commemorates — plus many more who fell in World War II — several were his boyhood mates. They died on the Somme, at Gallipoli, Passchendaele and Jutland.

In their memory the grateful villagers of New Milton did more than erect a cross. They collected £850 and bought the land that was to become the Recreation Ground. In a deed registered with the Charity Commission on April 16, 1920, they stipulated that the space was 'exclusively for the sporting amusements or pleasures of the inhabitants of the parish and for no other purpose.'

New Milton is my home town and I am but one of several generations of urchins who benefited from their foresight.

We learned our cricket and our soccer there, smoked our first Woodbine behind the pavilion, attempted to kiss our first girlfriends on its benches and collected a headful of stitches trying to ride a bicycle down the children's slide.

Mostly we managed to keep out of the juvenile courts and, since there was so much else to do, I don't think we went around gratuitously smashing up people or property.

Paragons we were certainly not but each Remembrance Sunday, in our best clothes, we used to line up in front of the war memorial in our playground and stand very still for precisely two minutes. It was small enough tribute to the men who had died to preserve our freedom and give us such fun.

I direct these thoughts to the boards of directors of a property development company called Trencherwood and the Gateway supermarket chain who are proposing to rip up New Milton's Recreation Ground and transform it into a £6½ million community asset which sells cut-price shampoo and has parking space for 250 cars.

True, they propose to compensate the inhabitants by providing alternative sporting facilities on the fringe of the town and, with a suitable show of piety, pledge that their temple of commerce will be so tastefully landscaped that the war memorial cross won't even have to be moved. All this appeared to be going quietly ahead until it came to the ears of two remarkable urban resistance fighters: 79-year-old pensioner Bob Gates and 52-year-old widow Doreen Fernie.

Gates tramped 64 miles of the parish streets to collect 5,170 signatures of protest and Mrs Fernie's petition is currently 4,000 signatures long and growing.

The Trencherwood-Gateway axis are smoothly countering this by proposing to finance a parish referendum proving that the majority of New Milton's 20,000 population would prefer cut-priced shampoo to a tree-ringed town-centre park where the elderly may doze while the kids play their sport and get up to innocent mischief.

The kids there yesterday were quite relishing

the prospect of a fight. 'We shall,' declared their spokeschild, 'lie down in front of their bulldozers.'

What may seem like a parochial hassle in a dot on the map between Southampton and Bournemouth is, of course, nothing of the sort.

Down the length of Britain the developers have rapacious fingers in dozens of pies.

They rely on community apathy to give them their breaks. Playing fields, sports clubs, open spaces disappear overnight while the winners of a very new game spend more and more time in Barbados or on the Costa del Sol.

In New Milton, Bob Gates, who played cricket on the Recreation Ground from 1927 to 1948, and Doreen Fernie, an attractive secretary, have taken on the invaders.

They have nothing to win but the status quo and I believe that is how the glorious dead of my small town would have wanted it.

My father, for whom life was a bonus after the Somme, should have written this story. He would have been much amused by a sentence on page eight of Gateway Foodmarkets Ltd's elaborately printed proposal to enhance New Milton's future way of life.

'The company,' it says, 'is a major sponsor of English Heritage and also contributes to needy local children through its Help the Child campaign.'

My dad would have pointed out that New Milton already has all the heritage it needs and that its children, by and large, are healthy and happy. I suspect the rest of his views could never be printed.

NEW MILTON: SEPTEMBER

FOUR weeks ago the Daily Mail took up the cause of a small Hampshire town whose War Memorial Recreation Ground was threatened by commercial desecration.

Those 3.6 acres of oak-fringed grass — once the home of New Milton's Cricket Club, still the headquarters of its football team and for 57 years a living tribute to local men killed in two world wars — are now safe.

The London-based property development company Trencherwood confirmed yesterday that it has abandoned expensive and advanced plans to transform it into a car park for a Gateway supermarket.

It must be said that Bruce Woodhead, the Trencherwood director in charge of the project, did not sound pleased. 'We are disappointed,' he said, 'that emotion clouded the issue.'

It certainly did. The emotion of a local population finally roused to the spectre of losing a town-centre recreation area bought by public subscription in 1920 to honour its war-dead was such that a dithering town council met in special session on Wednesday evening to reassess the issue.

Seventeen of the 18 town councillors turned up. They talked for only 15 minutes. They then voted 13-4 to send the developers packing. And by yesterday the developers acknowledged they had been beaten.

Let Britain take note. It can be done. No issue in Sportsmail's pages over the past 25 years — be it soccer hooliganism, the antics of Mr McEnroe or even Zola Budd — provoked such angry and prolific responses as the test-case of New Milton's little public recreation ground.

Letters arrived from all over Britain saying: 'The same is happening here.' Hundreds wrote offering to add their signatures to New Milton's public protest petition. We had letters from former New Milton residents in Australia, where the story was reprinted, and from the Falkland Islands. Above all, we had letters from ex-Servicemen, some whose relatives are commemorated on the Recreation Ground's war memorial, many more from the survivors of the Battle of Britain, Alamein and Arnhem, outraged that a park bought by public money to honour Britons killed in battle, should be threatened by the rattle of 30 pieces of silver.

Well, it is over now and the greatest of all tributes for a consummate victory must go to Doreen Fernie and Bob Gates.

They fought, certainly on emotional grounds, to preserve a small patch of British Heritage and protect the huge right of the British people to resist cynical land development by those who will never need the facilities they destroy. If the Daily Mail assisted in that campaign then we are very proud.

THE GREAT CHINA TEE PARTY

Discovering golf talent in Communist China was one of the thrills of 1987. Two years later, as the students' rebellion was cruelly repressed, one could only wonder what was to become of them.

CHUNG SHAN: NOVEMBER

ON a January morning just 34 months ago, Peter Tang walked to the dusty playing field of the Sanxiang Weisan High School, in Red China's Guandong Province and produced a slender metal implement that mystified the 50 students lined up before him.

One suggested it was a new fangled walking stick, another guessed it had something to do with fishing. All 50 split their sides when Tang then tossed down a ball, swung the instrument high above his head and struck the ball 150 yards.

So began one of the most fascinating experiments in the history of sport: the calculated manufacture of golfers out of young men and women who, until January 1985, were utterly unaware that such a game existed. The results have been staggering, not to mention humiliating, to those of us who have been hacking around golf courses for half a lifetime.

Last week, one of those students, a tall and slender girl named Huang Li Yu, went round the awesomely challenging 6,509-yard par 71, Chung Shan championship course in 69 shots. On Tuesday she was round in 70. She has a classic swing, hits the ball a mile and is just 20 years of age.

She took me to meet her parents in Banfu village. We were driven 20 miles, then walked two miles through streets too narrow for cars to penetrate. They teemed with chickens, ducks and wide-eyed children. 'You and your photographer will be the first Europeans they have ever seen', explained our interpreter. 'People are born and die here without ever leaving the village.

That would have been Li Yu's destiny were it not for Communist China's latest and most curious cultural revolution — the decision to take up golf. From chairman Mao to the Gang of Four, the game was reviled and banned as unproductive, ridiculous and decadent.

In lambswool sweater and fashionable slacks. Li Yu looked as removed from her birthright as a Paris mannequin in a scrapyard. Her tiny home, though spotless, was threadbare. The walls were papered with pictures cut from magazines. It was illuminated by a yard of strip lighting. There was a television set but it was broken.

We had to wait till darkness fell for Li Yu's parents to return. They had toiled all day, knee deep in water, in the paddy fields. Each earned £20 a month. Ignoring China's family planning dictum, they have five children, of whom Li Yu is the eldest.

Her father, Wang Bing Hong, is a sturdy, handsome man of 44. Despite his daughter's astounding talent for it, he has no conception of what golf is. He has never seen her play or visited the course just 22 miles away, which could be on another planet.

Li Yu is permitted to bicycle home to her parents only once a month. She lives in student quarters alongside the palatial Western-style Chung Shan clubhouse with its piped Glenn Miller music and fried egg and bacon brunches.

She is one of 20 chosen from the 50 who watched Peter Tang's initial demonstration to spearhead China's entry into the most capitalist of all sports. 'That number', says the 32-year-old director of the project, Aylwin Tai sternly, 'has now been reduced to 17. One was expelled for bad behaviour, and one man and one woman student fell in love and could no longer concentrate on the programme.'

The programme reminds one precisely of the sports regime established by East Germany to become, per capita, the most dominant sports nation on earth. It was based on relentless rehearsal, dedication, on threat of instant dismissal. It earned them the nickname of the Battery Huns.

Li Yu is a model student. She plays either 36 or 18 holes of golf every day. On the days she plays only 18, she then caddies for Western visitors. She has weekly lectures on golf's etiquette and history and takes English lessons. 'Without the English language', says Tai, 'she has no future in world golf.'

Li Yu's English is enchanting. It owes more to the assiduous study of Golf Monthly than Dickens. 'Eddup', she gently reprimanded when I lifted my head on frequent shots in a practice round with her at the second Chinese Open championship.

'Nizapa', she encouraged on the three occasions I managed to hole out in regulation figures. My aberrations were infectious. Li Yu drove the ball like a champion and hit long iron shots with maddening accuracy. But her putting was off colour and she took 80. Along the way, she suddenly imparted the startling information that, 'rast mon I was in Amelica and Canada'.

Indeed, last month 12 of the 17 Chinese vanguard golfers, all aged between 19 and 22, were flown to America and Canada to broaden their experience.

Playing the par 70 Vancouver Country Club within an hour of arrival. Li Yu shot a 77. Those acquainted with the iniquitous difficulties of the game will understand why, suddenly, the established world of professional golf will shortly be looking uneasily over its shoulder.

China's human resources are over-whelming, its discipline ruthless, its ambition boundless. That 77 by a slip of a girl, far more than her remarkable rounds on a home course she knows as well as the carpet on her study floor, was as alarming as it was brilliant.

Britain's hopeless tennis players may wish to know how it was achieved.

Peter Tang, their 38-year-old coach, said: 'For their first month they spent six hours a day, six days a week, simply learning how to swing the club. They never hit a ball.'

Aylwin Tai said: 'They are here to learn golf and if they succeed there is a whole new world out there for them.'

Tang and Tai were both recruited from Hong Kong. Tai has developed the Chung Shan golf club, designed by Arnold Palmer, into one of the foremost in the world. It is leased by a Hong Kong tycoon for 20 years to make as much profit as he can. It then becomes Chinese government property.

Its construction began in August 1984 with labour costs no serious problem. Chains of 1,500 workers simply shifted soil by hand. It has provided work as caddies for some 50 local school leavers, many of them girls, almost dwarfed by the bags they carry.

Unknown to most Westerners, five more courses have been laid in China, three in the Peking area and two here in the south. Each has young golfters under training. Each has players like the two leading male students here.

At 21, Zheng Wein Jun has a handicap of three and 19-year-old Xiao Cheng Han a handicap of four.

It was Zheng who guessed the slender metal implement he first saw 34 months ago — a seven iron — had something to do with fishing. His best score round Chung Shan to date is 70. On the recent American tour, playing the Princeton University course at Springdale, he was one under par without a practice round.

Those unacquainted with golf may view all this from a different aspect.

They may see the vast reshuffle of China's government in Peking last week as a not unrelated development. The old reactionary guard bit the dust and some new high flyers, looking suspiciously like apprentice capitalists were elected in their places.

Among them was a gentleman whom Peter Tang knows well. In fact, he has given him golf lessons. 'He's fanatical about the game. He plays two or three times a week and he has a golf net in his back garden which he uses every day. He's only 24 handicap at the moment, but his game is improving.'

One would expect Tang to be polite. The gentleman's name is Zhao Ziyang. And he is China's new Prime Minister.

1988

1988 came in on the clipped wings of Eddie 'The Eagle' Edwards, a ski-jumper who lent credence to the Biblical contention that the last shall be first, and went out with Ben Johnson, a sprinter who discovered that coming first can bring the world crashing around your ears. Neither did anything to enhance a year of unending Olympic controversy. Yet, paradoxically, the Summer Olympics in Seoul were a triumph for persistent diplomacy over politics. For the only time in the decade West and East shrugged off their differences and almost every nation in the world competed. Over the Seoul Olympics I made the worst misjudgement of my years in sportswriting. Six months before the Games I visited Seoul and predicted that a country threatened by ideological enemies north of the 38th Parallel and riven by internal political upheaval and student rioting had no hope of hosting successful Olympics. Though not alone in such pessimism, I was utterly wrong. Early in 1989, while covering the Tyson-Bruno fight in Las Vegas, a Daily Mail reader nabbed me and said: 'Damn you. I cancelled my trip to the Olympics because of what you wrote.' Occasionally a reporter is morally obliged to buy a reader a drink.

STAR OF THE EAST GOES WEST

A week after this idolatrous piece was written Katarina Witt won the most inevitable gold medal of the Winter Olympics.

CALGARY: FEBRUARY

IT was early morning in the echoing arena but at an hour many would have sagged with jetlag, Ice Princess was quite ethereal.

She had flown in only the previous evening from a distant ideology and was skating the prescribed contiguous circles of her compulsory routine with the supreme poise of a prima ballerina.

You can always tell the stars of sport. What we do with flurried haste, they perform in serene slow motion and Miss Katarina Witt won spontaneous applause from her captivated audience of 12 security guards, nine photographers and two reporters.

Even at that hour the light make-up had been carefully applied. Her hair drawn back into a neat bun. The earclips perfectly matched the gentian blue of her track suit.

Coquettishly she smiled in response to the small ovation and that, perhaps, was her undoing. Three times in her 45-minute practice session to retain the Olympic figure-skating gold medal she won four years ago in Sarajevo she was verbally assailed for invisible blemishes by a squat woman with tinted glasses, thin lips, wild hair and relentless frown.

Katarina started skating at the age of five. She is 22 now and for the past ten years, day in day out, this woman has been her coach, mentor, political tutor and in loco parentis.

Her name is Jutta Muller. It might have been Rosa Klebb.

When Katarina eventually skated off to collect her thoughts and handbag, she was close to tears. Rosa Klebb marched off arm-in-arm with a tall and elegant Soviet woman skating coach. As a mere man I did not know what to make of this.

I knew, however, that I had again witnessed what makes East Germany so ruthlessly successful at sport. Here at yet another Olympics, a tiny nation of only 19 million people is racing away with a harvest of medals, to which next week Katarina Witt is expected to repay her debt to the State with another gold.

But she has another role to play, too. That of international propagandist for which, as we were soon to see, she has been equally programmed to perfection.

Seven hours later, Katarina, still sleepless, was wheeled into a press conference theatre packed with 500 reporters. She looked as fresh as a Vogue cover model. She answered banal question after banal question in flawless English until *the* question came.

Katarina had been primed for this moment.

To her right, Jutta Muller's eyes bored into her brain. To her left, two East German State officials stared straight ahead, confident their protégée would get her lines right.

And so she did. Switching to her native German, instantly translated over earphones, she said: 'Of course, I could never have become a skater if I'd been born in a Capitalist State. My parents would never have had the money to allow me to express myself in such a way. Skating in your world is very expensive.'

She added, right on cue, that she was delighted that Messrs Gorbachev and Reagan were apparently making progress on the path to peace. No one had actually asked her about that but it was in her script.

Arguably the greatest skater, male or female, the world has ever seen, Katarina comes appropriately from Karl Marx Stadt, and is the daughter of what by Western standards would be classically middle class parents. Her father, Manfred, is director of an agricultural collective.

She is now at a critical crossroads in her life.

She has announced she will quit the rink after these Olympics and next month's World Championships in Budapest.

With her stunning looks, effortless command of English and vibrant personality she could easily follow skating trail blazers like Sonja Henie, Peggy Fleming, John Curry and Torvill and Dean to a professional fortune in the West.

An agent like Mark McCormack, who can guarantee to earn £2 million for a British Open golf champion in the 12 months after winning the title, could unquestionably make her £5 million in a year if she wins the gold medal here next week.

Katarina announced she intends to return to Karl Marx Stadt where her privileges begin and end with a one-room apartment of her own and a modest saloon car.

She glanced at Rosa Klebb to her right. 'I owe everything,'she said, 'to Fraulein Muller.' The two heavies beamed with satisfaction.

Fraulein Muller then explained that Katarina is a strong-willed girl with her own ideas who occasionally has to be restrained. 'I know when I can no longer give in to her and then I have to become the strict coach,' she said. 'I have to insist on what I believe in.'

What Fraulein Muller clearly does not believe in is Katarina defecting like Martina Navratilova to the West. Miss Navratilova has made £12 million from tennis since leaping the wall. But, then, she comes from Czechoslovakia.

In freestyle routine at these Olympics, Katarina Witt will skate Carmen. By amazing coincidence, so will her great American rival — possibly the only skater here who could deprive her of the gold and only then if she makes a colossal error — the bouncy Debi Thomas.

Miss Witt acknowledged yesterday that she had heard of Miss Thomas. She then emphasised that she, Miss Witt, is a far better skater now than when she won her last Olympic title four years ago.

As we all know, Bizet's Carmen came to spectacular grief.

What of Katarina Witt? There is a precedent. You will recall the enchanting Soviet gymnast Olga Korbut. She tried to leave Russia after her astonishing Olympic triumph to cash in on a Western tour. She was told that she could go, but that her baby would have to remain in Kiev. Olga stayed in Kiev.

Katarina has no such responsibilities. She is single and childless. She has Jutta Muller at one shoulder and the West beckoning her with inestimable wealth.

Soon we shall see the height of the Berlin Wall and the strength of East German ideology put to the test.

If Katarina stays, Communism will have won far more than a gold medal.

As you will gather, there is more to next week's Olympic figure skating than meets the eye.

THE EAGLE HAS BARELY LANDED

The Winter Olympics in Calgary were a disaster. Unseasonably mild weather, bad siting of the events and a schedule that dragged proceedings out over three weekends to scalp even more money from television rights, conspired to create a shambles. The media were mostly in a foul mood. Consigned to a Press Village of wooden huts, miles from a decent restaurant and served by a laundry that contrived to lose about 4,000 pairs of underpants, they conspired to make their own fun. I wasn't in a foul mood at all and joined wholeheartedly in the unspoken conspiracy to present The Eagle as the hero of the Games.

CALGARY: FEBRUARY

EDDIE 'The Eagle' Edwards, the Cheltenham plasterer, completed his Olympic campaign in glory last night. He jumped — and lived — and broke his British record.

A crowd of 60,000 roared their approval as the Eagle soared 71 metres, three metres better than his previous best and ten metres further than any other Briton.

In brilliant sunshine, with the violent gales of the past week abated, Eddie launched himself off the rim of the terrifying 90 metre ski jump, wobbled only fractionally and landed not quite on his backside to an ovation that will not be out-decibelled at these Winter Olympic Games.

That he thumped down at the 71 metre (237 ft) mark, a point which the world's ski-jump stars soar past like long-range bombers on entirely different missions, mattered not one jot.

The triumph was that Eddie was down on two skis without troubling morticians, surgeons, or even the anxiously-waiting stretcher bearers.

His position in the competition — 55th and last. But Britain's first and only Olympic ski jumper was jubilant, delivering his famous arm-waving salute to the gallery.

In the second and final round, Eddie decided to play it conservatively. His style was more confident and his landing more decorous at 67 metres. For the great eccentric, the Olympic Games were over. Now Eddie can get on with living, though clearly his life can never be the same again.

The supreme irony of all the Eagle fever was that almost simultaneously another Briton, Wilfred O'Reilly, was winning a gold medal in the short-track skating event and smashing a world record in the process, while virtually ignored by the Press and TV cameras who preferred to crowd round the foot of the ski jump.

Fears for Eddie's safety were such that despite his survival in coming an unchallenged last on the less intimidating 70 metre hill last week, concerted efforts were made yesterday to stop him jumping at all off the 90 metre Big Brother switchback.

'Eddie the Eagle has been wonderful world publicity for ski jumping,' said Torjborn Yggeseth, Norwegian director of the event. 'But all the time we have been worried what that publicity would turn into if he crashed and broke his legs.

'Under Olympic rules we did not have the power to ban him from making the first of his two jumps. But yes, we did go to the British delegation and asked them to withdraw him. Evidently they decided he could manage.'

Eddie's best effort left him a mere 47 metres behind the winner, Finland's Matti Nykaenen whose longest jump was 118 metres.

Britain's low flying Eagle was suitably modest in defeat. 'Perhaps I shall make a bit of money out of what has happened here,' he said. 'But to me jumping is the only important thing. I hope all the publicity will encourage a lot of British kids to take it up.'

He added that he was happy to have done his best for his new army of fans at home.

Aged 24 now, with years on his side, he confirmed he will definitely be jumping at the next Winter Olympics. 'By then,' he said, 'I think I have every chance of being the best in the world. Who knows?'

CALGARY: FEBRUARY

EDDIE EDWARDS woke up yesterday to the reality that he is now a household name from Vladivostok to Virginia.

He spent the morning making arrangements to jet down to Los Angeles and grant an interview to Johnny Carson on the world's most famous TV chat show, as well as discussing business affairs with his two agents, one here in Calgary and the other in London.

To date his only firm contract is a $2,000 deal for marketing Eddie the Eagle T-shirts but there should be at least another £250,000 in the pipe-line.

What bugged him — as it would perplex any young man of 24 whose status precisely two weeks ago was that of a jobbing Cheltenham plasterer — was what he's going to do with the rest of his life.

Eddie Edwards isn't a fraud. No man with the guts to switchback off a 90 metre ski-jump, which is nearly the height of St. Paul's, is a fraud. Nor is he a loser. No man who comes hopelessly last, and yet wins more attention from the world's media than any sports star at the Olympics, can conceivably be a loser.

What Eddie Edwards has become is the freak product of intense media hype. The serious Olympics were getting bogged down by the weather. Eddie, with his bottle-end glasses, wit, warm personality and abolutely no hope of winning anything was a godsent alternative.

The reporters, the cameras, the microphones moved in. Hype created more hype. More and more Press conferences were called. Star columnists were flown up from America merely to get a glimpse of him.

Eddie kept his nerve and sound west country common sense. He played up to the circus. But what, in the end, did he have to sell? Nothing. He remains without question, the worst ski jumper ever to appear at the Olympics.

'Eddie doesn't jump, he drops like a stone,' said a Norwegian with an anagram for a name. Torjborn Yggeseth controlled the ski jumping discipline here and earnestly tried to get Eddie excluded for his own safety.

He was confounded, of course, when Eddie leapt and survived. But he still maintained: 'In Norway, we have 1,000 eleven-year-olds who can jump further and better than Eddie. I think he should stop now before there is a tragedy.'

Eddie is an enigma. His honesty is so patent that as you listen to him trot out anecdote after anecdote about his boyhood escapades with girls and bicycles you just wonder if he could possibly be inventing it straight off the top of his head. His ability to handle the awkward question is devastating.

An American reporter asked him: 'Eddie, if you have made 1,000 ski-jumps, why is it that you're still so bad at it?'

'Have you ever tried it?' Eddie snapped back. End of discussion.

It is hard to see how he can settle back into plastering walls in Cheltenham and going to the cinema with his girlfriend, Hannah, whom he professes to love dearly despite the fact that he never once saw her when she was flown to Calgary by a British newspaper.

'I thought that was disgusting,' said Eddie. 'They were trying to exploit our love and I was having nothing to do with it.'

There have been oddballs in sport before. A Japanese runner once 'won' an Olympic marathon by leaping on to the course less than a mile from the end. A golfer named Maurice Flitcroft once conned his way into the British Open and hacked his way to an horrendous score.

Both were treated with unanimous derision as men who had desecrated great events.

Eddie is different. The sheer bravery demanded of any man hurtling headlong down a ski-jump insulates him from criticism. Eddie did what none of us writing about him would do for a million pounds.

It is just possible he is the oddest oddball ever to invade a sport. Was it a calculated quest for the international limelight or did it all happen by accident? I have been with him at length here and I honestly have to confess I do not know the true answer.

'Anything happen today, Eddie?' you ask.

'Yes,' he beams. 'I ran into Princess Anne when I was taking my dirty underpants to the laundry.'

Eddie the Eagle may just become the international celebrity with virtually nothing to celebrate. Before you decry the way the world is going, simply climb to the top of a 90 metre ski-jump and look down. It is the headlong route that has pitched Eddie Edwards into another world.

WHY CAN'T BOTHAM GROW UP?

Ian Botham bestrode the sports pages of the decade. All too frequently, and for all the wrong reasons, he made the front pages as well. Over the years I have eulogised and heavily criticised him in print. We still have a laugh when we meet.

LONDON: MARCH

EXACTLY a year ago I sat in a bar with Ian Botham on the Irish border. After four or five drinks I ventured the opinion that he was at last becoming a responsible member of the human race.

You take a small risk saying things like that to Botham when you've both been drinking. He could laugh. Or he could punch you straight to the floor.

Ian laughed. 'You're right,' he said. 'After all these years I think I'm just beginning to grow up.'

He was 31 at the time, the most talked-about cricketer of the age and currently engaged on a gruelling walk from Belfast to Dublin to raise money for leukaemia victims. During that march his personal efforts for the fund passed the £1 million mark.

The money impressed me far less than his evident genuine concern for those stricken by deadly illness.

He fretted that a small sufferer who had written to him hadn't been traced. He sent out scouts to find the boy, and his face lit up next morning when he was produced in a wheelchair. Botham resumed his march, pushing the young lad in front of him.

To my shame I have no idea whether the child lived or died. All I know is that his family will never hear a bad word against Ian Botham.

There are thousands in hospitals — doctors and nurses, as well as leukaemia patients — who similarly regard him as little short of an urchin saint.

There was not the remotest element of showboating about that Botham march. He wanted all the publicity he could get for his fund, not for himself. He took on bets of £100 and £200 that fellow walkers couldn't out-pace him, and cheerfully paid up when he lost.

After that Irish interlude I wrote the kindliest sports column of the many I have written about one of the most erratic but naturally gifted sportsmen Britain has ever seen.

I should have known better. Within weeks he was the central figure in an appalling public brawl and now, within a year, his loutish behaviour in Australia sees him threatened from re-entry to a country where the odd punch-up after a few amber nectars is seen as par for the social course.

Australia was to have been his brave new world among kindred souls far from the beetle-browed disapproval of the elders of the Marylebone Cricket Club, half a world away from the prim magistrates and Tory MPs who reminded him of his constant responsibilities to a young idolatrous fan club, light years removed from the many indiscretions of a brawling pot-smoking past, mercifully distant from the newshounds who dogged his footsteps from bar to boudoir and back.

Australia welcomed him as ready-made folk hero. He doubled the crowds wherever he played. He took his adopted state of Queensland to the very threshold of its first Australian championship.

Then, almost on cue, it all collapsed. The sleazy evidence poured out in court, and the single factor that might have swayed public opinion — his cricket — fell apart.

We have come this way so many previous times in the career of I.T. Botham that we know there are no simple explanations of the bewildering enigma of this man of bullish physical strength, immense generosity, enormous kindness and a seemingly undeviating talent for self-destruction.

He is no intellectual but nor is he unintelligent.

He is certainly impressionable, as evidenced by his naïve association with a fly-by-night business agent who promised him a motion-picture career on the scale of Errol Flynn and delivered nothing more than a tourist trip round a Hollywood film lot.

He has a propensity for showing off in social sporting circles, particularly when trials of physical prowess are in the air. He can't resist a challenge and generally wins.

And he drinks. So do I. So do most of my closest friends. But I know few of them so ready with their fists towards closing time.

Botham was only 19 and an apprentice cricketer learning his trade in Australia when he punched Ian Chappell, a famous Test cricketer 12 years his senior, off a bar stool.

Nor was he averse to recounting the episode for his biography.

His furious public quarrel with Somerset County Cricket Club — an instant decision to quit because they'd sacked his friend Vivian Richards — brought yet another new beginning at Worcester.

The crowds came flocking again. The bowling talent may have been on the wane but the stupendous, electrifying hitting, the capacity to win a match virtually single-handed, the miracle factor that had won Test matches for England when all seemed lost, were all still there.

But so was the flaw.

It is archetypically Botham that he returns to Britain almost immediately to hurl himself into a venture more ambitious than even his initial John O'Groats to Land's End walk.

Nine days from now, with elephants in tow, he is to cross the Alps by the Hannibal route, raising money every kilometre of the way for his friends stricken by leukaemia.

Police and French soldiers, press, TV and radio will accompany him, and a nation which has little knowledge of cricket and none at all of Ian Botham will become enthralled by the legend.

There will be herograms from statesmen, fan mail by the vanload, Hail Marys from simple ladies praying for his success, and another huge flow of money for one of the world's worthiest charities.

All for the man who was disgraced in an Australian courtroom yesterday for sheerly untenable behaviour on an airliner.

At 32, his sporting talent may hold up for another few years but what then? Like so many of the great icons of sport he should be capable of cruising into middle-age on the wake of his fame. But could it all end in shame?

With Ian Botham it is hard to tell. Will he ever grow up? This time I am making no predictions. But what a waste it will be if he cannot come up with a suitable answer of his own.

MEMORIAL TO A MASTER

The death of Henry Cotton, a hero and friend, provided an opportunity to suggest that resolution and impeccable behaviour are not incompatible. He read everything ever written about him and, though in no hurry, I nervously await his comments at some future date.

MAYFAIR: MAY

THE memorial service for Sir Henry Cotton was a glorious requiem mass in Mayfair which lasted almost two hours and required a 12-page order sheet to inform the likes of me when to stand, sit or kneel. Afterwards there were drinks in the drawing-room at Claridges at which there was much quiet laughter and fond reminiscence. Henry, a man of effortless style and wicked humour, would have adored it and probably did.

Discussion inevitably turned to an appropriate permanent memorial. A life-size bronze, perhaps, at Royal St George's where he won the first of his three Open Championships in 1934, or the renaming of the Penina course in southern Portugal on which he had lavished love and a lifetime's expertise.

'Quite unnecessary,' someone said. 'Henry's memorial is the health of the game of golf.' I wish I had been the author of that noble sentiment.

For those of us in daily contact with a broad range of sports, the past decade has been one of increasing uneasiness. Sport has rarely had the paragon virtues attributed to it by some of its more romantic chroniclers but for a century and more there had at least been inviolable codes of conduct.

Rugby men did not bite one another's ears off. Wimbledon champions did not scream obscenities at opponents and linesmen. Olympic athletes did not rattle with dubious pills. Cricketers did not shove umpires in the chest. Football teams were not pursued to the ends of the earth by brutual, xenophobic assailants. Now they do and are, with one notable exception. It is the game Sir Henry Cotton did so much to propagate, not only by technical mastery but by lifestyle, attitude and personal example. It is indeed his memorial: golf itself.

It is with joy, not apprehension, that we can look forward to another glorious summer of golf, highlighted by the 117th Open Championship at Royal Lytham St Anne's. It is not the most beautiful of our Open venues, flanked as it is by a busy commuter, railway line, but it was there, in 1958, that I witnessed one of those legendary tussles of wills which golf seems to be capable of resolving with courtesy instead of snarling rudeness.

A driver of one of those commuter trains, clearly indifferent to the timetables, drew his engine to an unscheduled halt alongside the second green just as the stately South African champion, Bobby Locke, was about to putt. Locke stood back and motioned the train driver to proceed. The engine driver signalled back that Locke should go ahead. Mr Locke repeated his gesture. So did the engine driver, clearly implying that he had absolutely no intention of moving until the great man had played his shot.

Locke conceded. He addressed an enormously difficult left-hand borrowed putt and sank it. The engine driver blew his whistle in salute and Locke raised his white cap in acknowledgement. Both men then proceeded about their business having fractionally enriched the game with another small anecdote of spontaneous chivalry. It still exists. I saw another example of it last year on the great Ailsa course at Turnberry, a magic place on a warm summer's evening as you walk out along the seashore to the lighthouse, passing on the way the decayed ruins of Bruce's Castle where Robert Bruce, liberator of Scotland from the tyrannical English, was born in 1274.

But on this day — the final round of the inaugural British Seniors Championships — both history and beauty were obliterated by rain driven in horizontally on the teeth of a blistering gale. In these awesome conditions, at the age of 52, Bob Charles, the New Zealand left-hander, muffled in waterproofs and frozen to the marrow, orchestrated one of the greatest rounds of foul-weather golf ever played. Only a dozen or so of us braved the elements to watch it and the privilege was entirely ours: imperious low-driving into the wind, undeviating long-irons, unflinching putting on treacherous greens.

It was a classic of golf, a one-under-par 69 on a day when champions would have settled for 80.

The irony was that as he sat in the locker-room in an expanding puddle of water, Charles discovered that he had lost the Championship, and thus a large sum of money, by a single shot. It did not remotely concern him. To England's Neil Coles the title, to Charles the joy of sheer academic achievement of taming a Scottish links course in a tempest. 'That,' he kept grinning, 'was the best golf I've played in my life.' Consolation for the loss of an additional £8,600 would have been intrusion into private celebration.

That is golf: a quiet squeeze on the shoulder

for the vanquished, a handshake for the victor. It is the Henry Cotton inheritance. He didn't invent courtesy and good manners and etiquette, he simply knew they were highly marketable commodities. And so it has proved. Consistent winners at golf now become very rich men.

It is contended that vast prize purses ring the death knell of sport but golf proves it a fallacy. In 1987 alone the tiny Welshman, Ian Woosnam, won £1,086,829. Nick Faldo's purse for winning the Open Championship at Muirfield was £75,000 but shrewd commercial exploitation of his title probably grossed him another £2 million. England's Howard Clark, who finished 56th in the global pecking order, made £204,084. But the most revealing statistics are these: in 1966 the world's top 200 players shared £2,936,537 in prize money. In 1987 they split £34,335,769 between them.

It is heartening evidence of world confidence in golf by commercial sponsors clamouring to associate themselves with a game they know to be free from shop stewards, cheats and intolerable egos. They know it to have a heritage of discipline, self-discipline, mature social conduct and ultimate respect for the rules. They know that the rare transgressor may expect no mercy. When a young British professional was conclusively proved to be cheating in recent times he was suspended for a little matter of 20 years. There was no mechanism for appeal. In career terms it was capital punishment. By such draconian sentences golf protects its greatest asset: integrity.

The other great development Sir Henry Cotton just lived to see was the balancing of power across the Atlantic, thus creating in Britain the greatest boom the game has ever known.

He was to see two British players win Britain's own Open Championship in the space of three years. That had not happened for almost four decades. He was also to see a combined British and European team achieve what many had previously deemed unachievable: a first Ryder Cup victory on American soil.

There, at Columbus, Ohio, we had the ultimate proof that money is not the lone incentive, for there was none at stake. What we saw there on the middle day was golf of such stunning intensity — Americans firing long irons to 15 feet, Europeans getting 10 feet inside them and sinking the putts — that I feel resigned never to witness such inspired team play again. The next evening's victory party would have seen off the Borgias yet not an incident occurred that could have offended the primmest member of that episcopalian community.

The contrast with recent behaviour in other sports is inescapable and is not something I wish to dwell on here. Too much sportswriting these days confirms that a sport gets the press it deserves. So does golf: a generally urbane caravan of reporters. the occasional elegant essayist and a complete absence of peeping toms. The New York Times recently examined their lifestyle and concluded they had the softest option in journalism. It is certainly not as soft as writing leisurely lifestyle articles for the New York Times but, admittedly, is the most agreeable way of life.

To drive round the last bend into St Andrews on a summer's morning, to process the fairways of Wentworth as the leaves turn gold above the World Matchplay Championship, to dine with Arnold Palmer, to interview Jack Nicklaus, to stand behind Ballesteros on the practice ground, to be engulfed in an Open Championship's last hour is to be part of a privileged world.

That too, is what we were celebrating at Sir Henry Cotton's memorial service: a man's determination to make the world a better place. It's not a bad epitaph.

TOAST TO A CHILDHOOD HERO

My hero and friend Denis Compton reached 70 during the year. Colleagues and opponents came from all over the world to honour him at an unforgettable dinner in London.

LONDON: MAY

STATISTICS kill any damned story so here is a handful to get them over and done with.

In Benoni, South Africa, he once scored 300 runs in 181 minutes. In the English summer of 1947 he scored 3,816 runs and hit 18 centuries. In the 1950 Cup Final he played left-wing for Arsenal when they beat Liverpool 2-0. By his third marriage he has daughters named Charlotte and Victoria, aged ten and three. He was born in Hendon on May 23, 1918, which means that next Monday will be his 70th birthday.

The subject of that thumbnail biography is also averse to statistics, largely because he can't remember his own or anyone else's. Records were for Bradman, not the greatest all-round British sportsman of my lifetime.

Denis stamped the hallmark on his golden talent at an unusually early age. At 14, playing at Lord's for London Elementary Schoolboys, he scored a century memorable less for 100 runs than the sheerly luminous manner of their making. Tousled, athletic, impish, assured and happy, he radiated the persona that years later was to cause his disciples to start queueing at daybreak to watch him bat.

Image, a phoney modern word, is that which the moderate would wish upon themselves. Style is the genuine article, a God-given grace to accomplish without apparent effort.

Compton had style. He had such style that an entire generation of schoolboys, of whom I was one, tried to walk, run and throw like him. We ladled on the Brylcreem because that's what Denis used and we neatly turned our shirtsleeves two folds back because that's what Denis did. No caning hurt when you'd played truant and cycled miles to watch him bat: it was a privilege, a mere percentage of the admission price.

He was immensely courteous to the kids who worshipped him. I have to this day the autograph he signed for me at Dean Park, Bournemouth, in 1946. Some 50 of us milled around him as he came off for lunch. He promised he would sign for all of us provided we formed an orderly line. We did and he kept his word and thus, without effort, he created not fanship but idolatry.

Denis scored 115 that day. I can remember two shots now, an off-balance sweep that only Vivian Richards could emulate and a cover drive he fashioned by coming down the wicket to a slow left-arm spinner who had yet to release the ball. His hair, Brylcreem or not, was in a tangle and his shirt was open down to the fourth button and he was the nearest thing we'd ever seen to God.

It must have been hell going in to bat in front of him as Jack Robertson did for years. Robertson, a consummately elegant player capable of making 200 every time he batted, could hardly have been unaware that all but his close relatives wanted him to get out so that God would come in and start orchestrating lightning and thunder. Of course these are the recollections of an impressionable schoolboy but fanciful they are not.

In a contemporary essay called Genius Unrationed, Neville Cardus, the master of our game, wrote that in the immediate post-war years 'Compton's cricket symbolised the hopes and renewed life of a nation that had emerged from the dark abyss of war...They sat in the sun and the strain from those heavy years fell from all shoulders as Compton flicked the ball here, swooped it there, drove it right and left.'

It wasn't all roses. In the Old Trafford Test of 1948 he was two not out when he nicked a blinding no-ball bouncer from Lindwall into his face. He went off to be stitched, consumed a restorative brandy and returned to score 145 not out.

He also drank a large brandy at half time in the 1950 Cup final. It was his last football match and he played a storming second half but wishes it to be known that this was not necessarily the stimulant upon which his career was fuelled.

In life he was, and still is, charming and scatter-brained. The legendary stories of him scoring centuries with borrowed bats and arriving for the start of play in last night's dinner jacket and advancing down the ground at the height of a Test match to discover the result of the 2.30 at Ascot are all true, and I am delighted that Peter West is at this moment occupying his retirement from television by assembling them into a long-due biography.

Inevitably there is the temptation to compare him with some of the present day sportsmen but that could introduce an unwanted jarring note to his 70th birthday celebrations.

Denis Compton doesn't qualify as a paragon. He has about as much commercial acumen as the average Poet Laureate. He was simply a genius of a ball-games player who has lived comfortably with celebrity, laughed at life and endowed us with vivid memories that many will carry to our graves. It would be a serious oversight not to wish him a particularly happy day on Monday.

LET'S HAVE A TANTRUM

By 1988 John McEnroe was getting a little long in the tooth. But his legacy to the next generation was distinctly on display at Wimbledon.

WIMBLEDON: JULY

ONE of the better matches at Wimbledon yesterday was between the lady tennis correspondent of the New York Times and a male sports columnist of the London Sunday Mirror.

The Mirror man took his Centre Court seat and lit a cigarette. The New York Times lady coughed theatrically.

The following conversation then occurred:

'Would you mind putting that thing out?'

'No. Anyway, your chewing gum stinks.'

Tolerance is becoming increasingly conspicuous by its rapid disappearance from the world's premier tennis championships.

If you don't bitch, blaspheme, winge, whine, chuck rackets, bash the turf, mouth obscenities either silent or otherwise, curse umpires and linesmen, abuse opponents and punch clenched fist uppercuts into the air when you hit a decent shot, you are now seen as weak and devoid of motivation.

Junior Wimbledon is now in progress on the outer courts. There is plenty of motivation out there. At an age when they should be addressing the umpire as 'Mr', the kids are bitching, blaspheming, whingeing, whining, etc. I watched a French child yesterday who looked like Bugs Bunny with delirium tremens.

They catch it, obviously, from the senior players who in turn have been sold it by psychologists and psychiatrists who are making an industry out of 'motivation' and also have no other way of getting free tickets for Wimbledon.

I must write with circumspection about psychiatrists since my next door neighbour is one. Happily his field is persuading recidivist rapists to submit themselves to chemical castration-motivational therapy which has yet to reach Wimbledon but will probably become

quite popular if proved to accelerate a male first service by 10mph.

However, I met one of these tennis shrinks once. He was an extremely nervous man probably because he was constantly petrified of exposure and the fact that his client kept losing by scores like 3-6, 0-6.

I asked him how guys like Wellington, Churchill and Fred Perry got on without personal motivators?

In lieu of a comprehensible answer, one suggested it may possibly have been because they have talent.

In Perry's case could it conceivably have been that he was a Northerner, son of a Labour politician, socially shunned in his early days, who was just as determined to win a trophy with no cash prize attached as today's combatants are for a cheque for £165,000.

Obviously there is enormous talent this year, as every year, at Wimbledon. But, heavens, they do make such a fuss about it.

KEEPING OUT OF THE BUNKER

Security at the Seoul Olympics surpassed anything ever seen at a State, political or sporting occasion. To convey its intensity I played what might loosely be described as a round of golf with one of our protectors under unusual circumstances. The final paragraph was not written in vain. A proud artefact at Camp Boniface Golf Club today is a framed letter from Michael Bonallack, secretary of the Royal and Ancient, St Andrews.

PANMUNJOM: SEPTEMBER

MEANWHILE, just 32 miles north of the Olympic pool where Mr Moorhouse was swimming the race of his life, 43,000 American soldiers were on Red Alert across the 38th Parallel.

When you pass the sentries on the way into Panmunjom, where the fragile peace treaty to seal off Communist North Korea from capitalist South Korea was signed 35 years ago, they shout 'Stand Alone.'

It is an eerie place, the four kilometre-wide demilitarised zone between these Olympic Games and the sulking Kim Il Sung's brainwashed regime to the immediate north.

But stand alone it literally does. Without round-the-clock military vigilance these Games would not be proceeding.

All leave has been cancelled. The soldiers stare steadfastly to the north while the world focuses on the playgrounds just down the road.

Very few of those troops have a hope of witnessing a single Olympic event. I am happy to report, however, that they are not entirely bereft of all sport. In stand-down hours they may indulge in a game which, pray God, will never again feature on an Olympic agenda. Golf.

One must confess that the Camp Bonifas Golf Club does not instantly remind one of St Andrews. But it does have certain advantages.

It levies no membership fees. There is no waiting list to join. And all women are banned for the reason that no women are permitted to serve there.

Admittedly there are some disadvantages too.

Teeing up at the first — correction, *only*

hole — there yesterday I was rudely disturbed at the critical top of the backswing by two gentlemen clattering firepieces. They emerged from a hole beneath my very feet and trudged on without a hint of apology.

'Sorry about that, they're not golfers, I'm afraid,' murmured my opponent, Captain George Geczy III, United States Army. 'While I'm about it, I might as well tip you off about a couple of other eccentricities of this course.

The first was that if, being left-handed, I sliced my tee shot out of bounds and attempted to retrieve the ball, I would undoubtedly have both legs blown off.

The second implied that I would be unwise to hook my ball into the close vicinity of the two camouflaged gentlemen still burrowing their way along the trench to my right. 'They're hand-picked sharp shooters,' explained George, 'and very fast on the trigger.'

Under these relaxing circumstances we drove off. You don't play a round of golf at Camp Bonifas. You play the same hole 18 times. To liven matters up a bit they've constructed four different tees, the most distant of which is 170 yards from the flag.

I have desecrated some bizarre golf courses in my time but none to compare with this. The wire fence down the left denotes the start of the demilitarised zone.

It is the most heavily mined and fortified frontier on earth. Venture into that no-mans-land and your chances are less than even that you will come out alive.

To get there you drive up Highway One from Seoul through evocative landmarks of modern history. The Glorious Glosters fought up a hill here with terrible casualties. Speakman won his VC over there.

All around millions of Koreans died, ignorant of which warring ideology they were supposed to live for.

When the guns fell silent in 1953 they settled for cold war instead. The atmosphere remains as frozen today. Just occasionally it hots up.

Camp Bonifas, from which the cramped one-hole golf course proudly takes its name, is so called because on a morning in 1976 Captain Arthur Bonifas ventured out to lop a branch off a tree that was obsuring his line of fire at potential North Korean infiltrators. He was shot dead and posthumously promoted to major.

The golf course commemorating him could certainly benefit from a little top dressing on its green.

It would also be delighted, of course, to receive a brief note from the Royal and Ancient commending it for perpetuating the game under mildly difficult circumstances.

Perhaps someone will draw the attention of Michael Bonallack, secretary at St Andrews, to these few words. A line or two from him would give them tremendous heart as they stand alone to protect us at the XXIVth Olympics.

LIBERATION ON COURT

The last lip service to amateurism died when tennis returned to the Olympics. It is true that Steffi Graf received only a gold medal for her trouble but she created a sensation, in more ways than one, among the gentlemen of Korea.

SEOUL: SEPTEMBER

WOMEN's liberation is still so many light years from Korea that Steffi Graf's appearance at the Olympic tennis came close to causing mass male cardiac arrest.

For much of the morning they had been watching a pat-ball match between a French girl and a Korean that would hardly have graced a Surbiton Lawn Tennis Club's ladies section quarter-final.

Back-hand return shots floated four feet above the net, attempted overhead smashes flew off the woodwork, double faults rattled so consistently into the netting that those like me who regard the return of tennis to the Olympics as a ridiculous intrusion were feeling thoroughly smug. It was daylight larceny to charge admission money.

But then came Graf. She strode in like Tarzan. Not Mrs Tarzan, but the genuine article. She is only 5ft 9ins but that, in Korean terms of feminine altitude, is the Empire State Building. Anatomically endowed in areas where Korean ladies are not, on mahogany-tanned legs that could have been muscled up no further had she ridden in the Tour de France, with her sheepdog hairstyle and friendly boxer's face, she looked as though she'd just heard about the D-Day landings.

Korean menfolk, many of whom could walk under the average European dining table without ducking, were mesmerised by private thoughts. What fazed them utterly was that this object from another sporting planet is just 19, a multi-millionairess from tennis, now the undisputed finest woman player in the world and still getting better.

When she started playing the great stadium was filled by the sibilant sounds that are esperanto for sheer astonishment. They had never seen a woman hit a ball so hard. Few were to know, of course, that nor has anyone else.

Steffi, being very young, played to the staggered gallery to her own detriment. She dropped the first five points of her opening games against Russia's Leila Meshki and was so determined to flatten her shots to within a millimetre of the net to demonstrate what pathetic rubbish the earlier match had been, that she made error after error.

However, to win that set 7-5, she served an ace that would have drilled a sideways hole through an entire set of the Encyclopaedia Britannica.

The Korean males looked at one another with alarm.

Do such women exist? How is some future husband going to cope with that? They settled down for the second set, visibly focusing on Steffi's powerful legs.

The newspapers don't have Page Three tarts here but the photographers were snapping away like mad. There was a positive air of sexuality about it which the Korean hostesses — omnipresent at all Olympic events in ankle-length national costume — ignored by staring steadfastly at their gilt-sandalled feet.

Steffi's opponent offered no such threat. The 20-year-old Meshki, born in Stalin's home town of Tblisi, Georgia, has the look of a ballet dancer who didn't quite make it. Prim, demure, pony-tailed, she is ranked 34 in the world largely due to a resilient two-fisted return which will make money for the Soviet Union but will never win her major championships.

Graf, who has just won the Grand Slam and in the whole of 1987 lost only 14 sets to anyone, proceeded to wipe her out.

She won the second set 6-1 in Panzer style. Imparting back-spin on her backhand she looks as though she is destroying vermin with a single blow. Down the forehand she hits like Mr Tyson. Korean tennis fans simply sat there, watching a game they never knew existed. As in boxing, the ferocity of tennis never comes through on television.

Steffi, whose on-court tennis earnings throughout the year work out at around £800 a minute, walked off after 66 minutes without a pfennig to add to her bank account.

At least, that is what the Olympic authorities would wish you to believe. She is actually here on her own account to promote the footwear of the Adidas company and on the International Olympic Committee's account to earn more money from television coverage.

In due course, she will win the individual tennis gold medal here for West Germany. The destiny of none of the 237 gold medals on offer at these Games is more simple to predict.

Many are called this time and most will be humiliated. Confronting club tennis players with professional stars is wholly alien to what the Olympics are supposed to be about.

Steffi got away with it yesterday for reasons that have nothing to do with tennis. She played like a man and it disturbed Korean manhood greatly.

THE UNFORGETTABLE GAMES

Even the Ben Johnson drugs scandal, which provoked the suspicion that you could no longer believe what you were seeing in sport, could diminish Seoul's triumph as stage managers of the Olympics.

SEOUL: OCTOBER

LAST evening, as the darkness came, Korea bade us farewell with the most staggering and emotional closing ceremony in the history of the Olympics.

A nation flattened by recent war, took as its theme global unity and peace. With immense dignity, with dance and song that reached back into a millenium of culture, with the greatest pyrotechnic display ever to transform a night sky into day, they told us how pleased they were to have played host to 160 nations united once again by sport.

It transcended the cynicism of drugs, the curse of commercialism, the strident nationalism some nations brought here. It invited us to hold this fragile Olympic movement together. There was hardly a dry eye in the house.

The most glittering old medal of all at these Games goes to South Korea. I was one of thousands convinced they couldn't do it in the face of superhuman odds. They did. No Olympics have been more graciously staged. None, in these seething days of political discord, has been more secure.

Three weeks ago, South Korea was on the fringe of the Third World. Its elevation to the First World is confirmed by a simple question: which future Olympic city can follow that?

Their success was due more than anything to the pride and calmness of Seoul's people. In almost a month here I have not seen a scrap of litter in the streets or a smear of graffiti on any wall. Twice, searching for taxis in a hurry, private motorists have pulled up and driven miles out of their way to drop me at my destinations. Last night brought the ultimate test.

The closing ceremony, rehearsed for months, was choregraphed as an exercise in perfect symmetry. It was severely disrupted when the athletes broke ranks and overran the stage. There was no bad behaviour — it was their Olympics anyway — but it was rather like a bunch of tourists squatting on Horse Guards during Trooping the Colour.

We watched with fascination as the plain-clothes security guards handled it. With gentle persuasion, never touching anyone, they controlled what could have degenerated into an almighty shambles.

If Ben Johnson deigned to watch it all on television back home in Canada, I hope he was ashamed. He and many other athletes dragged the Olympics to the brink of disaster here. It took the Koreans to remind us that the Games are greater than the cheats.

On that score, these were the finest Olympics I have ever attended. You could not move a yard, of course, without being searched. Security was as tight here as in Crossmaglen. The justification was that as the Olympic flame flickered and died last night not one person had been touched by international terrorism. A miracle.

South Korea, heroically, has done its part. It is now for the Olympic movement to purge itself of the poisons that endanger it. It must launch an all-out war on drugs. And it must realise that the vast sums offered by rival American television networks to become 'host broadcaster' of the Olympics with all the privileges that entails, must be resisted.

Much of the world takes the American TV feed. Much of the world, therefore, has been given to understand that these Games were a hick-town sports meet.

Why? Because the United States seen as head-to-head rivals with the Soviet Union, got their severe comeuppance there. They were run into the ground not only by the Soviet Union but by East Germany, population 19 million.

American television stumbled over any foreign name of more than two syllables, made it perfectly obvious that it had no idea where countries like Senegal and Surinam actually were, concentrated on American athletes running tenth, moved gear from screech to hysteria, when America won anything, offered commentary of ignorance and near illiteracy and generally patronised the world.

There have been moments of disillusion here, no more so than when it was proved that a British performer had fallen into the drug trap. It is to be hoped that he will be banned for life, just as a British pole vaulter thankfully was a few weeks before he was due to come here.

The war against drugs must be ruthless and uncompromising. That is one message of these Seoul Olympics. The other is that, given a host nation with the will to move mountains, the Olympics are still alive. Only just, badly dented, an endangered species. But what other international movement in this world of turmoil could have got 160 nations together under one roof for a fortnight of deadly competition?

We leave Seoul on a note of delicate optimism, sincerely thanking our hosts on the way out.

NOW IT'S BLAZING SADDLES

Towards the end of the year I wandered, not quite by accident, into a polo ground in Australia. There, on a pony, was a gentleman whom many, 11 years earlier, would have cheerfully murdered.

MELBOURNE: NOVEMBER

IN the old days, had he seen a bright light on the road to Damascus, Kerry Packer would have either bid for the generating station or cut the power lines so no one else would.

Now uncontestably the richest man in Australia, his own conversion has been quite dramatic. Three stones lighter than the hulking figure who hijacked world cricket, the horrendous chain-smoking cut back to one low-tar pack per day, ruddy of complexion and utterly relaxed in stained jodhpurs and rumpled shirt, he leaned back in his chair in a paddock outside Melbourne and announced: 'I don't give a stuff about business any more.

'I've been going to the office every day for 30 years and I was getting fat and out of condition and very bored. I'm surrounded by a whole lot of people who keep telling me how absolutely brilliant they are, so here's their chance to prove it.

Some will glibly diagnose a classic bout of mid-life crisis. In the case of Kerry Packer, aged 51, it is not that simple. Firstly, he has recently been given a clean bill of health following major surgery. Secondly, with the shrewdest foresight, he sidestepped the Great Financial Crash. Thirdly, he has discovered polo.

Polo is the keynote. He has, by his own admission, become totally obsessed by it. So obsessed that every waking hour these days is devoted to honing the team he is bringing to England for four months next summer to play thrice weekly at Smith's Lawn, Windsor, Royal Berkshire, Cowdray Park and Cirencester.

The very name of Kerry Packer, of course still causes many British Establishment figures to become apoplectic and spill their drinks.

You will recall that a decade ago, denied the Test match television contracts he wanted, he virtually bought the game by signing up every leading player in the world.

It was the most ruthless hijack in the history of world sport and when Packer subsequently won a dramatic three-week High Court action in London to prove he was within his legal rights, his name was bracketed by many alongside those of the Yorkshire Ripper and Al Capone.

'How do you think England will react to your return?' I asked him. He laughed. 'I wasn't aware,' he said, 'that they play polo at Lord's.'

Cricket may never forgive him but the world of polo may relax. Packer has no intention of buying it, changing it or influencing it in any way. He simply wants to play it.

To this end he is currently in the saddle four hours a day. This week he is playing five matches in six days at a tournament near Melbourne. At Ellerston, his vast country property north-west of Sydney, he is laying out Australia's most luxurious polo complex. It has five full-scale pitches already.

He has bought 150 ponies. He has signed up seven of Australia's finest high-goal players and appointed Jim Gilmore, a six-handicap international, as his polo manager. He has already leased stabling and team quarters in Windsor for his assault in England next year.

Shortly, two of his three personal pilots will fly him in his private Gulf Stream jet to Buenos Aires, Argentina, the mecca of the game. He merely wants to see the world's top stars in action and is as excited in his anticipation as any schoolkid.

'Funny isn't it,' he said with a rare flash of humility, 'for such a bloody awful player. I rode as a kid but then I didn't get in a saddle for 25 years. I wasn't much good before and I'm no better now. But I'm working at it. I've got to shed another stone.'

Currently handicap one on the international scale of ten, he rode six seven minute chukkas with immense determination and aggression here yesterday. His team won 10-7.

I asked him how much all this was costing him. 'Get stuffed,' he replied. The radical change of lifestyle does not extend to any moderation in his extensive usage of the Australian vernacular. 'Put it this way, it's worth every bloody dollar I'm spending. I'm frustrated I didn't start younger but, then, I had to make the money to take it up later on.'

Taking up polo past 50 is not unlike taking up boxing at 40. My guess is that so far is has cost him between £15 and £20 million.

Kerry Packer can probably afford it and, even if he couldn't, would have done it anyway. In the first interview he has given since his major operation — performed secretly at a far-distant clinic to avoid rocking the share market — he spoke intensely about a tycoon's confrontation with mortality.

'It brought me up with a jolt,' he said quietly. 'I'm not a great ponderer, but the operation made me realise that life isn't a dress rehearsal. Hang on a minute, this is it, the only one I'll ever have. How much time have I got? Okay, let's get out of here and do what I want to do.'

Australia's biggest TV owner, inheritor of an enormous media empire, a man who could exert powerful political influence and revolutionise world cricket on a whim, simultaneously spotted something else. The world's commercial markets were over-heating to explosion point.

'I can't claim to have pinpointed the date of the Crash,' he said, 'but it was obvious something bloody awful was going to happen. So what was I do do? Sell? Get out?'

On Boxing Day, 1985, he began secret negotiations to sell his vast TV holdings to Alan Bond, the high-flying London-born entrepreneur who became Australia's idol when his yacht won the America's Cup.

'What I was being offered was a ridiculous, absurd price. It was a deal I would have been an idiot to refuse. So I sold,' said Packer.

Twenty-two months later the world markets were holed beneath the water-line. Several of Australia's biggest-name businessmen instantly drowned. Packer was in the lifeboat, reading up the rules of polo.

'That's all I think about now,' he said. 'Polo. I still have business interests but I resent having to waste a minute on them. I'm spending more and more time at Ellerston with polo people. They're a fantastic group and I love their company. They wouldn't know what a take-over bid means.

'They're country people. They're much nicer than city people. They have bush fires and droughts and they have to help one another. They suffer or prosper together. Me? I've always been a city person. Always realised that if I'm doing well at business then I'm cutting some other bastard's throat.'

THE CRUCIAL DRIVE

Nigel Mansell, the Grand Prix driver, is a very tough man. So it was almost reassuring to discover he has nerves like the rest of us. With some help from his close friend Greg Norman he secured a place in the Australian Open Golf championship. He failed to make the half-way cut the following day, but his opening round was not without merit or humour.

SYDNEY: NOVEMBER

NIGEL Mansell didn't sleep a wink the night before his debut in big golf.

Well, that's not entirely true. He nodded off around 6am and dozed fitfully till eight o'clock.

That was probably the saving of him because it meant he missed reading the Sydney Morning Herald which featured across five columns in its sports pages an article modestly headed 'How to Whip Up a Perfect Round in the Open.'

Its author was one Charles Pettit, resident professional at the Royal Sydney Golf Club where the Australian Open Championship is being played, and thus the man above all others who knows the geography of this gracious yet most testing of golf courses, 6,807 yards long and par 72, better than the route to his own front gate.

Had he seen the article, Mansell would have undoubtedly last-minute swotted it like some panic-stricken non-achiever on the morning of his O-levels.

'Grand Prix driving has it own particular stresses, but the thought of playing out there with all those stars really got to me,' he admitted. 'I'm virtually a tee-totaller but I had a double brandy before I went to bed. It didn't send me to sleep at all. I just tossed and turned.'

In due course his moment came to step up on to the elevated first tee at Royal Sydney.

His playing companions for the opening round were Billy Dunk, a wizened gnome of an old-timer Australian professional, and — so help me, wait for it — none other than Charles Pettit, emeritus professor of all that lay before them and author of 'How to Whip Up a Perfect Round in the Open.'

Nigel's opening shot was not the most distinguished ever played in an Open Championship. In fact it was terrible.

It came out of the heel of the club, marginally missed decapitating a lady testing her theory that all Formula One drivers look like Martians, rocketed through the roots of some paper bark trees about 180 yards distant and came to rest on broken ground one yard from a wire-netting fence.

Legal adjudications were sought. It was deemed Mansell had driven into ground under repair and was thus due a free drop. He hit a terrific recovery shot on to the green and was down in par four. He scrambled a par five at the next without once touching the fairway. He was par three on the third and then, at the fourth, sank a 15-footer for a birdie.

Mansell punched the air like his friend Greg Norman: one-under after four holes. It was not only star scoring. It was one of the greatest triumphs you could have witnessed of sheer iron-will determination over some decidedly dodgy technique.

'Not only that,' conceded Mansell, 'I was so uptight I could hardly breathe. I was panting. I was gripping the club as tightly as you grip a racing car steering wheel.

'But gradually the tension eased off and I began to enjoy it.'

But where, meanwhile, was Mr Charles Pettit?

Quite remarkably Charlie Pettit was rarely seen throughout the entire round except during fleeting appearances on tees and greens.

The author of 'How to Whip Up a Perfect Round in the Open' drove into areas of Royal Sydney even he never knew existed. He occasionally found himself hitting over entire forests from neighbouring fairways. Whenever glimpsed he appeared to be behind tree trunks, fighting bushes last seen in films about war behind the Japanese lines and changing clubs like a man demented.

At the height of his distress he walked on to yet another tee to be confronted by a spectator dressed in canary yellow. It was Mr Geoffrey Boycott, that most sensitive of English sportsmen, who appears to be here on some mysterious assignment and seemed to know Mr Pettit from pleading with him on previous visits for a free round on the course.

'Eee oop,' bellowed Boycott cheerfully within earshot of many, 'get on with it Charlie. Tha's played this course 'oondreds of times.'

Mr Pettit needed little reminding of that. That's why he'd written a guide to it in the Sydney Morning Herald. He was so upset that at the final hole he smashed his drive into distant undergrowth yet again.

Mansell hit his drive left-fairway on the final 410-yard par four and then struck an eight-iron into a green back-dropped by thousands lining the clubhouse balconies. An enormous roar went up. His ball had stopped nine inches from the hole.

Mansell sank it for a birdie three. He was round in 77. Charles Pettit, author of 'How to Whip Up etc' finished with 87.

Neither will survive the halfway cut of this great championship. Neither expected to.

All that Mansell did was gently rebuke a few chip-shouldered Australians who said he'd never break 90. And all that dear Charlie Pettit proved was that golf, an eternally lovely game, reserves the right to reach up and grab you just where it hurts.

CORNER SUITE

Sandy Lyle was going through a traumatic period of his life when he complained about Australia. In fact they gave him the ten-star treatment and he beat Greg Norman in a thrilling head-to-head.

PORT DOUGLAS: NOVEMBER

PORT DOUGLAS is almost where Australia runs out of land at the top right-corner corner. It is a long haul from anywhere, let alone Pebble Beach, California, where two days ago a jaded and homesick Sandy Lyle publicly announced he didn't want to come here. In fact so fed up was Sandy with the remorseless travel of professional golf that this normally most imperturbable of sporting paragons flew off the handle about Australia, Australians and Australiana.

'I've been there three times in the past and it's always been a hassle,' he groaned. 'I'm fed up with the Australian scene. When I've gone down there I've only been given tiny corner rooms and not been treated in the same way as, say. Ballesteros or Langer.'

Inevitably there were journalists in earshot. Inevitably his reported sentiments were blazed across yesterday's Australian newspapers. And inevitably the interminable history of the Whingeing Pom was instantly enriched. Australians, deeply sensitive about what others think of them are having a field day at Sandy's expense and you can guarantee the columnists and cartoonists will be sharpening their wits for days.

Well, I was already here yesterday when Sandy Lyle flew in from California and have to admit, damn them, that once again they've lumbered him with corner quarters.

It is called the Presidential Suite.

It is decorated in powder blue, it has its own dining room, drawing room, bed-room and two bathrooms. It has a private jacuzzi and its own six-shelved bar with enough booze to see the most dedicated dypsomaniac past Christmas. It looks out on to the bluest of blue shark-proof lagoons and beyond that is the Great Barrier Reef. Its usual rent per day — though not, of course, for Sandy — is almost exactly £1,000. Sandy just grinned when he saw it. He knew that the Port Douglas Mirage Resort, a complex of ultimate luxury, had called his bluff.

They had already sent their private jet to collect him from Sydney Airport and fly him to Cairns where his personal helicopter was waiting to convey him the final 40 miles to his latest Australian corner room. His mood last evening was benign.

This was just as well. This coming weekend he is to captain five other United Kingdom players in an inaugural sporting event: the first Golf Test match against Australia.

More of that later in the week. For now it might just be worth recalling that the first Poms to come here for Test matches were cricketers who sailed from England on ships scarcely faster than the early prison hulks, travelled trans-Australia on trains which gave the impression they were going backwards and were frequently transported to the Big Match by horse and cart.

They didn't whinge. Cricket was their profession, their privilege, their pride. They made scarcely more money at it than the farm labourers they'd left behind but they had played for England and, a century ago, seen the world.

Sandy Lyle, in extremis in California, swore this would be the last time he would ever visit Australia. It was a most uncharacteristic remark from a man of usually impeccable composure.

Threatened with legal action if he didn't turn up — his photograph appears in all the glossy publications surrounding this event — Sandy arrived. He is not exactly enduring terminal hardship. Whingeing may now cease.

1989

1989 brought the third major soccer tragedy of the decade: 95 spectators killed on the terraces of Hillsborough. Instead of provoking concerted determination that it could never happen again it produced only further embittered and dogmatic bickering between football fans and officialdom and the government. That was the most disturbing aspect of a year of much disillusion. Internationally Ben Johnson's craven admission that he had achieved his world sprint records on drugs — thus vindicating those who had risked libel actions by pointing that out months previously — laid bare the enormity of drug usage in sport. Nationally journalistic intrusion into the private lives of prominent sports personalities reached unprecedented depths. Happily the gloom was relieved by Nick Faldo proving himself a golfer of historic significance and the tennis courts being invaded by teenagers of precocious genius and far better manners than many of their immediate predecessors. Unhappily, it was not the year England simply lost the Ashes at cricket; it was the year England even lost its cricketers to South Africa in a massive defection.

ROUGH DIAMOND MBE

The New Year brought honour for darts and Mr Eric Bristow MBE. The only way to catch up with him was to get the golf clubs out again.

STOKE-ON-TRENT: JANUARY

IT must be said that membership of Her Majesty's Most Excellent Order of the British Empire has definitely not gone to Eric Bristow's head.

Squeezing several sachets of tomato sauce over his liver and bacon in the Little Chef diner just outside Stoke-on-Trent, Mr Bristow said: 'Change? I'll never change. Some blokes went to Eton, but I was educated in the saloon bar of the Arundel Arms in the East End of London and there's no changing that, is there?'

His mates, Trev and Rees, nodded vigorous support for such profundity. Rees is 22 and services fire extinguishers when he isn't playing golf with Eric, which is almost every day. Trev is somewhat more than a mate being also Mr Bristow's driver. Mr Bristow can't drive a car and doesn't propose to learn since he is occasionally seen in public in close proximity to pints of lager.

'Remember that pop star what got drunk and run down a kid and killed him?' said Eric. 'Finished, wasn't he. Public didn't want to know him after that. I mean, you can't go around killing kids and think that nobody notices.'

Trev and Rees growled deep-throated appreciation of such sagacity. So did I. Mr Bristow, whose new Mercedes is being delivered next week, reveals many qualities — in addition to not drinking and driving — that make nonsense of the shock-horror reaction to the preferment of a darts player in the New Year's Honours List.

Eric affects not to be wounded by it, but is. 'I don't care that they keep writing about me as some pot-bellied, lager slob. But I'm not, am I?' Indeed, on the bitingly-cold links of Wolstanton Golf Club in The Potteries he cut an athletic if not quite sylph-like figure.

But what hurts him more, as five times World Champion and five times World Master, (a record not even approached by any other darts player in history), is that so many of his own countrymen don't recognise him as a winner.

'Look at Steve Davis, the snooker player. He wins everything but they don't like him. Look at me. I win everything and they don't like me. But who do they love? They love Frank Bruno, who shouldn't be allowed in the same ring as Mike Tyson, and they love that Eddie the Hopeless Eagle. That's the British public for you.'

'Yes, I'm a winner,' said Eric, smashing his

first drive into a distant hedge. The only place you can catch up with Eric Bristow MBE these days is on a golf course. He plays seven days a week, mostly with Trev.

They've had this arrangement for the year since Eric ended his long live-in liaison with Maureen Flowers, the world's woman darts champion. Maureen, 11 years his senior, used to drive him everywhere from their base in Stoke. 'Didn't work out,' explained Eric. 'Living in one another's pockets, you see.' Trev and Rees muttered their sympathy. Eric has a new girlfriend, Miss Jane Higginbotham, but she doesn't live in. She lives in Middlesbrough. 'Means I've had to learn to use a washing machine and do my own ironing,' admitted Eric, 'but I've had a smashing year.'

Mr Bristow's ambivalent attitude to women became apparent when we discovered our 18 holes coincided with ladies' foursomes day.

Thus etiquette decreed the ladies had preference on the course. We had to stand aside in the chilling wind to allow four matches to pass us uninterrupted. 'Just look at them,' observed Eric. 'I mean, some of them can't hit the ball at all. What are their husbands doing even allowing them out here? They should be back home doing the ironing.' Ironing seems to be preying on Eric's mind. Visibly irritated by the long delay, Eric smashed his next drive into some trees on the left before resuming his dissertation on distaff attitudes.

'They're not all like that, you know. Take Margaret Thatcher. I've always liked Margaret Thatcher. She's a hard one, that, and I like hard people. I've never met her, but I'd like to very much.'

Mention of the Prime Minister, since her influence on the New Year's Honours List is considerable, prompted me to ask whether the absence of any English footballer or football official from the List, while both a darts player and lawn bowler have been honoured, could be construed as a slap in the face to a game which is giving the Government such a hard time about membership registration cards? Eric didn't think so. 'They shouldn't get nothing, should they? What have they done? Nothing.'

Viewing the wider aspects of his own award, Mr Bristow said he was pleased for the game. He was most pleased of all, however, that the award had been made to him personally. 'It was for me', he said, 'because I'm a character and I get all the mentions when the game is discussed.'

He is greatly looking forward to going to Buckingham Palace to receive his decoration and will not be troubling Moss Bros. He is having his own suit tailored. 'I mean', he said 'these things have got to be done proper, haven't they?'

Eric ends a lot of sentences with questions except where golf is concerned. 'No putts are to be conceded,' he decreed severely. He hit some wonderful shots from time-to-time, but Trev the driver beat us all. Mr Bristow paid up cheerfully and promptly.

Yesterday Trev drove his employer down to the Lakeside Country Club in Surrey where for the next week Mr Bristow will be embroiled in the Embassy World Professional Darts Championships.

The spotlight will be on him as never before. 'It doesn't worry me at all,' said Eric. 'I was educated in a hard school from the moment my dad took me into the Arundel Arms at the age of 14 to play darts.

'I knew what I was going to do with my life. Well I've done it and I'm not ashamed about that. I make plenty of money and I spend it. My idea of a great holiday is a month in Las Vegas. That's the object of education, isn't it? To give people happy and successful lives.'

It was less a rhetorical question than irrefutable statement. There were moments when I thought I'd been playing golf with Alf Garnett, but there is more to Eric Bristow than prejudiced and envious eyes perceive.

He is a patriot, a buccaneer, an egotist, a multi-decorated world champion and a sporting if indifferent golfer. Last month he was in America promoting the sales of British darts and soon will be in Canada on a similar mission.

I loved his company and am among those who congratulate him on his MBE. There would never have been an empire in the first place if such characters did not exist.

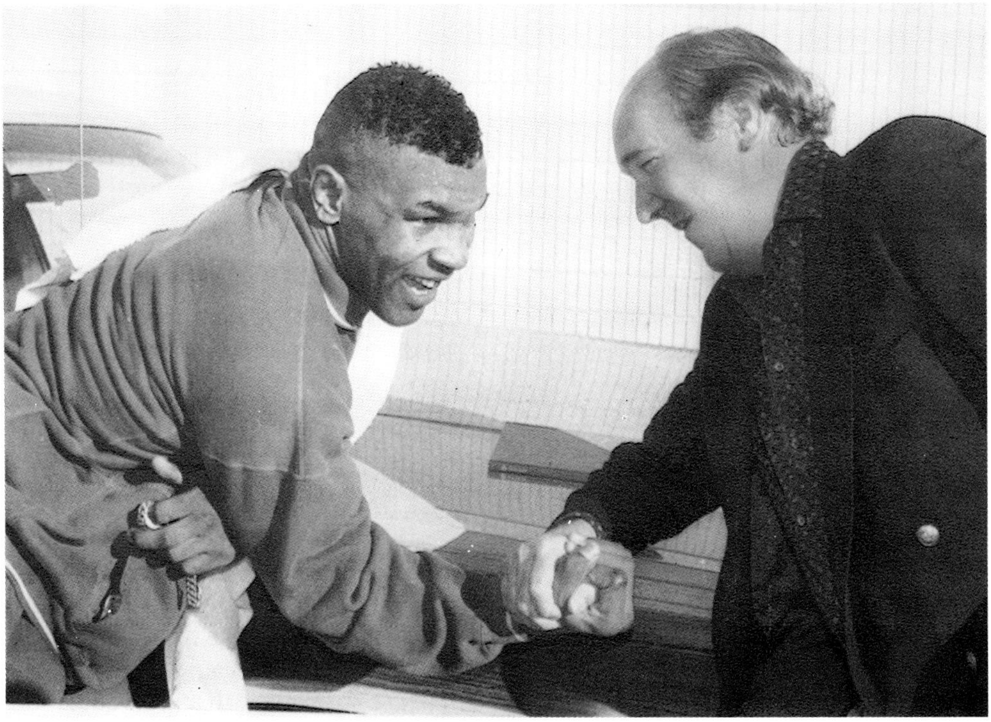

THE PRISONER

Interviewing Mike Tyson was no more difficult than talking to any other mixed-up man of 22. Getting access to him was the problem.

LAS VEGAS: JANUARY

WHEN you finally get him on his own, away from all the hoodlums and the hoods, Mike Tyson turns out to be the strongest puppy in the world.

He has this engaging habit of emphasing exciting points about Duran or Ali or Joe Louis by stabbing you in the shoulder with his right forefinger.

Since this is made of teak and has the diameter of a broomhandle it not only endangers your collarbone but truly makes you wonder what it will feel like when he sticks his thumb and the other three into a boxing glove and lets Frank Bruno have it.

He is shy and wary, particularly of the British press whom he has clearly been given to understand are only interested in his sex life, his rocky marriage and such wild antics as breaking training to rush up to Canada to do something about one or the other or preferably both.

When we settled to talk about boxing he immediately relaxed. Boxing is the only world in which he is equal to its historians and superior to all contemporary exponents.

It transpired that he actually wanted someone fresh to talk to. He is bored. Bored most of all by being virtually a prisoner of his own handlers in a hotel suite in a ghastly town in the middle of the Nevada Desert.

They give him new toys to play with, like the 175,000 dollar Lamborghini he now uses to drive the two miles to the gym, but when you observe him struggling with the mysteries of a manual gear shift you wonder why handlers so disciplinarian in one respect can be so irresponsible in another.

'Bored, bored, bored, man, is what I am of this place. Stuck in here all the time drives me crazy and I've got another five weeks of it.'

Actually it's rather more than five weeks and it's not strictly true he never gets out. Now back in training he is leaving the hotel at 4 o'clock each morning to run in streets as yet unpolluted by traffic fumes and the human hassle world heavyweight champions invariably attract.

Later, around 1 pm, he drives to the gym accompanied by a convoy of vehicles containing security guards, sparring partners and other men of dubious countenance and unspecified employment.

One appears to do nothing more than bring Tyson's ghetto-blaster, a three-feet long instrument of torture which is likely to inflict more damage on Tyson's eardrums than any opponent ever will.

Although his recent sparring sessions have been conducted behind the bolted and grilled doors of Johnny Tocco's windowless training establishment, the wild noise can be heard a block away.

I must explain that such direct quotations I use from Mike Tyson in this story are heavily expurgated. The reason for this is that on average every fifth word he utters would tend to cause offence in print. Frequently he splits a word into syllables and slips the other word in between.

It is utterly innocent because it is the argot of where he came from and also where he is. Boxing's brutality is not confined to the ring.

I asked him if he's afraid of anything: snakes, spiders, heights, cocktail parties full of Ivy League socialites, things like that.

'I ain't afraid of nothing,' he said instantly. 'I ain't afraid of getting hit or hurt but that don't mean I'm not nervous. I'm as nervous as hell before the start of any fight. Nervous that something might go wrong. Nervous I don't do as well as I should. It's adrenalin, ain't it. Pours through you like fire. You can't wait to get started and then all the nerves go and you're in there, hoping you'll do it right.'

He giggled slightly before amending this declaration. 'Yeah, I do get scared. I get scared at night when I get chased by monsters. Happens all the time. I dream a lot and I'm always getting chased by monsters.'

Is he ever scared that with his phenomenal strength and aggression he could kill a man in the ring? The casual question shocked him. He took some time to reply, as though the possibility had never occurred to him before. 'God forgive an accident, man,' he said, and this time he went a whole sentence without swearing.

Then he got annoyed. A legendary fighter called Joe Louis finished up in this very town of Las Vegas as a celebrity 'greeter' at a huge casino-hotel. Mr Louis's greetings were often less than convincing since he was in a wheelchair, frequently with his once-noble head lolling from side to side. And then there was Muhammad Ali, of magnificent physique and wit, now reduced to human wreckage by going many fights too far.

There was no time to ask the question. Tyson pounced 'That's **** man, 'that's ******* **** I hate hearing people speak that ****. You can tell people who speak like that to **** off, man. Boxing is a business that is totally different to any other business. Why it's **** is because people who talk like that don't come up with no solution. They just sit there and say how lousy it is that those boxers finish up bad. They don't realise a lot of us started bad so where's the ******* difference? When you go in there you're going to get hurt. Everybody gets hurt. You talk to me about Ali. Do you know that Ali really needs the money?'

Tyson angry is an awesome sight. The eyes, brown around the pupils, blaze. There was no question that he threatened violence but there was also no question of your correspondent provoking him still further by asking him what happened to the 40 million dollars Ali earned before descending into a living hell?

Tyson was much happier refuting a rumour I reported in last Friday's Daily Mail. It was to the effect that such is his passion in a fight that he has no recollection of knocking any opponent out, that he merely comes out of a trance to see them lying at his feet.

'Are you crazy, man? How could I fight like that? That story is rubbish. I know everything that goes on in a fight. I can tell you afterwards when everything happened and how it happened and I can tell you almost every punch. I know this game man, I really know this game.'

He knows its history, its legends, its unsung heroes, its cowards because he studies nothing else. The long hours of his lonely vigil in the Las Vegas Hilton are filled watching filmed fights of all of them back to the days of Carpentier.

'I don't read books. I don't watch much television. I sit there and I study boxers.'

So who were the greatest? Which ones would have given him the hardest fight? Was there one among them who would have beaten him?

Tyson was now intense, concentrating on getting the words right because this was the only question of vital importance. His integrity was at stake because his opinion was genuinely sought.

'That's a great question, man. I'm telling you there ain't no answer. How the hell can there be one? How can you ever tell about Marciano versus Ali when you don't know how either man was feeling on the night or whether he made a mistake he wouldn't make in a million years. I'm in this game and I know about it and I'm telling you again there ain't no answer. No-one will ever know.

'But if you ask me a different question, nothing involving heavyweights and who'd give me the hardest fight, I'll tell you and nobody can argue because Duran, as a lightweight, was the greatest fighter ever seen. I've watched him for hours and hours on film and I'm telling you he was so tremendous that nobody could live with him.'

Returning from the sublime to Frank Bruno, Mr Tyson declined to say anything derogatory or provocative about his next opponent, thus casting grave suspicion over the publicity handouts which quote him as saying he will crush Bruno like a British egg.

But are they friends?

'Stupid question, man. We're just about to fight. What do you expect me to say, that we're going to finish up hugging one another? I hardly know him. I ain't saying nothing one way or the other about Bruno. We'll just fight, that's all. It's stupid to think that boxers love one another just because they've fought. It's you writers who make up things like that. Some fighters hate other fighters for the rest of their lives after they've lost. I ain't going to get drawn into it.'

Of course he will get drawn into it. For two weeks before the fight, after Bruno has joined Tyson in Las Vegas, they will give frequent press conferences and, at the behest of publicity agents, mouth all the familiar banal rhetoric that gives boxing such a bad name.

Statements like 'I'm feeling great' will be accorded the most profound significance. Tyson is worth much more than that. He is a fascinating member of the human race, terribly unhappy here as a young man of 22 is entitled to be when he has already grossed in excess of 50 million dollars, knows where none of it is, is being sued by his estranged wife for 125,000 million dollars and comprehensively ripped off by businessmen who reassure him they're his friends.

I asked him what career he would have liked had he not been a boxer. 'Nothing, man,' he said. 'I'm just a fighter. It's the only job I have.'

I asked him what he most wanted in the world. 'Some peace man,' he replied, 'just some ******* peace.' The man who is scared of nothing looked furtively around to see if the hoods had overheard him.

Later, outside the gym, our photographer, Monty Fresco, asked him if he'd indulge in an utterly spurious picture allegedly involving an arm-wrestling match between the world heavyweight boxing champion and a Daily Mail sportswriter of indeterminate age. His handlers pointedly looked at their watches, but Mike insisted.

'Jeez, I can't stand the pain,' drawled the man who could have snapped my arm like a matchstick. 'You British guys, are you all like that?' This remark may not significantly shift the betting on the Tyson-Bruno fight. But it was an interesting insight into the mind of a lonely genius who has the world's admiration but is craving for simple love.

THE AMBASSADOR

Returning to Las Vegas for the Tyson-Bruno fight I could only marvel at Frank's composure in an atmosphere of unrelieved hysteria. He was to lose, of course, but surviving five rounds conferred him with heroic status.

LAS VEGAS: FEBRUARY

REPORTERS don't write for posterity. They write to daily deadlines, well knowing tomorrow's story will insulate the next day's take-away.

Yet somehow I hope that years hence someone may produce a fading dog-eared cutting of this column and show it to Frank Bruno's children.

Not, I swiftly add, to suggest it has the remotest literary merit but to let them know how their father comported himself when the time came to secure his, their mother's and their futures.

So, young ladies, here goes:

Your father did not have the most privileged of upbringings, as I am sure he won't have told you.

As far as you are concerned there have always been large cars to transport you to good schools and bring you home again to toys, books, your own bedrooms and the family swimming pool.

But these things have to be earned. They don't fall into your lap. And your father earned them just about the hardest way I know.

He went into professional boxing, acquitted himself with much distinction and then, to the astonishment of many and the horror of some, was negotiated into the position where he could fight an American named Mike Tyson for the world heavyweight championship.

Your father, probably with you and your futures in mind, accepted the challenge.

So I must tell you a little about this Tyson. Only 22, bull-necked, ghetto-hardened, street-educated, as at home in the fight ring as though he had been born in one, with a punch in either hand that could literally kill a man, he stalked the world looking for his next opponent.

Very few would fight him. And those who did, even those if you will forgive me saying so with credentials greater than your father's, regretted doing so.

This Tyson was incapable of losing fights. He won them with such frightening violence that their duration was no longer registered in rounds but seconds. Your father, Frank Bruno, volunteered to become the next contender. Either that or someone talked him into it. Whichever, your dad went off to train and get himself supremely fit in the wilds of

Arizona. He should have stayed there until just hours before the fight but regrettably, under some contractual agreement, he was required to present himself in Las Vegas, a 20th century Gomorrah.

The idea was that your father's presence at a number of press conferences would boost the sale of tickets which, for all the furore in Britain, were not selling all that well.

In fact, they were going so badly that if you had the nerve to sit it out at a roulette table, someone would have given you a free one, so keen were officials to show a global TV audience the place was packed.

So, initially, your Dad was dragged into a meeting with the Press to apologise for his utterly justified remarks about being kept hanging around like a hick punter when he arrived at the huge hotel where the fight was to take place.

Although your father conducted himself with dignity, I have rarely witnessed anything more embarrassing. Until, that is, they stage-managed for a massive attendance of TV, radio and Press, a conference with both fighters.

The Tyson entourage, 14 in number, arranged themselves on the left-hand side of the podium. Some wore caps. Most wore track suits, chewed gum and looked extremely menacing. Heading the British delegation was a man from Savile Row. Superbly dressed in understated bespoke tailoring, with a subdued and beautifully knotted tie, he looked like an ambassador, which indeed he was.

This man was your father.

For an hour he was forced to listen to a banal harangue, embracing world politics, apartheid, Greek philosophy, Shakespeare, quotations from Winston Churchill and quite slanderous allegations about his business rivals in the world of boxing, by a man named Don King.

Had I been your father I would have walked out, I would particularly have walked out when this odious self-appointed windbag warned Mrs Thatcher gratuitously — though it was hard to understand quite where she came into it — that early next week 'Frank Bruno will be returned to Britain in an incapacited state'. To compound this appalling remark he added: 'Funny things happen in boxing rings and we don't want to be responsible for them'. Even Mike Tyson, sitting four yards from your father, was stunned by the sinister implication of that statement. He shook his head slowly, dissociating himself from it.

In many years of writing about sport, I have never heard anything quite so evil. Well, your father took it, staring straight ahead. The sickening thing about boxing is that the men who do the fighting are discussed as though they are so many pounds of horseflesh.

When, finally, his turn came to answer questions, none remotely intelligent, your father handled them with admirable brevity. Being a fighting man he is no master of the English language, but even so his replies were gems of dignity.

Obviously he said he was here to win the world heavyweight title, to which Tyson obviously replied: 'I'm the best fighter in the world and he's going to be in a lot of trouble on Saturday.' Press conferences before big fights are arranged to provoke exchanges like that. They are designed to make headlines and capture the opening minutes of the television news, thus generating the interest which sells seats in the arena or closed-circuit TV venues across the world.

Your father went along with all that. His voice was firm, his composure under provocation quite superb. I wrote earlier that he looked like an ambassador. Well he is. He is probably the best sporting ambassador Britain has sent into foreign fields for many years.

The only problem is that beautifully mannered, elegantly dressed, self-controlled ambassadors are hardly expected to prevail in the murderous fire of a world heavyweight boxing ring. Especially when a man called Mike Tyson is advancing from the opposite corner.

I snatch this opportunity to write positively and affectionately about your father before the contest because, deep down, I believe his only motive for being here concerns his love for you.

Frank Bruno is a brave man and, as Mr Dave Allen used to say, may his God go with him.

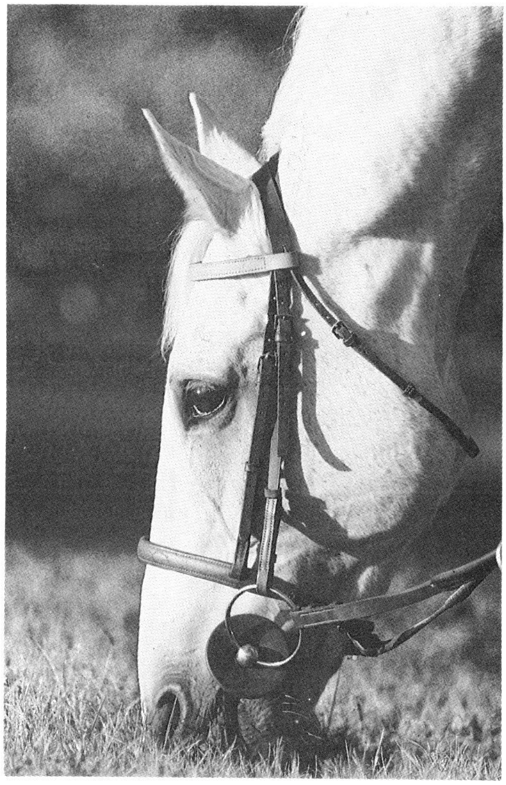

DON'T CALL ME DESSIE

Was there a more stirring sight throughout the decade than Desert Orchid winning the Cheltenham Gold Cup? But then, he always was a horse with a mind of his own.

CHELTENHAM: MARCH

LOOK, this is frightfully irregular but since you're here I'll give you ten minutes. But I must warn you that I hate being misquoted. It's bad enough reading what those hacks from the sports pages write about me, but these past few weeks have been intolerable.

Every damned glossy magazine and colour supplement seems to have send down some wordsmith to do what they call a 'piece' on me. They all read the same because they carry pocketfuls of one another's cuttings, re-write them and charge about £500 expenses.

If it's not long after breakfast or lunch I can generally orchestrate a prolonged coughing fit to put them off, but I don't expect many of your readers will know what that means.

What appals me is their familiarity. They call me Dessie. I simply detest being called Dessie. I mean, they wouldn't call the Prime Minister Maggie to her face and then go away and write about her as Thatchie, would they?

I find this a most deleterious trend, particularly among the commentators. 'Goochie', 'Cloughie,' 'Barnesey' . . . they do in in all sports. I'm told that Peter O'Sullevan called me Dessie on one occasion, but I can hardly believe it. He went to Charterhouse, you know.

And they ask such banal questions. 'Does he enjoy it?' I've heard them say.

Enjoy it? Well, put it this way. I could, without inordinate intellectual strain, nominate a number of alternatives to coming up the last three furlongs at Cheltenham on a freezing Thursday afternoon in March with lungs bursting and what feels like a ton of turnips on your back.

Not that I have a word to say against my present partner, Simon Sherwood.

Thoroughly well-spoken young man — went to Radley, you know, like Ted Dexter — but I do have a quiet smile when he says it hurts him more than it does me when he gives me the occasional crack across the hips.

Do I hate Cheltenham, you say? What a stupid question. I love it. Racing people, you see. Queen Mum always there, looking a million dollars and having a gin or two and thoroughly enjoying it. Thousands of Irish and English people mingling together and getting on like a house on fire. There surely has to be a lesson there.

But just imagine if I'd had the same talent for the Flat. Honestly, I think I'd have feigned pneumonia rather than go to Royal Ascot with all those woofters in hired top hats and the dreadful women with their phoney accents.

Admittedly Cheltenham does give me the willies in one respect. As you know, only one of my 26 wins had been on a left-handed track and Cheltenham is left-handed.

So much junk has been written about this that I'd better explain it once and for all. It's like you suddenly landing in Madrid or Los Angeles and having to drive on the wrong side of the road. It's like the trouble left-handed people have opening wine bottles with a corkscrew.

You don't feel natural for the first few minutes and, of course, the Cheltenham Gold Cup only lasts a few minutes, although I don't mind telling you that when you're doing it, it feels like bloody hours.

Anyway Simon and David Elsworth, my trainer, have been working on it and I'm now feeling considerably less dyslexic.

Must tell you a funny story about that. As part of the remedial training they showed me several films of my earlier races on left-handed tracks and at the end of one of them John McCririck, of ITV, suddenly came on the screen and I have to tell you I was simply riveted. Wearing a pink suit, he was, that looked as thought it had spent all winter rolled up in the golf bag. I mean, I simply fell about. Hasn't he got a wife or mother or anyone to advise him? Also he was waving his hands about like a demented crow. But shall I tell you something? I liked that chap because he really got stuck into the bookies.

We horses have a pretty ambivalent attitude to bookmakers. They live off our backs. Some are more appreciative than others.

I mean, have you ever met that Ron Pollard from Ladrokes? What a card. He must be the only Socialist bookie in captivity.

He'll quote you odds on anything — even 500,000 -1 against Zola Budd runing five miles on the moon this century.

But they're not all like Ron. Not only have they lumbered me with ridiculous odds for the Cheltenham Gold Cup but they will be praying for me to lose. So how can I respect them?

I have not the remotest idea how I shall do in the big race. Obviously, like Seb Coe and Daley Thompson at the Olympics, I shall be running my guts out. This is the big one as they say in soccer and I am very conscious of it. I was not all that sad when Kribensis blew it on Tuesday because, like television newscasters, we secretly hate to see a rival performing well. It leaves the stage to me and I hope to fill it.

How will I celebrate if I win? Dear boy, how innocent you are. Many moons ago they decided that if I were to have a future in steeplechasing I should undergo a certain operation to concentrate the mind.

I am to modern sport what the great 40-year-old male sopranos of the 17th century were to opera singing. I am a gelding, the end of a line, a one-off who will forever dine alone on Father's Day.

Good heavens, just look at the time. I said ten minutes and you've been here half an hour. You must go now while I get my oats, in a manner of speaking.

SPORT'S SONG FOR EUROPE

Suddenly, as the decade drew to a close, we were informed there could never be another like it. Brussels was calling in the team shirts. We were Europeans now.

LONDON: APRIL

I AM lobbying my local European MP to solicit his support for a few bright ideas I have for the 1992 Olympic Games in Barcelona.

These include the introduction of the Adolf Hitler Memorial 1,500 metres, the Klaus Barbie Appeal Fund long jump and the Eva Braun Testimonial marathon for women.

Of course, that is offensive. It is meant to be. Its object is to shock you into pestering your local European MP until he pledges to strangle at birth the latest brainchild of his Brussels Commissioners.

It is, so help us, to scrap 'God Save The Queen' when a British victor stands on the gold medal rostrum and replace it with another anthem which starts like this:

Freude, schoner Gotterfunken,
Tochter aus Elysium,
Wir betreten feuertrunken,
Himmlische, dein Heiligtum.

Sportsmail readers will instantly recognise the words of Friedrich Von Schiller which, as set to music by Ludwig von Beethoven and played by the Berlin Philharmonic under Herbert von Karajan, compound a breathtaking concert hall experience.

However, to render it when the likes of Daley Thompson or Virginia Leng stand there as a dark blue flag of economic convenience rises slowly to the masthead would be as emotionally appropriate as playing Colonel Bogey to commemorate a German victory.

Indeed, it's worse than that. What the European Community Commissioners, in their arrogance and at their interfering worst, are advocating is that all EEC Olympic victories should be celebrated by the raising of their gold-starred banner and the playing of the von Schiller verse from Beethoven's Ninth Symphony. Jacques Delors, the EEC president, admits he is eager 'to give the EEC a higher profile at international events.' You bet he is.

What next? A united Western European soccer team for the World Cup? Probably.

There seems no limit to their insistence that European tribalism can be vaporised on a whim from Brussels and clearly, drawing the fangs of competitive inter-European sport would contribute mightily.

Well, they've gone about it with a blunderbuss.

There's nothing wrong with 'Ode To Joy.' Lovely tune, nice lyrics for the drawing room when translated but hardly appropriate, perhaps, for some sweating weightlifter bubbling with anabolic steroids:

Joy, bright spark of divinity,
Daughter of Elysium,
Fire-inspired we tread
Thy sanctury.

But the crassness of the selection is its totally Germanic origins. Would the great German hurdler, Harald Schmid, enjoy standing there while the band played Elgar? Or would the Italian marathon champion, Gelindo Bordin, be greatly moved by a few bars of Berlioz?

I have long harboured the Utopian dream that to deaden the strident nationalism and defuse the political overtones, all flags and anthems should be eliminated from the Olympics.

But that is flogging a dead horse now that a new money-mad Olympic movement actually trades nationalism as a television selling product.

So why, in such circumstances, should the EEC nations be neutralised while the anthems of the Soviet Union, America and Kenya continue to ring out?

It is one of the battier ideas to emerge from Brussels and hopefully Britain's newest member of the International Olympic committee will campaign against it the moment she gets a chance. After all, it's her mother's tune they are scheming to sling out.

THE HOUNDING OF BOBBY ROBSON

Bobby Robson telephoned me a few days after this column was published. I was able to tell him that, apart from two abusive letters, the large postbag it provoked entirely supported the contention that the personal life of a sportsperson should be his or her own affair. It was fascinating that most of the supportive letters were written by women.

LONDON: JUNE

BOBBY ROBSON called a press conference yesterday to explain certain developments in his private life. I did not attend. I have no interest in Bobby Robson's private life.

What does interest me is the sudden sanctimonious wave of puritanism that is sweeping our nation, insisting that we all know about Bobby Robson's private life. And those of Mike Gatting, Ian Botham, Ronnie Ferguson and the rest of them.

It is not, of course, puritanism at all. It is

vicious intrusion to gratify the prurient appetities of those whose lives are so boring that they buy certain newspapers for the kicks.

Sometimes the revelations are accurate. Sometimes they are not. Always they are presented with coy opprobrium implying that adultery was invented yesterday. Some lady readers will react to that from a male writer by echoing the celebrated High Court response of Miss Mandy Rice-Davis during the Profumo scandal a quarter of a century ago: 'Well, he would say that wouldn't he.'

Of course I would. That is why I was not interested in anything Bobby Robson had to say yesterday. Or his wife. Or their dog. If there are problems in the Robson family, for God's sake let them settle it behind closed doors. Marital problems are not exactly exclusive to the famous.

Ironically, if Bobby Robson wished to turn the tables on one of his persecutors I could tell him precisely how to do it. I won't immediately, but reserve the right to do so if this becomes a protracted business.

It may go without saying that Bobby Robson is a friend. Not close. Just a man I have known as a footballer and football manager for almost 30 years. I no longer watch football, for reasons that have nothing to do with this debate, so I have no idea whether he is the right man for the job or not.

But what I do know is that newspaper campaigns to destroy him have moved so far from fair criticism to sheerly hysterical vilification that it was quite obvious he had enemies in high journalistic places who wanted him out. Appalling England performances in last year's European Championship gave them the rocket-launching platform. They blasted him with everything to the point where his hair turned from mostly black to very grey inside twelve months.

Robson then did an unforegiveable thing.

In the winter and spring that followed he controlled an England team that went 11 matches without defeat, played with great fire and, for all the internal problems he suffered about not getting the players he really wanted, blasted its way to the threshold of entry to the next World Cup in Italy.

It was a tremendous performance but, in his long overdue hours of satisfaction, Robson never once attacked those who had made his life such a misery in the fallow times. He remained urbane, courteous, co-operative, forgiving.

So, having failed to nail him in the dressing room, there were those determined to catch him, allegedly, in the wrong bedroom.

It must be some decades now since I have agreed with any decision emanating from the Football Association's headquarters at Lancaster Gate. But how right they are to stand back, hands raised in utter indifference, to any spurious, pontificating demand that he should be sacked. Sacked for what?

Anyone who believes that Bobby Robson should be sacked for any reason other than steering England's football team into calm waters should consult history.

There wouldn't be an England, there would never have been an Empire, there won't be a European parliament in future if the new moralistic strictures espoused by newspapers with no morals at all were applied.

I am sorry to tell you this, ladies, but I have lived long enough now to know that quite 50 per cent of the successful men in this country have, to put it euphemistically, put their marriages at risk.

Most intelligent wives are aware of it and exact compensation in one way or another. Very few marriages fail because of it unless it is gossipped about by the neighbours. Then pride is involved and the goalposts are moved. When the newspapers get hold of it the sky can fall in. But the hypocrisy about it has become so appalling that someone, sooner or later, has to bring it into the open.

The only way to beat the peeping-tom predators is to laugh them all the way back to their miserable little puritan redoubts where, under cover of darkness, their mistresses will join them for furtive encounters.

This is not to advocate unrestrained licentiousness. It is to suggest that when moral restraint is the message of newspapers for whom no-one has respect, we can all relax.

AN UPSIDE DOWN DAY

In the lazy days before Lord's and Wimbledon there was time to test out the ultimate hangover cure.

HENLEY: JUNE

HENLEY was a picture yesterday two weeks before the Royal Regatta.

Chimney pots clean on the inside. TV aerials burnished brightly. Hardly a loose slate anywhere. For this bizarre information you are indebted to Nigel Lamb, who insisted on showing me the place his way.

This involved two sorties along the Grand Challenge Cup course at a height of 500ft flying upside down in the open cockpit of a biplane at 145mph. Not to be recommended after a farmhouse breakfast but an enriching experience when you finally force your eyes open.

The nervy bit for the newcomer is fixing the safety belts: two straps over the shoulders, two under the crotch, one round the waist which all clunk-click into a central hasp.

Nigel tightens all these for you, comfortingly explaining that you should now feel like a trussed chicken. Then he suggests you might like to fasten another single red belt round your middle. 'What's that for?' you ask suspiciously. 'That's in case something goes wrong with the others,' he says, bumping down the grass runway of Booker airfield and banking away towards Henley.

He's already confiscated your loose change and cigarette lighter. 'Don't want these falling out and jamming up the works, do we?' he says reasonably. Nigel seems to spend half his life flying upside down. He and his wingman, Richard Manning, once flew the 22 miles from Calais to Dover completely upside down in close formation. Actually it is terrific fun when you get used to it. So were the rolls and the loops. What wasn't such fun was when Nigel stood the plane on its tail and threw us into a stall turn. It's then that you understand the brilliance of these stick-and-rudder aerobatic pilots.

He warns you that it's coming. 'Tense your leg and stomach muscles,' he advises. 'It'll stop the blood rushing to your head.' All the same the universe suddenly goes mad. Utterly disorientated, conscious only of an engine that sounds like a thousand sheets of ripping calico, a split second of total blackness and you've come through seven-G, which momentarily transforms your body weight from 13st to 91st.

The tyro simply cannot comprehend how these men do it. Nigel and Richard Manning do it all the time in tight formation. In the loops they are just six feet wing-tip to wing-tip apart.

They will be doing it at 85 airshows and sporting events throughout Britain this summer in the scarlet and white livery of the new Toyota aerobatic team. You wouldn't dream of going up with them, of course, unless you knew their pedigree. In fact, you are as safe as houses. Nigel Lamb, 32, has flying in the blood.

He is the son of a World War Two Spitfire pilot and trained with the Rhodesian Air Force. Richard Manning, 41, is an ex-RAF fighter pilot and instructor to the Red Arrows display team. They can fly anything. For Toyota they fly immensely high-powered Pitts Specials with a 200 horse-power Lycoming engine.

The planes are so small you could park them in a domestic garage, so light they are only half the weight of a saloon car, so manoeuverable they can roll through 360 degrees in one second. They fling them about all over the sky, utterly under control despite G-forces even greater than those felt by the Red Arrows pulling out of big dives.

'How can you think straight in circumstances when I think my skull is going to burst?' you ask. Nigel methodically explains the physiological workings of the inner ear, the speed at which messages can pass from eye to brain. I understand none of it, comprehending only that it's rather like ball-sense in other sports: either you have it or you haven't. 'Well, you don't pull five or six-G the first time you go up,' reasons Nigel. 'You step it up gradually. If you flew with us every other day for a month, you'd be used to it.' I rather doubted that.

They work immensely hard. Some days in this frenetic summer season they will zig-zag across Britain to fly up to five displays in different locations in a single span of daylight. They are professionals, of course, but they are not businessmen. They are sportsmen of the highest calibre.

Both could have become staid civil airline pilots. But their affinity is with the great seat-of-the-pants barnstorming aviators of war and peace, from Baron Manfred von Richthofen above the trenches of the Somme to the mad Russian, Kharlov, who flew under three successive bridges of the Moscow River for a lark.

They will entertain millions of spectators this year not only to keep their overdrafts in check but for the sheer joy of flying. 'Luck,' says Nigel Lamb, 'is finding someone to pay you for what you love doing best.'

Both were trained as military pilots and Nigel says: 'For me the greatest pilots of all were the pioneers, the fantastic air aces of World War One who discovered all these things we do today with better planes.'

Back on land after seven-G we had lunch on Booker Airfield where the restaurant is named the Red Baron, the *nom-de-guerre* of Baron von Richthofen. It rather made the point.

ROYAL TIGRESS

The Seventies saw Princess Anne as an Olympic competitor. The Eighties saw the Princess Royal as an Olympic administrator. The irony was that those who elected her as an elegant figurehead had another think coming.

LONDON: JUNE

EIGHT months ago when the Princess Royal was sworn in as a member of the International Olympic Committee, I wrote that, for all the wrong reasons, they had elected a tigress to their think tank.

The IOC, with its absurd observance of near-Ruritanian protocol, loves titles.

Her Royal Highness the Princess Anne, progeny of a genuine royal household untouched by two centuries of social revolution, was a terrific catch.

Hers was a big name to drop, a password even to that room in Buckingham Palace where they hand out decorations.

They read the lady wrongly.

They discovered that when Princess Anne, for all her exhausting global travel for the Save the Children Fund and her 500-plus official engagements in Britain each year, announced that she is to stand against Italy's Dr Primo Nebiolo for the presidency of the Association of Summer Olympic International Federations at its October elections.

It is safe to infer that she less wants the job for herself than to see the odious Nebiolo stripped of the power which jerks the purse-strings of the vast income the summer Olympics now generate from worldwide television.

Nebiolo, whose profligate use of after-shave and other potions is said to shorten business meetings in confined spaces by hours, is the most hated man in sport.

Thwarted in his ambition to become a member of the IOC, the tactics he has employed in the International Amateur Athletic Association — of which he remains president — have affronted almost everyone.

But in the late summer of 1987 Nebiolo made a terrible mistake. From his president's box in the Olympic stadium in Rome he watched Italian stewards cheat an Italian athlete to a medal at the World Athletics Championships by wrongly measuring his long-jump.

For weeks, even after the deception had been proved beyond doubt, he did nothing to denounce it.

Brazenly he turned up to chair the 25-member council of the Association of Summer Olympic International Federations in Barcelona in April with the familiar leave-it-all-to-me tactics. But this time he'd met his match.

The president of the International Equestrian Federation coolly demanded: 'Why is the council persistently denying the will of the meeting? Why are we still talking?' Applause broke out. Someone had at last tackled Nebiolo head-on.

The president of the International Equestrian Federation is the Princess Royal.

She will, on the ticket of integrity, beat Nebiolo in the October elections, thus adding considerably to her huge commitments and raising hopes among the Anglo-Saxon nations that the most significant trend in international sport since the war — the rise of the Latin countries to positions of supreme authority — may be arrested.

The Olympics are run by Juan Antonio Samaranch of Spain. World soccer is run by Joao Havelange of Brazil. Athletics is run by Nebiolo of Italy.

These organisations are now the clearing houses for billions of dollars in their four-year trading cycles, and all the money comes from the contracts they have the power to confer on everyone from television networks to stadium contractors.

The Princess Royal will not have the power to change these arrangements by becoming president of the Summer International Olympic Federations, whose function is not to generate money but to apportion it among the 25 sports which now contribute to the spectacle of Summer Olympics.

Nebiolo's method, clearly to cling on to the votes that would hopefully keep him in office, was to split the sum total equal ways.

This may have been popular with wrestling, which received as much as athletics, but is patently ridiculous.

I have no doubt these anomalies will be sorted out, but where will this leave the Princess Royal, who in her eight short months as an IOC member, has so stirred up its comfortable self-satisfied, luxurious way of life by demanding to know how everything works that several of its senior executives must now be deeply regretting they ever invited her to join?

The tigress in the think-tank, who lives to a schedule measured by the minute, is less than ecstatic about the way Olympic meetings are convened in five-star hotels so that members and their wives can relax in exotic places while matters that could have been settled by telephone are discussed at inordinate length.

She is also so appalled by the expensive freebie gifts that land on her doorstep in the hope of influencing her vote to designate this or that city to host the next Olympics that she sends them all back.

This is not the way most IOC members behave.

The curious thing is that her father, Prince Philip, never wanted her to join the International Olympic Committee.

He was happy for her to succeed him as president of the International Equestrian Federation and wanted her to concentrate on that.

He was dealing, of course, with a strong-headed daughter who can recognise sycophancy, social-climbing and possible corruption when she sees it.

He was dealing with a woman who looks down at yet another Olympic banquet for 500 invited guests eating five courses and swilling fine claret well knowing that the bill would have kept 5,000 Ethiopian children alive for another year.

She can advance no further in the Olympic movement.

To go beyond what she has taken on would be to embroil herself in world politics, which are what the Olympics are now about.

The protocol of the British Royal Family forbids that, but this quite remarkable woman is pushing it as far as she can.

Just ask Signor Nebiolo, whose seductive after-shave on this occasion has failed to impress.

ARNIE'S ARMY

He returned again to score 82-82 in the Open Championship and miss the half-way cut by miles. But as he proceeded down the 18th fairway for the last time, they stood and roared. There will only ever be one Arnold Palmer.

TROON: JULY

THE American equivalent of a knighthood, which is a front cover of Time Magazine all to yourself, was conferred on Arnold Palmer in 1960 when he was hitting a golf ball like a raging bull.

The purists winced. The public roared. The television cameras zoomed in and stayed there, transfixed by a man who continually had to blast desperate recovery shots out of pampas or jungle but kept winning tournaments. Thus grew Arnie's Army, the legendary thousands-strong fan club that craned and tiptoed merely for a glimpse of this man who had not only invented the art of the impossible but came up with solutions.

Thus, too, golf soared from an elitist game into a public spectacle and there is not a multi-millionaire star on the circuit today, even a couple who were cuttingly jealous at the time, who would not acknowledge their debt to the Palmer persona.

Without television it would have been impossible. With television it was inevitable. For what he brought to the screen, with that swing of minimum elegance and maximum theatre, was an unprecedented sense of drama.

A year after his Time front cover he came to Royal Birkdale and won the Open, hitting at one juncture a recovery shot from thick undergrowth of such outrageous optimism, let alone execution, that the club elders rightly commemorated it with a nearby plaque at which you may either lift your hat or cross yourself.

The following year, 1962, he came to Royal Troon to defend his title.

At the 577 yard sixth, the longest hole in

British championship golf where many obituaries will be written these next four days, he struck two one-irons into the heart of the green.

At this point even elderly Scots, who had averted their gaze at the sheer awfulness of his ungainly follow-through, were forced to acknowledge that the laddie showed a certain promise.

Palmer, with rounds of 71, 69, 67, 69, carried off the Open again with a record score and a modest speech.

On Tuesday, 27 years later, he flew into Prestwick to play Troon again. He won't win the Open — though it may be ill advised to suggest that to his face — and he's unlikely to hit the sixth with successive irons. But his mere presence here, little short of his 60th birthday, invests the championship with a dignity and authority that will be missed when he decides no longer to come.

It is hard to convey to a British reader the status this man has attained, but, along with Ronald Reagan and the late John Wayne, whose views about life did not widely conflict with his own, he is probably the man Corporate America would most like to have at its dinner table.

Some may think this would make him unbearable. In fact, if there is a mentor whose public conduct the tyro sports stars should study in this new era of whinging complaint and raucous abuse, it is Palmer.

Just watch him at the end of a round as the back-slappers and autograph-hunters close in. Very carefully, fingertip by fingertip, the golf glove is drawn off. It is presented to some delighted recipient with a few kindly words. Then come the autograph books, all handed back with — from Palmer, not the autograph-hunter — a grave 'Thank you.'

What no-one ever notices in the mayhem is that Arnold Palmer has never stopped walking to the sanctuary of the locker-room. When the door closes behind him he has probably signed his name no more than a dozen times, but the reputation for utmost courtesy whatever the provocation is unimpaired. I defy anyone to send me a newspaper cutting of the last 30 years even hinting that Palmer has ever been rude to a fan.

It is why, when you open any one of a dozen American glossy magazines these days, you will still see Arnold Palmer in advertisements endorsing everything from limousines via luxury watches to salad dressing.

Two years ago, when Nick Faldo won the Open at Muirfield, Palmer struck a disaster. At the 14th hole he was trapped in a bunker, took five shots to get out and finished with a ten.

At the end of that round he was besieged by reporters. This time he didn't attempt to move. He answered every question, a model of constraint at a time when many would have either blamed their caddie for over-clubbing or brushed past to kick the locker door to matchwood.

Down all the years of Arnie's Army there has also been a Supporter's Club of One. Even legends have to have a home base and for Arnold Palmer there is Winnie, the wife with the marvellously debunking sense of humour whose biography, which she will never write, would take America by storm.

She is with Palmer at every big event. She walks outside the ropes with the fans and such is their affinity that should she cross a fairway and miss a single hole, Palmer senses that she is not there. He does not approve of this. Public paragons have their peculiarities too.

Winnie will be walking outside the ropes at Royal Troon this week. Arnold Palmer will be playing inside them, possibly for the last time in an Open Championship.

Never mind if the odd tee-shot goes astray or he tangles with another bunker on this gloriously bleak terrain where golf was born. You wouldn't want to miss, would you, the swansong of the man who determined that the game was given to the world?

DON'T SHOOT THE PIANIST

For English cricket it was a cataclysmic summer. We barely had time to blink before the Ashes were gone and the hue and cry for a scapegoat was on. The irony was that within 24 hours it was mass defection, not merely defeat, that dominated the front pages. South Africa the sporting outcasts, had had the last word of a turbulent decade.

LONDON: JULY

THE debacle is so complete that it really doesn't matter whether it rains solidly from now till the end of August. It is no longer merely English cricket that is under scrutiny. It is the English character.

For almost 600 years, from Agincourt via Dunkirk to the Falklands, our track record has been pretty good, born as it was of an esoteric code of honour and a sheer bloody-mindedness in adversity.

Many foreigners found this unattractive. About as unattractive, that is, as I found the sarcastic but quite justifiable roar that greeted England reaching the towering heights of 50 for the loss of only five premier batsmen yesterday on a blameless Old Trafford wicket. After all, a counter-attack was in progress. At one juncture we had been 38 for five.

It would be unpardonable to proceed further without offering unstinted congratulations to the Australian team which has simply murdered us. They have played to the extreme limit of their limitations and deserve our thanks for making the proceedings watchable.

Coupled with that is the name of their captain, Allan Border, an undemonstrative man who suffered such calumny and derision from his own countrymen over four lean years that his triumph here with a side conspicuously nowhere near the best in the world must give him immense satisfaction.

Border moulded an average-to-good touring team into a commando raid, thereby suggesting that probably the most fatuous thing England could do at the moment would be to sack David Gower from the captaincy.

The only thing worse that could happen would be for Gower to resign voluntarily when

the Ashes, weather permitting, are rightfully handed over to Australia today.

To fire Gower would be to renege on a pledge Ted Dexter made at the start of the season and plunge us back into the chaos of last summer when four captains in a single series gave us the stability of an Italian government. Gower's resignation would merely convince a watching world that we now simply quit when the going gets tough.

One cannot assess a man's leadership capacity, of course, unless you are there in the dressing room with him when the bails are hitting the fan. But simply to cry for his head, without considering the implications or the alternatives, is as illogical as it is absurd. We have been through all that with Bobby Robson, the England soccer manager, and no-one to this day has had the grace to apologise to him.

Gower's problem may well be an egalitarian approach to a team comprising old lags cynically playing from memory, desperately anxious newcomers easily out-psyched by moderately talented Australian bowling, a couple of complete no-hopers who should never have been chosen at this level of firepower and some men who have made it abundantly clear — though not yet in public — that they have no intention of getting involved in next winter's hellfire tour of the West Indies when they can pay off the mortgage by playing some low-key and extremely lucrative cricket in South Africa where, for spurious political reasons, they will be treated like heroes.

Gower looked like death when he walked to the wicket yesterday. This was sad, because he is a quite brilliant player. Furthermore, unlike so many of the critics demanding his head on a tabloid front page, he has a great record of physical courage.

I have immense respect for a man who has faced the sheer brutality of various West Indies attacks in 19 Tests over the past decade and, during his winters off, has chosen to hurtle head-first down the terrifying Cresta Run.

It is not Gower who should be sacked. It is the players who have so shamefully let him down. Gower, after 104 Test matches, remains one of the few class players in the country.

Instead of reminding him of this a large section of the British Press has chosen to assail him not for his shortcomings at the crease, which would have been perfectly fair, but for failing to attend some crapulous Press conference on the middle Saturday of a Test match which would have yielded some easy copy.

At Lord's he walked out and at Old Trafford he simply didn't show up, and I find that as utterly reasonable as it was quite unreasonable of the Test and County Cricket Board to commit him to attending in the first place.

The TCCB now have three paid men — Ted Dexter, Micky Stewart and Peter Smith — to handle all the nonsense that would distract a man's thinking while he was still out in the field. The problem is that David Gower is paid, which rather undermines his position.

I relish the story of Douglas Jardine, a former England captain, being confronted by a similar predicament many years ago. It occurred on the afternoon of December 1, 1932, when a deputation of Australian sportswriters politely confronted him on the practice area behind Sydney Cricket Ground and requested him to name the team he proposed to field the following morning in the opening Test match of what became the Bodyline Series.

Jardine, a Scot, a Wykhamist, an amateur, a not over-gifted batsman and a wonderful snob, was outraged. 'I never,' he replied, 'speak to the Press. And on principle, I never speak to Australians.'

Jardine won his series and wrote a wonderfully thoughtful book about it called *In Quest of the Ashes*. It is a bible of leadership, of one-upmanship, of how to harness limited resources with discipline and cunning.

Gower's problem is that of persecution rather than legitimate criticism. Sack him, for God's sake, and who else have we got? It isn't our cricket we have to get right so much as our entire attitude to sport. Shooting the pianist has always been an expedient measure. Shooting the orchestra, in this case, might help.

ACKNOWLEDGEMENTS

Were it not for Lord Rothermere and Sir David English, respectively owner and editor-in-chief of the Daily Mail, I would probably have spent The Eighties writing unreadable novels. My thanks to them for saving me.

Thanks also to my sports editors of the decade: Tom Clarke, Peter Lea and, posthumously, Arthur Firth, a great newspaperman who came to sport and then, sadly, died so suddenly.

For correcting the occasional clanger I thank the Daily Mail's sports sub-editors as I do its photographers who did extraordinary things to achieve some of the pictures in this book.

For reasons they will understand my thanks also go to Julie Ivelaw-Chapman, Denis Compton, Ian Buchan, John Mitchell and my secretary, Hilary Michell, saintly saviour of the disorganised.

Above all my thanks to my wife, Sarah, who puts up with it all and still has the gracious gift of laughter.

Wherever possible the photographs in this edition appeared with Ian Wooldridge's original articles and the publishers wish to thank the Daily Mail for giving permission for their use. Thanks also go to the staff at the Mail's photo library who were so cheerfully cooperative in helping to 'sort and search' in spite of the timing coinciding with preparations for a move to new offices.